FIREPOWER

Princeton Studies in American Politics

Historical, International, and Comparative Perspectives

Suzanne Mettler, Eric Schickler, and
Theda Skocpol, Series Editors
Ira Katznelson, Martin Shefter,
Founding Series Editors (Emeritus)

A list of titles in this series appears at the back of the book

Firepower

How the NRA Turned Gun Owners into a Political Force

Matthew J. Lacombe

PRINCETON UNIVERSITY PRESS

PRINCETON AND OXFORD

Published by Princeton University Press
41 William Street, Princeton, New Jersey 08540
6 Oxford Street, Woodstock, Oxfordshire OX20 1TR

press.princeton.edu

All Rights Reserved

Library of Congress Cataloging-in-Publication Data

Names: Lacombe, Matthew J., author.
Title: Firepower : how the NRA turned gun owners into a political force / Matthew J. Lacombe.
Description: Princeton, New Jersey : Princeton University Press, 2021. | Includes bibliographical
    references and index.
Identifiers: LCCN 2020039432 (print) | LCCN 2020039433 (ebook) | ISBN 9780691207445
    (hardback) | ISBN 9780691207469 (ebook)
Subjects: LCSH: National Rifle Association of America. | Republican Party (U.S. : 1854–) |
    Gun control—United States. | Firearms ownership—Political aspects—United States. | Firearms
    owners—Political activity—United States. | Pressure groups—United States.
Classification: LCC HV7436 .L334 2021 (print) | LCC HV7436 (ebook) | DDC 363.330973—dc23
LC record available at https://lccn.loc.gov/2020039432
LC ebook record available at https://lccn.loc.gov/2020039433

British Library Cataloging-in-Publication Data is available

Parts of this manuscript are adapted from Matthew J. Lacombe, "The Political Weaponization
of Gun Owners: The NRA's Cultivation, Dissemination, and Use of a Group Social Identity,"
Journal of Politics 81, no. 4 (2019): 1342–1356.

Editorial: Bridget Flannery-McCoy and Alena Chekanov
Production Editorial: Natalie Baan
Jacket Design: Jessica Massabrook
Production: Erin Suydam
Publicity: Kate Hensley and Kathryn Stevens
Copyeditor: Hank Southgate

Jacket images: Shutterstock

This book has been composed in Adobe Text and Gotham

Printed on acid-free paper. ∞

Printed in the United States of America

10 9 8 7 6 5 4 3 2 1

CONTENTS

ACKNOWLEDGMENTS

This book would not have come to fruition without the support of so many generous people. As my advisor and the chair of my dissertation committee, Dan Galvin has been involved with this project every step of the way, consistently offering insightful feedback, friendly encouragement, and invaluable guidance. Dan's a model scholar and mentor; I'll always look back fondly on the time we spent thinking through the puzzles explored by this project and strategizing how to address them. I hope the clarity of his thinking and the positivity of his disposition have rubbed off on me. I also benefitted from the insights and advice of three other tremendous committee members—Tony Chen, Ben Page, and Jay Seawright. Tony consistently pushed me to clarify the stakes of the project for the field and routinely offered helpful suggestions—both big and small—about how to improve it. Ben's deep commitment to democracy has inspired me to take on questions related to political power and representation in the United States. His guidance of this project and the wisdom he's imparted as a coauthor have been both a pleasure and a source of great learning for me. Jay went well above and beyond the standard duties of a committee member; he helped shape numerous aspects of the project, was exceptionally generous with his time, and frequently pushed me to improve the quality of my work. Finally, beyond my committee, Kristin Goss deserves special recognition for graciously mentoring me as part of a fellowship program at the University of Virginia's Jefferson Scholars Foundation; her advice improved the book and her encouragement motivated me to work on it.

Numerous others also assisted with the book's development. This project began as a dissertation at Northwestern University, where I was exceedingly lucky to have benefitted from the support of a tremendous community of scholars; beyond just my committee, I thank the many mentors and classmates there who provided me with inspiration, encouragement, and guidance, as well as the staff members who facilitated my progress. For help related to this project, I especially wish to thank classmates Ethan Busby, Sean Diament, D. J. Flynn, Laura Garcia Montoya, Adam Howat, Rana Khoury, Sasha Klyachkina, Jake Rothschild, Richard Shafranek, and Warren Snead, as well as faculty members Ana Arjona, Sarah Bouchat, Jamie Druckman, Laurel Harbidge-Yong, and Chloe Thurston (who was particularly generous with her time and insights). I'm also very grateful for the support of my talented and kind colleagues at Barnard and Columbia; their insights and friendship were crucial as I finished this book. I thank them for warmly welcoming me to the community and for sharing their wisdom with me. I especially appreciate the insightful comments Alex Hertel-Fernandez and Kate Krimmel gave on parts of the book, and the helpful advice on navigating the publication process that I received from Séverine Autesserre, Kim Marten, and Mike Miller.

Outside of Barnard, Columbia, and Northwestern, Hans Hassell and Tim LaPira made crucial suggestions on a paper that forms the basis of chapter 3, as did David Karol, who also offered helpful advice. Jeff Broxmeyer, Lindsay Cohn, and Sam Jackson gave very detailed comments as part of an especially helpful MPSA panel. Heath Brown and Boris Heersink provided friendly advice and encouragement about the project (and warmly welcomed me to New York). Patrick Charles shared numerous archival finds, and Ken Benoit, Christopher Farris, and Brandon Stewart provided helpful advice regarding text digitization and modeling. I had the good fortune of being assigned Ruth Bloch Rubin and Phil Rocco as mentors during lunches at the Northwestern CAB workshop and am grateful for their friendly insights and encouragement in the years since. Many others whose own work inspired and informed this book provided encouragement that motivated me at (unbeknownst to them) crucial times, including (but I fear not limited to) Don Haider-Markel, Hahrie Han, Mark Joslyn, Michele Margolis, Lily Mason, Sid Milkis, Hans Noel, Eric Oliver, Dan Schlozman, Theda Skocpol, and Bob Spitzer. I'd also like to acknowledge four current and former Allegheny College faculty members—Brian Harward, Shanna Kirschner, Dan Shea, and Ben Slote—for developing my sense of intellectual curiosity and helping me navigate entry into the academic world.

I also benefitted from the input of participants at the 2017 and 2018 APSA and MPSA meetings, the Cornell Democratic Resilience conference, the Northwestern Applied Quantitative Methods Workshop, the Northwestern Comparative-Historical Social Science Workshop, and the Northwestern American politics student workshop, as well as during talks at Allegheny College, Barnard College, Columbia University, the University of Chicago, the University of Kansas, and the University of Oregon.

Suzanne Mettler read the entire manuscript in her capacity as an editor of the Princeton Studies in American Politics series. I so appreciate her careful attention to and enthusiasm about the project; the direction she provided substantially improved the book. Three anonymous reviewers for Princeton University Press (and two at the University of Chicago Press, along with editor Chuck Myers) provided tremendously detailed feedback for which I'm very grateful. At Princeton University Press, I owe a great debt of gratitude to my editor, Bridget Flannery-McCoy; working with Bridget was a great pleasure, and her guidance of and attention to the book strengthened it in myriad ways.

The Jefferson Scholars Foundation at the University of Virginia funded my final year of graduate school and provided me with numerous other intellectual and professional resources. I thank Brian Balogh and the other fellows for their support. This project was made possible by generous funding from the APSA Centennial Center, Barnard College, the Dole Institute of Politics, the Gerald Ford Foundation, the Moody Foundation through its association with the Lyndon B. Johnson Library, and Northwestern University. Special thanks go to Northwestern's Institute for Policy Research for its support, along with the Interlibrary Loan Staff, whose hard work locating NRA magazines is very much appreciated.

Last but not least, I'd like to thank my family and friends for their support. Kelsey has been exceptionally supportive as I've completed this project—always there to celebrate the good times and to talk me through the bad. Moreover, she's been patient when my mood has been—as she might put it—"less than ideal." Finally, none of my successes would be possible without my parents (and stepparents), whose sacrifices, encouragement, and love have made me who I am.

FIREPOWER

1

Introduction

In April 2015, the annual meeting of the National Rifle Association brought nearly eighty thousand gun rights supporters to Nashville, Tennessee. The three-day conference offered seminars on topics ranging from home defense to doomsday survivalism planning to cooking with wild game, and a massive exhibit hall featured the latest firearms and firearms accessories (customized holsters, specialized apparel, and so on), along with live product demonstrations and a chance to meet celebrities like controversial rock star—and NRA board member—Ted Nugent. There was a prayer breakfast, a family-friendly indoor shooting range, and free country music concerts every afternoon.[1]

Yet the most prominent event of all was the Leadership Forum hosted by the NRA's Institute for Legislative Action (NRA-ILA), which since 1975 has served as the organization's primary political advocacy and lobbying branch. The forum featured speeches by more than ten Republican presidential hopefuls, including Jeb Bush, Ted Cruz, Marco Rubio, Ben Carson, and, of course, Donald Trump. Taking place long before the 2016 primaries began, the event was clearly an important part of the GOP's so-called invisible primary—the very early, informal jockeying that occurs among each party's presidential aspirants as they attempt to court elites, donors, activists, and the party faithful.[2]

Accordingly, the speakers not only touted their pro-gun credentials, but also spoke to their broader conservative beliefs across a range of issues, harshly criticized the Obama Administration, and warned of the specter of a Hillary Clinton presidency. Many took hawkish stances on terrorism and mocked President Obama's reluctance to use the term "radical Islam";[3] Wisconsin Governor Scott Walker, for example, said that he wanted "a Commander-in-Chief who will look the American people in the eye and say that radical Islamic terrorism is a threat and we're going to do something about it."[4] Louisiana Governor Bobby Jindal, speaking in support of businesses that refused service to same-sex couples on religious grounds, warned that if "Hollywood liberals and editorial columnists" could "conspire to crush the First Amendment, it won't be long before they join forces again to come after the Second Amendment."[5] Criticisms of Obamacare were also common, as was support for restrictive immigration policies. Texas Senator Ted Cruz, touting his legislative record, challenged voters to ask other Republican candidates, "When have you stood up and fought to stop Obamacare? . . . When have you stood up and fought to stop the president's illegal and unconstitutional executive amnesty?"[6]

For future President Donald Trump, the appearance previewed not just the themes but the rhetorical style that would characterize his campaign. He made populist appeals against free trade while criticizing the negotiation skills of Obama Administration officials. He opined that Vladimir Putin and ISIS had no respect for President Obama, and went on to say that Obama was "just not a good person."[7] Trump also emphasized the threat posed by illegal immigration, calling the United States' border with Mexico "a sieve" and saying that "it's not what the country's all about. . . . Millions of people coming in illegally. We've gotta stop it at the border and we have to stop it fast."

The 2015 meeting stood in stark contrast to the organization's first annual membership convention. Held in 1948—seventy-seven years after the association was founded—the inaugural event brought around seven hundred NRA members to the Shoreham Hotel in Washington, DC, for what it described as a "4-day gunner's get-together." General Jacob L. Devers from the US Army kicked things off with a welcome address in which he emphasized the importance of rifle training for national defense and thanked the NRA for its assistance during World War II. In keeping with the association's focus on marksmanship, subsequent sessions covered competitive shooting, management of local gun clubs, and recruitment of "junior riflemen." Politics were not absent from the event—NRA Executive Director C. B. Lister led a session on "The Legislative Picture" to explain what the organization was doing to combat gun control laws and to encourage attendees to write personalized pro-gun letters to politicians and newspaper editors—but politicians were. No presidential aspirants made an appearance, and there was no mention of political parties.[8]

Barry Goldwater famously said that politicians should "go hunting where the ducks are" while seeking votes.[9] For Republican candidates in the twenty-first century, the NRA—which reports having five million members—is unquestionably important hunting grounds. But, as the scene from its 1948 meeting suggests, this was not always the case. As we will see, NRA supporters have participated in politics at unusually high rates for a long time, consistently—and typically successfully—opposing gun regulations since as early as the 1930s. Yet, despite this durable political engagement, it has taken the NRA a long time to cultivate the powerful conservative constituency that supports its agenda today and that helped carry Donald Trump into the White House in 2016. Why are gun rights supporters so politically active—and when and how did they come to occupy such an important place in the Republican Party? How has their behavior shaped gun policy, and, crucially, what role has the NRA played in all this?

These are the questions this book seeks to answer. I contend that the NRA has played a central role in driving the political outlooks and political activity of its supporters—activity that has had both direct and indirect influence on federal gun policy in the United States.[10] Even from its earliest days as a relatively small organization dedicated to marksmanship, competitive shooting, and military preparedness, the NRA cultivated a distinct worldview around guns—framing gun ownership as an *identity* that was tied to a broader, gun-centric political *ideology*—and mobilized its members into political action on behalf of its agenda. When the time was right, it joined forces with the Republican Party and eventually became the right-wing political juggernaut that it is today. How a group can construct an identity and an ideology, and what happens when it aligns these behind a single party: that's the story of the NRA, and the story this book aims to tell.

The Power of the NRA

The focus of this book is on the political power of the NRA: What is the source of its power? How does it operate? How has it shaped gun policy and the broader political system?

Central as it is to politics, power can be difficult to pinpoint. We may have a general sense that certain groups are powerful because the observed political or economic environment seems to reflect their preferences and interests; weak gun regulations, for instance, suggest that the NRA is powerful, just as high levels of economic inequality suggest that big businesses and wealthy individuals have power. However, even when we have good reason to suspect that particular groups are powerful, the ultimate *source* of a group's power isn't always easy to determine. From where, exactly, does a group like the NRA derive influence? Similarly, it can be challenging to identify the *forms* a group's power takes. How, exactly, do business groups translate their resources into preferred political outcomes (such as the election of industry-friendly politicians and the adoption of industry-friendly regulations)? This difficulty is reflected in a lacuna in the field of political science, which acknowledges the importance of power but has struggled to explain how groups can build and use it over time.[11]

The power of the NRA—although widely acknowledged by scholars and observers alike—is no exception to this challenge. Some politicians and commentators assert that financial resources—taking the form of outsized campaign contributions and expensive lobbying efforts—are the primary source of its influence. Others—focusing on financial resources in a different way—argue that the NRA's true purpose is to serve as a front for firearms manufacturers who are interested in weakening gun laws in order to boost sales; these arguments typically don't specify how, exactly, the money of gun manufacturers is translated into policy change, but they imply that financial resources play a central role. In short, the NRA—which operates in a political system that many Americans believe is dominated by large corporations and wealthy elites[12]—is seen by some as another example of the power of money.

Yet these financially focused arguments cannot fully—or even mostly—explain the NRA's influence within American politics.[13] NRA members are mostly working-class individuals, not financial elites.[14] And although the NRA does have an ongoing relationship with manufacturers, this relationship is neither a defining characteristic of the group nor a sufficient explanation of its political power. For one thing, the NRA's incentives are not always aligned with those of gun manufacturers. Given their interest in selling *new* firearms, manufacturers have no reason to oppose—and actually have good reason to support—laws that make it more difficult for individuals to sell existing guns to one another. These sorts of laws, however, are strongly opposed by the NRA. Moreover, there is evidence that the NRA can actually overpower manufacturers when disagreement exists. For example, when Smith & Wesson made an agreement with the Clinton Administration in 2000 to alter its products and sales processes to improve safety, the NRA initiated a crippling boycott against the company: its production declined by over 40 percent in just two years.[15] So while manufacturers may (and do) still contribute to the NRA, this suggests that the NRA controls the relationship and is not a tool of the industry.

Moreover, the NRA's spending does not stand out: groups that make comparable campaign contributions (e.g., environmental groups like the League of Conservation Voters and labor unions like the Service Employees International Union) do not appear to have influence comparable to the NRA's, while groups that do appear to have comparable influence (e.g., business groups like the Chamber of Commerce) spend much more money than the NRA on lobbying. Further, despite periods when gun regulation advocates have outspent the NRA—including in the aftermath of the Sandy Hook massacre, when billionaire Michael Bloomberg put his full financial weight behind gun control—there have been no major shifts in federal gun policy (which remains, as we will see below, far more lax than in any other similarly developed nation).[16] And finally, there is compelling evidence that the NRA successfully persuaded policymakers on gun policy long before it began spending substantial sums on politics. Taken together, all this suggests that other factors besides money are in play.[17]

In this book, I will look beyond the NRA's use of financial resources and turn instead to what I describe as *ideational* resources: the identity and ideology it cultivates among its members, which have enabled it to build an active, engaged, and powerful constituency. From existing accounts of important gun control policy battles, we know that a crucial aspect of the NRA's influence is its ability to translate the political intensity of its supporters into influence over policy. Gun rights supporters—especially NRA members and those whose status as gun owners is an important part of their personal identity—are very politically active,[18] both generally and relative to individuals who support gun control: they're more likely to write letters or donate money on behalf of their cause,[19] more likely to participate in electoral campaigns,[20] and more likely to join advocacy organizations like the NRA.[21] Further, a remarkable 71 percent of individuals who favor less restrictive gun laws reported in 2014 that they are unwilling to ever vote for political candidates who support gun control; among those who favor stricter laws, only 34 percent said that they are unwilling to vote for candidates who do not share their gun preferences.[22]

As the following chapters will demonstrate, there is compelling evidence that this engagement gap has had major effects on gun control policy. As early as the 1930s, the NRA helped thwart some of the first federal attempts at gun control by leading a letter writing campaign against proposed gun regulations.[23] This became a favored strategy, and an effective one; another campaign in the mid-1960s against strong gun control proposals being debated in Congress generated such a flood of mail that numerous policymakers credited the letters with the bill's defeat.[24] Privately, politicians have acknowledged that pressure from gun owning constituents has altered their behavior as policymakers (with one senator, for example, saying that he'd "rather be a deer in hunting season than a politician who has run afoul of the NRA crowd"[25]); these accounts are supported by quantitative analyses demonstrating how an "intense minority" on gun control has caused elected officials to vote against the will of an "apathetic majority."[26]

Indeed, part of what makes the NRA's success so striking is the extent to which the American public favors new gun regulations. Americans have voiced support for gun control—both in the abstract and in terms of specific policy measures—since the advent of public opinion polling.[27] In what appears to be the earliest polling data on guns, Gallup found in 1938 that 79 percent of Americans favored gun control. Between that year and 1972, many polls were conducted by Gallup and Harris; not one found that less than 66 percent of Americans favored gun control, with support peaking in 1969 at 84 percent.[28] More recent polling has continued to demonstrate strong support for gun control policies: a 2017 Pew poll found that 84 percent of Americans support mandatory background checks for all gun sales, 89 percent support laws to prevent the mentally ill from purchasing guns, 71 percent support a federal database to track gun sales, and 68 percent support a ban on "assault" weapons.[29]

These high levels of support for gun control are perhaps unsurprising given the state of gun violence in the United States. Horrific, high-profile mass shootings are unfortunately neither new nor rare phenomena. The Labor Day 1949 murder of thirteen people in Camden, New Jersey, is considered the first mass shooting in US history,[30] and a shooting at the University of Texas at Austin in 1966 took the lives of sixteen individuals. Although not new, mass shootings have become even more deadly in recent years; the 2016 shooting at Pulse Nightclub in Orlando—in which forty-nine people were murdered and fifty-three injured—was the deadliest in US history until the fall 2017 Las Vegas concert shooting, which claimed the lives of fifty-eight victims and caused injuries to hundreds of others.

Moreover, while mass shootings command the greatest media attention, they are actually only a small part of the US gun violence story. Between the beginning of 2001—the year of the infamous September 11th terrorist attacks—and the end of 2016, guns were used to kill over 500,000 Americans.[31] In that same timespan, terrorist attacks—which, unlike episodes of gun violence, almost always lead to swift government action—resulted in the deaths of around 3,200.[32] Guns are involved in the deaths of more than 30,000 Americans annually—a number that rose to nearly 40,000 in 2017.[33] As Nicholas Kristof pointed out in 2015, more Americans have died from guns since 1970 than in all US wars combined.[34]

Put in comparative perspective, the United States is an anomaly. It was the site of 31 percent of the world's mass shootings between 1966 and 2012, despite comprising only 5 percent of the world's population.[35] Moreover, the US rate of gun-related deaths—at over 10 per 100,000 people as of 2016—is exceptional among advanced countries; nearby Canada, for example, had only 2.1 gun deaths per 100,000 in 2016, Japan had just 0.2, the United Kingdom had 0.3, Switzerland (which has a high rate of gun ownership) had 2.8, and France 2.7. Along with Brazil, Colombia, Guatemala, Mexico, and Venezuela, the United States is among six countries that accounted for slightly more than half of the world's gun-related deaths in 2016.[36]

One factor that separates the United States from most other industrialized countries is the lack of strong legal restrictions on the ownership and use of guns. Mandatory, universal background checks—which the United States does not require—are very common throughout the world. Some countries outright ban the private ownership of handguns. Federal licensing is also common, with many countries requiring individuals to take a safety course to obtain a license. Although the purpose of this book is not to determine the effectiveness of gun regulations, the nearly inverse relationship that exists between a country's level of gun ownership and its rate of gun violence suggests that gun control works.[37]

And not only does the United States lack restrictions on firearms that are popular around the world, it has also witnessed the proliferation of laws that have in various ways weakened prior regulations. In fact, contrary to the claims of gun rights advocates, the United States had strong state level gun regulations for most of its history—regulations that have been eroded in recent decades by laws explicitly protecting and expanding gun rights. Some form of stand-your-ground laws—which, with slight differences across jurisdictions, allow individuals to use deadly force to defend themselves with no duty to retreat—now exist in thirty-four states as of early 2020. Similarly, individuals are increasingly allowed to carry concealed firearms; in sixteen states (as of early 2020), gun owners are not even required to obtain a permit to do so, and in most other states, it is easy for anyone who legally owns a handgun to get a permit.[38]

These factors—broad public support for gun control, high rates of gun-related deaths, and the relative weakness of existing US laws—underscore the high stakes of the gun debate, make the NRA's long-term political success all the more notable, and suggest that the US policy landscape would be substantially different in a world without the NRA. Understanding how the NRA has evolved over time is essential to understanding the success of its political strategies; I offer a brief sketch below, and many more details in the chapters to come.

A Very Brief History of the NRA

The NRA was founded in 1871 by military officials who hoped to promote rifle shooting and marksmanship as a form of war preparedness. Chartered in New York—the home of one of its cofounders, Captain George Wingate—the NRA enjoyed some initial success. The popularity of shooting matches enabled the organization to gain members, and its founders' connections with public officials helped it earn a subsidy from the state government. This popularity, however, eventually faded, as did political support in New York for marksmanship training.[39] By the turn of the twentieth century, the NRA was very small and, after losing its subsidy, nearly defunct.[40]

The organization was reinvigorated, however, during the first two decades of the 1900s—a period in which it became, in its own words, a "quasi-governmental" organization.[41] A group of military officials who were displeased with the shooting skills of American troops in the Spanish-American War sought to create an organization that could offer marksmanship training to civilians; in lieu of a new organization, the NRA—at Wingate's suggestion—became the vehicle for this renewed effort. President Theodore Roosevelt, himself a gun enthusiast and NRA member, soon urged Congress to establish the National Board for the Promotion of Rifle Practice and the Civilian Marksmanship Program. These programs would be closely associated with the NRA and would provide it with federal funds for decades to come.[42]

Around this same time, the government also established a program that allowed NRA members, exclusively, to purchase surplus military firearms at low prices.[43] Another program provided funds for NRA shooting competitions.[44] These developments—a product of good timing and close relationships with powerful public officials—cemented the NRA's shooting programs and competitions as "the law of the land."[45] The group grew rapidly, benefitting not just from its relationship with the federal government but from the military buildups associated with both world wars. The NRA surpassed ten thousand members by 1924 and fifty thousand by 1940.[46]

Throughout this early period, the NRA and its supporters staunchly opposed gun control laws and actively worked to prevent their passage. Later in the book, I explore both the nature of these efforts and their effects on gun policy during the NRA's "quasi-governmental phase" (as I've termed the organization's first hundred or so years) through case studies of two periods when new gun laws were debated and, eventually, passed.

The first case focuses on the federal government's initial attempts at gun control—the National Firearms Act of 1934 and the Federal Firearms Act of 1938—which were spurred by increased crime rates and the rise of organized criminal syndicates. The case shows that the NRA's development and use of ideational resources—consisting of the identity and ideology discussed earlier—enabled it to substantially weaken both laws prior to their passage, mostly through mass-mobilization campaigns (and the desire of politicians to *avoid* such campaigns by writing bills that aligned with the NRA's views).

After these 1930s battles, gun control mostly left the national agenda for the next two decades. Violent crime rates were down and the country's attention was turned to world affairs. The NRA, meanwhile, continued to expand, maintaining its robust relationship with the federal government and consistently adding additional programs to attract new members. Following World War II, for example, as soldiers returned home with a newfound interest in firearms, many veterans took up hunting as a hobby. Sensing an opportunity—and also hoping to preempt new controls on guns—the NRA developed hunter safety programs. Since their inception in the 1950s, these have been the primary outlets through which outdoorsmen receive training, drawing in millions of participants.[47] These and similar offerings enabled the organization to surpass one million members by the end of the 1960s.[48]

The 1960s also witnessed the return of gun control to the national agenda in response to surging crime rates and a string of high-profile political assassinations, including those of President John F. Kennedy, his brother Robert, and civil rights leader Martin Luther King Jr. The NRA and its supporters, as they had in the past, fiercely opposed the numerous gun control proposals that were developed in the mid-1960s.

This period of debate—which eventually culminated in the Gun Control Act of 1968—is the second of the two case studies mentioned above. The NRA's efforts to cultivate an identity and ideology among its supporters had continued to build on each other over time, and enabled it to fend off numerous gun control proposals over the course of the 1960s and to then—as it had in the 1930s—substantially weaken the legislation that eventually did pass. In general, the NRA's influence in this early period relied on its ability to mobilize its members and on the reputation it gained as a result; this reputation caused policymakers—in the hope of avoiding the NRA's wrath—to give the organization a role in crafting new bills and to develop weaker legislation than they would have otherwise preferred.

Despite the NRA's political activity throughout its quasi-governmental phase, the organization remained nonpartisan; it did not endorse candidates, rarely mentioned parties when discussing politics, and mostly invited military officials to speak at its events. Gun control was not a cleavage issue dividing Democrats and Republicans at this time, so the NRA lacked a clear home in the party system.

All of this would change, however, starting in the 1970s—a decade of organizational turmoil that ultimately led to a major turning point for the group, ushering it into a new, politically partisan role. This "partisan phase," as I have termed it, is the one it remains in today.

The shift into this new phase started with fracturing in the NRA's relationship with the government. Although the NRA had stayed out of partisan politics in the 1960s, its political activism nonetheless made it an increasingly controversial group. As the controversy surrounding it grew, its relationship with the government (and the status of its federal funding) began to deteriorate. As federal funding dried up, the organization had to decide how to move forward.

The conversation about the NRA's future direction pitted its "old guard"—a group of leaders who favored a nonpartisan approach to politics and resisted additional investments in the organization's political infrastructure—against its "new guard"—a group of activist members and lower-level leaders who sought to ally with the insurgent New Right conservative movement and take the organization in a more partisan direction. This conflict came to a head at the now-infamous 1977 annual meeting in Cincinnati (discussed further in subsequent chapters) when the new guard staged a dramatic organizational coup and seized control in what has come to be known as the "Revolt at Cincinnati."

The new guard sent the NRA down a dramatically different path—developing new ways to recruit members, substantially expanding political operations, and, perhaps most importantly, aligning the group with the Republican Party. These changes marked a new chapter in the

NRA's history and eventually resulted in the organization becoming the political force that we observe today. The NRA could still mobilize its members to shape gun policy outcomes, but this mobilizational power was now joined by partisan influence. This has deepened the NRA's power and expanded the forms this power takes.

Later on, I explore the nature of the NRA's influence in this new phase over four additional case studies. The first case—focused on the passage of the Firearm Owners' Protection Act of 1986—demonstrates that the NRA's partisan influence now gave it much more power over the legislative agenda. The law substantially *weakened* existing gun regulations, and that it was on the legislative agenda at all was in part a reward for the electoral support NRA members provided Republicans in the early 1980s. As subsequent chapters show, the bill would not have made it to the floors of Congress without Republican leadership prioritizing it.

The second case considers the debates that occurred in the late 1980s and early 1990s over what became the Brady Act and Assault Weapons Ban. While the Brady Act of 1993 and the inclusion of a ban on assault weapons in a 1994 crime bill were no doubt legislative losses for the NRA, they were much weaker than gun control advocates had hoped. They could only be passed during a brief window of unified Democratic control of government—and were immediately followed by Democratic losses in the 1994 midterm, which discouraged Democrats from pursuing gun control laws for years afterward. The episode demonstrated how the NRA's position in the Republican Party worked in conjunction with its mobilizational power to hinder the passage of strong gun control laws.

The final two cases pertaining to the NRA's partisan phase examine gun regulation efforts following the Columbine tragedy of 1999 and several prominent gun violence episodes in the 2010s. They document the NRA at the height of its power. Even in the wake of national tragedies, gun control efforts went nowhere. Whereas the 1986 law demonstrated *positive* agenda setting power (i.e., the ability to get something on the legislative agenda), these instances demonstrate strong *negative* agenda setting power. The NRA's Republican allies in Congress have frequently been able to kill gun control before it's voted on, even when there is tremendous pressure to pursue it. This has enabled the NRA to prevent new gun regulations without even having to launch mass-mobilization campaigns; in these most recent cases, the mere threat of such a campaign has been sufficient to discourage meaningful legislation from being proposed.

Outside of politics, the NRA's partisan phase has seen it balance its newer position as a hardline, partisan political group with its long-standing position as the central player in the US firearms community. This latter status continues to provide the organization ways to recruit new members, raise funds, and—as a result— expand its political base. The NRA continues to oversee shooting sports in the United States, holding over eleven thousand tournaments and fifty national championships per year.[49] Membership in the NRA is, as one writer involved in the hobby put it, "virtually inevitable for anyone desiring to participate in the target shooting sports."[50] Moreover, as state laws legalizing concealed carry have spread across the country, for example, the NRA has positioned itself as the primary—and in many cases the *only*—source for training. More than 75 percent of states with "shall-issue"[51] concealed carry laws require training to obtain a license, and more than 50 percent require training that, in practice, only the NRA can provide.[52] As a result of its roles in politics and American gun culture, the contemporary NRA[53] maintains a robust membership, which it reports at approximately five million people,[54] and has active affiliate chapters in all fifty states.[55]

The NRA, around the time of this writing, faced several legal challenges and dealt with some heated internal conflict among its leaders. Short of the organization being forced to shut down as a result of the lawsuits it faces, however, there is little reason to believe that its devoted pro-gun following is going anywhere. As the following chapters demonstrate, their ties to the group and its cause are deep and durable. These ties do not depend on the presence of a single NRA leader. They remain strong even when the organization faces financial difficulties. And, if anything, they only become deeper when gun owners believe that they are under attack.

Previewing the Rest of the Book

Two of this book's central concerns are explaining why gun rights supporters are so dedicated to their cause and why the NRA and its members have such an important place in the Republican Party. Chapter 2 lays out a framework for answering these questions that guides the rest of the book. It discusses how the NRA has crafted a worldview around guns consisting of both a gun owner social identity and a broader political ideology. When its supporters adopted this worldview, the NRA reaped substantial political benefits—including, ultimately, its alignment with the Republican Party.

With this framework in place, subsequent chapters look more closely at each piece and, in so doing, address questions that lie at the heart of gun politics. How has gun ownership become such a central part of how NRA members view and participate in politics? How does the NRA mobilize them into politics at unusually high rates? Why do many gun owners see gun rights as central to a broader set of political beliefs? When and why did support for gun rights become a conservative issue stance?

Chapters 3 and 4 answer these questions by closely examining nearly eighty years (1930–2008) of editorials from the NRA's *American Rifleman* magazine, along with gun-related letters to the editor of four major newspapers covering that same period. I use the *American Rifleman* as a measure of the organization's views and priorities and treat pro-gun letters to newspaper editors as a measure of the attitudes and views of NRA supporters; because no historical surveys exist that are well equipped to answer the questions posed above, I instead use the letters from gun owners to measure their feelings about guns over time. (Chapters 3 and 4—along with the appendix—provide more details about these data sources.)

Chapter 3 analyzes these materials to document how the NRA created a distinct social identity built around gun ownership, charting the NRA's assiduous, long-term efforts—through not just its membership communications but also its popular firearms programs—to cultivate such an identity and to connect it to politics. This identity took hold among many gun owners and shapes how they view the world. The chapter demonstrates how the NRA has used this identity to mobilize its supporters into politics by portraying gun owners' way of life as under threat from gun control proposals and imploring its members to take action in defense of it.

Chapter 4 uses the same data and analytical approach to explain how the NRA has created a gun-centric political ideology, in which gun rights are central to a broader set of issue positions, and thus how gun rights became so closely related to contemporary conservatism in the United States. As with the gun owner identity, this gun-centric ideology originated with the NRA and subsequently took hold among gun owners. These two aspects of the NRA worldview work in tandem; the ideological connections made by the NRA reinforce the identity it has created.

Chapter 5—consisting of the first two case studies discussed above—explores how the NRA used this worldview to influence gun policy outcomes during its quasi-governmental phase. It digs into a wide range of archival materials to identify how the NRA mobilized gun owners to defeat or weaken gun control legislation in the 1930s through the 1960s.

The book then shifts to a slightly different set of puzzles: When, why, and how did the NRA become a central pillar of the Republican Party, and how has this alliance altered both the NRA and the GOP? Using a rich collection of archival documents, chapter 6 documents the party-group alignment of the NRA and the GOP, detailing the constellation of factors that collectively facilitated this alignment, which began in the 1960s, culminated during the 1980 election, and has deepened in the decades since. It shows how the NRA's cultivation of a group social identity and gun-centric political ideology made its supporters an attractive demographic group to conservative politicians, and laid the foundation for the group's eventual incorporation into the Republican coalition. Chapter 6 also digs into the NRA's motivations for entering the realm of partisan politics, showing how funding challenges and internal conflicts led to the 1977 "Revolt at Cincinnati," after which the NRA quickly became an active player in GOP politics. Finally, the chapter analyzes public opinion polls to document gun owners' increasingly close relationship with the Republican Party—especially following the election of President Donald Trump.

Chapter 7—consisting of the four additional case studies mentioned earlier—then explores the NRA's influence on gun policy outcomes in its new, partisan phase. Picking up where chapter 5 left off, it examines the gun debate from the 1980s to the 2010s, showing how the NRA's position in the GOP coalition has enhanced its political power, most notably by providing it with more leverage over the contents and timing of the legislative agenda.

Finally, the conclusion looks toward the future of both the NRA and the gun debate more broadly. It discusses potential threats to the NRA's political influence, including its own internal struggles, the rise of more effective gun control advocacy organizations, and the potential downsides of its close relationship with the Republican Party. Finally, it discusses the potential generalizability of the book's findings to other groups and policy areas, notes its implications for our understanding of interest groups and political parties, and reflects on the NRA's place in American democracy.

2

Explaining the NRA's Power

In early 2018, the *New York Times* ran a frontpage story headlined "The True Source of the NRA's Clout: Mobilization, Not Donations." It described how America's foremost opponent of gun control had advanced its agenda not by buying off politicians, but by encouraging its members to punish policymakers who failed to support gun rights. The argument wasn't new; by that time, close observers of gun politics increasingly recognized that much of the NRA's power came from to its ability to rally gun owners into action.[1]

Yet there is relatively little understanding of *why* the NRA is so unusually successful at mobilizing its members into politics. Most interest groups, if not all, ask their members to take action on behalf of their agendas; what is it, exactly, that sets the NRA apart from these other organizations?

My argument is that an important source of the NRA's power is the gun-centric worldview it has crafted, consisting of two separate but related streams: a distinct, politicized group social identity built around gun ownership, and a group-centric political ideology that connects gun rights with a range of other issue stances and beliefs. Each of these streams can be thought of as *ideational* resources in the sense that—unlike tangible, material resources such as money— they exist in the realm of ideas, and are manifest in their impact on the political views, preferences, and values of NRA supporters.[2] And they operate through *mass* (rather than private, insider) channels; unlike lobbying or campaign contributions—which use financial resources to influence politics behind-the-scenes—their effects on policy outcomes come, either directly or indirectly, as a result of their impact on the political behavior of mass-level gun rights supporters.[3]

Beyond powering mobilization, ideational resources also played a crucial role in facilitating the NRA's entry into the Republican Party coalition. This chapter introduces (and future chapters expand) the concept of *party-group alignment* to describe the confluence of factors that together led to the NRA's close alliance with the GOP. The NRA's identity and ideology are two such factors; they made gun owners a very politically attractive demographic to a broader coalition of conservative politicians, which—in conjunction with other developments—was (and still is) a key reason for the NRA-GOP alliance.

In this chapter, I go into greater detail about each of these central ideas: the ideational resources of identity and ideology, and the party-group alignment that has been so central to the NRA's more recent political power. I end by circling back to last chapter's discussion of political power, exploring what the NRA can teach us about how power is built and exercised.

Identity

In the aftermath of Donald Trump's election in 2016, "identity politics" became key buzzwords for those trying to make sense of his unexpected victory. On the left, debate erupted about whether Democrats had faltered in paying too much attention to identity issues, while many on the right credited the success of Trump's politically incorrect campaign to the rejection of such politics. Underlying these discussions was an implicit assumption that identity politics referred to an emphasis (or, in the view of some, *over*emphasis) on the perspectives of individuals from historically marginalized groups. The presumption was that identities related to race, gender, sexual orientation, and so on were the only ones that existed.

Yet a rich tradition in social psychology demonstrates that individuals hold a wide range of distinct and potentially overlapping identities. Meaningful identities can exist whenever individuals are aware of their membership in a group and attach some personal significance to that membership;[4] these groups can be based around race or gender, but they can also be based around a person's hometown, college, occupation, or even his or her favorite sports teams. Most relevant to this book: they can be based on shared characteristics like gun ownership.

These identities are very important drivers of an individual's political attitudes and actions. Political decisions, that is, are a product of the particular identities that are most relevant to them at the time of those decisions.[5] In other words, *all* politics is identity politics, and understanding political behavior is a matter of figuring out when, why, and how particular identities are salient. In this view, Trump's election was not a rejection of identity politics, but instead a triumph of a different *kind* of identity politics—one focused on, among others, white racial identity, rural identity, and, yes, gun owner identity.

Studies of identity and group-based political behavior have provided insights into a wide array of topics. Foundational work on voting behavior, for example, has clarified the important role that partisan identity plays in shaping individuals' political decisions.[6] Other, more contemporary examples have tackled questions around race (e.g., what explains high levels of political unity among African-Americans?),[7] partisanship and political participation (e.g., how do individuals' identities and group memberships shape their party affiliation and political involvement?),[8] rural consciousness (how does attention to a distinctly rural identity help us understand why many low-income voters oppose government redistribution?),[9] and political polarization (what role do social and political identities play in widening the divide between Democrats and Republicans?).[10] In fact, an identity-driven approach has even been previously applied to some aspects of gun politics.[11]

But despite broad acknowledgment of identity's political potency, a crucial question remains unanswered. If membership in an organized group can be a basis for an identity, is it possible for such groups to actively cultivate—to *create*—these social identities among their supporters?[12] Drawing on insights from social psychology, I argue that it is indeed possible, and I explain how through an examination of the NRA. This topic is not just of academic interest; understanding how a group like the NRA is able to use identity as a political weapon can help us understand why US gun regulations are relatively weak and why gun politics are so central to American politics today.

HOW TO BUILD AN IDENTITY

So, how has the NRA gone about constructing a group identity? A useful example comes from a 2002 editorial written by longtime NRA CEO and Executive Vice President Wayne LaPierre, which was published in the organization's longest-running and most widely circulated magazine, the *American Rifleman*. In it, LaPierre expresses opposition to a proposed bill that would have extended background checks to cover a greater proportion of gun sales made between private individuals, including at gun shows.

Throughout the editorial, LaPierre describes gun owners in positive terms—calling them, for example, "law-abiding" and "peaceable Americans"—while deriding gun control supporters as "gun prohibitionist[s]" running an anti-gun "propaganda machine" that is paid for by their "billionaire backers." Rather than arguing about flaws contained within the bill (for instance, making the case that the proposed regulations are unlikely to actually reduce crime), LaPierre consistently frames his opposition in terms of its potential impacts on the personal lives of gun owners. He calls it an "attempt to put private sales of firearms between peaceable Americans—you, me, our families and friends—under the total control of the Federal government." "Our very culture," he says, "is the target." Finally, LaPierre compels his readers to take political action. Arguing that the bill would create a slippery slope leading to more restrictive legislation, LaPierre tells NRA members to "Write, call or e-mail your Senators and Members of Congress and tell them: No gun control.

No gun show bans. No private sales ban. No transfer ban. If you do it now, and keep up the heat, we can stop the . . . [gun control] machine cold."[13]

LaPierre's editorial illustrates the process through which groups like the NRA can build identities. This process can be broken into four specific steps, which grow out of related studies from social psychology: (1) cultivation, (2) politicization, (3) dissemination, and (4) political mobilization.

The first step is the creation of a collective identity built around group membership. The goal is to create a situation in which those who share a particular characteristic—such as NRA membership—see themselves as a distinct social group and feel emotionally tied to the group. In practice, this involves associating the "in-group" with positive characteristics and members of perceived "out-groups" with negative characteristics.[14] The NRA does this by linking gun owner-ship to a number of desirable traits. Gun owners are average, "law-abiding" citizens, as LaPierre emphasizes; they are self-sufficient, patriotic, freedom-loving defenders of the American tradition. And the NRA juxtaposes gun owners with several different out-groups, including the media, politicians, and lawyers. In general—and in clearly populist terms—the opponents of gun owners are portrayed as radical, out-of-touch elitists (the "billionaire backers" whom La-Pierre evokes) who support collectivist policies and want to impose tyranny through bureaucracy.

Second, for a group identity to be politically useful, it needs to be perceived as related to politics. Recall that individuals have mul-tiple, overlapping social identities, many of which are not relevant to politics; devotion to a sports team, for instance, often involves a shared identity, but that identity (hopefully) does not inform indi-viduals' political attitudes.[15] The goal for the NRA, in this case, is to politicize this identity so that it's salient not just in contexts related to recreation and self-defense, but also when members engage with politics. To do this, groups can frame policies in terms of how they impact the identities and values of group members, as opposed to only discussing their specific policy impacts. LaPierre demonstrates this in his editorial, framing gun control as an attack on gun owners as a social group and depicting the gun debate as a battle between a "good" in-group and "bad" out-groups.[16]

Third, groups can then more widely spread identities they have developed by consistently emphasizing particular identity characteristics in their communications with members (communications like the LaPierre editorial discussed in this section). They can also develop activities and offer programs that encourage their supporters to gather together in person and associate participation in such programs with desirable characteristics. The NRA does this through both its membership publications—such as the *American Rifleman*—and its highly popular firearms-related programs. Indeed, although its programs and events are nominally apolitical, a closer examination (included in the following chapter) indicates that the NRA has used them to spread its politicized gun owner social identity, describing the programs as an initial route into "all else that the NRA stands for."[17]

The final step is for a group to actually use an identity to mobilize its supporters. Individuals are motivated to take action when they believe that their identities are under threat.[18] Given this relationship between perceived threat and political action, groups can attempt to mobilize their supporters by depicting the group's identity as under threat from its enemies. LaPierre, for instance, combines threatening language with a call to action on behalf of gun rights. Moreover, LaPierre's slippery slope argument is an example of a common refrain in which the NRA asks its supporters to take action after telling them that even seemingly innocuous gun laws will eventually lead to universal gun bans and confiscation.

HOW A GROUP IDENTITY ENHANCES THE NRA'S POWER

The identity the NRA has developed around gun ownership has helped it overcome the sorts of collective action—or "free rider"— problems that are endemic to the creation, maintenance, and mobilization efforts of organized groups. The NRA, like many other political groups, seeks to provide its members with benefits—such as the protection of gun rights—that can't be restricted only to those who have actually joined the organization and contributed to its cause; although it needs dues-paying members who are willing to take political action to produce these benefits, the NRA cannot stop other, noncontributing gun owners from enjoying them. NRA members are subject to the same regulations as everyone else. The NRA, then, must find ways to encourage individuals to do their part despite a temptation to free ride off of others. By providing a sense of belonging to its supporters, the NRA's identity offers a strong incentive for individuals to join the group and a compelling reason for them to take political action when they think it is threatened.[19]

This collective political action in the face of perceived threat matters, as it enables NRA members to directly affect legislative outcomes. By producing a flood of pro-gun constituent letters and phone calls directed at politicians, for instance, NRA mobilization campaigns have consistently helped it defeat or weaken gun control regulations in those (increasingly rare) moments when they are debated in Congress. The NRA uses identity-based mobilization to advance its agenda outside of the legislative process as well, most notably during elections when it deploys the same threat-based, identity-driven techniques to mobilize its members in support of (or opposition to) particular candidates. Since NRA supporters are such a politically active group and since the NRA is so effective at guiding their behavior, many politicians are eager to receive an NRA endorsement and do so by supporting its gun rights agenda. Indeed, the NRA's creation of a gun owner social identity and the related political intensity of its supporters have made them an attractive group to ideological activists and political parties; this attractiveness, as I'll discuss more later in the chapter, has helped the NRA achieve a prominent place in the Republican Party coalition—another key source of its power.

Relatedly—but a bit more broadly—the gun owner identity helps explain the well-documented but nonetheless perplexing political engagement gap that exists between gun rights supporters and gun regulation supporters; despite being in the majority, gun regulation supporters—who do not share a collective identity—are much less likely than gun rights supporters to take political action. This engagement gap in turn helps explain why Democratic politicians who claim to support gun control have often deprioritized it: they may perceive gun control as an issue that can *lose* them votes, but that probably will not *gain* them many. This gap may also make gun rights supporters seem more numerous than they are; when surveyed, policymakers systematically overestimate public opposition to gun control. This misperception could be a consequence of the frequency with which elected officials are contacted by gun rights supporters relative to gun control supporters.[20]

Over time, the widespread mobilization of gun rights supporters helps the NRA advance its agenda in ways that are more difficult to directly observe, such as agenda setting. Policymakers, anticipating the reaction of NRA supporters, are discouraged from proposing new gun control laws in the first place—knowing (sometimes firsthand) what happens when the NRA turns gun owners against elected officials. These anticipatory agenda setting effects are one explanation of the seemingly stubborn—and, to many Americans, frustrating—hesitance of veteran politicians to pursue stronger gun regulations, even in the wake of horrifying instances of gun violence and despite public opinion polls suggesting that they're very popular—sometimes even among gun owners themselves!

Many gun owners, in fact, claim to support particular regulations—such as mandatory background checks on all gun sales—in the abstract, but then often actively oppose pieces of legislation containing these same measures.[21] This occurred in 2013 when gun rights supporters flooded the phone lines of Congress in opposition to the Manchin-Toomey bill, which came in the wake of the Sandy Hook shooting and would have expanded background check requirements to cover a greater proportion of sales between private individuals.[22] When policy proposals like Manchin-Toomey are seen as battles between the pro-gun in-group and anti-gun out-group, opposition to them is more related to group identity than it is to policy content or individuals' abstract policy views.[23]

Finally, the NRA's cultivation of a group identity may also enhance its use of more traditional political resources, like money. Much of the money the NRA spends on campaigns, for instance, goes directly toward mobilizing its own supporters, typically through advertisements that appeal to its gun owner identity. Given how responsive NRA members are to these sorts of identity-based appeals, it's possible that the NRA's ads are more effective at mobilizing gun rights supporters than most campaign appeals are at persuading their target audience. If so, then the NRA's campaign spending may, as a result of the gun owner identity, be unusually productive.

Ideology

First held in the 1970s, the annual Conservative Political Action Conference (CPAC) is a multiday event that brings together conservative leaders and activists for speeches, training courses, and networking. Gun rights and the Second Amendment are frequent topics of discussion among the event's long list of speakers—a list that now regularly includes the NRA's top officials. The NRA's presence at events like CPAC is not surprising given both the conservatism of NRA members and the fact that support for gun rights is now widely considered a conservative issue stance.[24] In today's politics, we often take for granted that gun rights and gun ownership are associated with conservatism.

Yet this ideological configuration is not automatic or organic; one could even imagine an alternative in which conservatives *support* strict gun control laws as a way to address crime. Why, then, is support for gun rights viewed by many as one part of a broader conservative worldview?

One reason is that—beyond the gun owner social identity—the NRA has simultaneously crafted a gun-centric political *ideology*. As discussed below, this ideology is distinct from but nonetheless related to the gun owner identity, and portrays gun rights as closely interconnected with other issue stances—stances that are now, in contemporary politics, associated with conservatism. In addition to reinforcing its identity, the NRA's cultivation of an ideology also laid a foundation that enabled its eventual alliance with conservative activists and politicians.

Ideologies package together stances on a range of political issues—gun control, abortion, Social Security, healthcare, and so on—and tie those stances to particular values and ideas about the purposes of government. Contemporary liberalism in the United States, for example, values equality, believes that government should play an active role in achieving it, and, as a result, advocates for issue stances that would expand the social safety net, such as requiring paid sick leave or enhancing Social Security benefits. A bit more technically (and following the lead of other scholars), I define ideologies as sets of interrelated issue stances (which can also be referred to as issue positions), along with the broader beliefs and values associated with those stances.[25]

By grouping stances on distinct issues into coherent bundles, ideologies help structure politics for both voters and politicians. These bundles sometimes align with and help define partisan divides; this occurs when members of each party adopt similar ideological perspectives, as is currently the case in the United States, where liberals are mostly Democrats and conservatives mostly Republicans. This isn't always the case, however; for much of the twentieth century, for example, the Democratic Party coalition included both liberals (especially in the northern states) and conservatives (especially in the southern states). Moreover, ideologies can and do exist even when they haven't been fully adopted by a major party, as is the case with libertarianism in the United States.

When an ideology includes an issue stance—such as support for gun rights—that is central to the mission of an organized group, it can help shape that group's relationship with both other groups and political parties. When NRA leaders go to CPAC, for example, they're joined by the leaders of other groups that also advocate conservative issue stances—like the anti-abortion Susan B. Anthony List[26]—as well as conservative GOP politicians; these groups and politicians are allies due in part to their shared ideology.

Ideologies can also shape which groups *oppose* each other politically. Because support for gun rights is a conservative stance and environmentalism is a liberal stance, for example, gun rights groups and environmental groups find themselves on opposing sides of the ideological divide (even despite the fact that many members of both groups enjoy the outdoors). And because liberalism—and, along with it, support for environmental protection—has been adopted by Democrats, and conservatism—and, with it, support for gun rights—by Republicans, these groups also find themselves on opposing sides of the partisan divide.

Ideologies, in other words, help form groups into coalitions and structure their relationships with parties; they're one way of dividing politics into teams that act collectively to advance their individual goals.[27]

In this sense, ideologies help explain groupings of issues and politicians that might not otherwise exist. Take, for example, a conservative T-shirt and bumper sticker slogan from the Obama years, which read, "I'll keep my guns, money, and freedom. You can keep the change!" The slogan unites two issue stances—support for gun rights and opposition to taxes—with freedom as a value. "You can keep the change," mocking President Obama's 2008 campaign slogan, "change we can believe in," connects these ideological views with opposition to the Democratic Party. There is no inherent connection between gun rights and low taxes, but they're linked together—and tied to a belief in freedom and support for the GOP—by the conservative ideology associated with the contemporary Republican Party.

Ideologies, in short, play a crucial role in structuring the political landscape, which means that understanding both their contents—the set of beliefs that comprise them—and their development—how, when, and why they come together—is important for explaining how various organized groups fit into that landscape. Although prior scholarship has focused on the role of politicians[28] and political thinkers[29] in building ideologies, I argue that organized groups can also play a role in their development. Along these lines, I focus on how the NRA has connected support for gun rights to other issue stances, as well as the personal values and beliefs about government that are associated with those stances.[30]

THE NRA'S GUN-CENTRIC IDEOLOGY AND ITS DEVELOPMENT OVER TIME

When combined, the set of issue positions to which the NRA has connected gun rights closely resembles contemporary conservatism in the United States. These include opposition to "big government"—of

TABLE 2.1. Issue Sets Connected to Gun Rights by the NRA

Issue Set	Brief Description
Crime	Gun rights are a solution to crime because the personal ownership of firearms is the best defense against criminals. Harsh sentencing and, in general, incarceration are preferable to what the NRA refers to as "prior restraint"—limiting access to guns prior to misuse of them. (Not included here are editorials that discuss crime but argue exclusively that gun control measures aimed at it are unlikely to work.)
Liberty	Gun rights are crucial to Americans' social and political freedom, broadly conceived; they are necessary as a means to prevent government tyranny and are also a fundamental end of freedom. The Second Amendment is America's "first freedom" because it is necessary to protect all other freedoms.
Limited Government	Infringement on gun rights is one example of government interference in individuals' lives, among others. Gun control is a form of "big government." (This topic focuses more on specific policy issues than it does on the inherent rights of free societies, which is the focus of the "Liberty" category.)

which gun control is one form—and support for crime policies that focus on harsh punishment and incarceration while emphasizing the usefulness of firearms for defense against criminals. They also include support for a strong military and opposition to international organizations like the United Nations (UN). Finally, the NRA and its supporters argue that the protection of a broad range of liberties requires a constitutionally protected right to own and use guns. The three primary issue sets to which the NRA has connected gun rights are summarized in table 2.1; these higher-level issue sets, which are based on the contents of NRA editorials in the *American Rifleman* (a data source discussed more in subsequent chapters), enable me to examine the NRA's ideology across different points in time, even as the narrower, more specific issues of the day changed.

The three major issue sets to which the NRA has connected gun rights have remained stable over time—going all the way back to the beginning of my study in the 1930s—but their relative emphasis and how they have been discussed have changed in response to sociopolitical events and developments within the NRA itself. The extent to which these issue connections have aligned with the positions of the United States' major political parties has also changed over time, as discussed throughout the remainder of the chapter.

In the 1930s and early 1940s—when gun violence rates were high, and the gun control debate was active—the NRA and its supporters frequently tied gun rights to crime and to both individual and collective liberty, emphasizing the right of individuals to use guns for self-defense and the collective importance of guns for defense against foreign threats. During World War II and its aftermath, including the Korean War and the start of the Cold War, emphasis shifted squarely to the importance of guns to national defense and the preservation of collective liberty. This emphasis on collective liberty—which tied gun rights to a worldview likely shared by many former service members—fit well with the NRA's widespread recruitment of WWII veterans.

Later, in the 1960s and 1970s—with crime rates rising following a period of decline and gun control back on the national political agenda as a result—gun rights were once again frequently connected to self-defense and individual liberty. The NRA and its supporters also began to support harsh "law and order" crime control policies, arguing that severe criminal sentencing was preferable to restricting individuals' access to guns. As the NRA's previously strong relationship with the federal government deteriorated, the linkage of gun rights to liberty began to change. There was a gradual movement away from an emphasis on *foreign* threats to liberty and toward an emphasis on the threat of *domestic* tyranny imposed by one's own government, with gun control depicted as a form of "big government." This shift coincided with a dramatic increase in the discussion of the Second Amendment, which was portrayed as a mechanism for protection against an intrusive state. During the 1980s and 1990s, as the NRA fully transitioned into its partisan phase, the issue sets it advanced remained relatively steady, but were increasingly reflected in the positions of the Republican Party.

Notably, the NRA began advancing a nationalistic, right-wing brand of populism in the early 2000s. It accused globalist elites—including billionaires like George Soros—of conspiring with liberal politicians and international organizations to take away Americans' guns and destroy their heritage. These arguments previewed the future of GOP politics by advancing a worldview strikingly similar to the worldview advanced by Donald Trump during his campaign and subsequent presidency; although I cannot conclusively demonstrate that Trump adopted these viewpoints directly from the NRA, the similarities suggest that he may, at the very least, have learned from its approach to politics.

HOW A GROUP IDEOLOGY REINFORCES THE NRA'S IDENTITY AND FACILITATES COALITION-BUILDING

Unlike identity and (as discussed next) party-group alignment, ideology plays a less direct role in the NRA's efforts to advance gun rights. It is nonetheless crucial, however, because it strengthens the group's identity and, in various ways, helped facilitate its entry into the Republican Party coalition.

A group ideology can buttress a group's identity when its stances reinforce the positive personal characteristics associated with being part of the group. When the NRA, for example, portrays gun control as a form of big government and ties support for gun rights to limited government, it reinforces the notion that gun owners are self-sufficient people who don't have to rely on others—an important part of the group's identity. Moreover, by linking together issues, ideologies can also sometimes link together otherwise distinct identities in a mutually reinforcing way.

Take, for example, the NRA's aforementioned support for a strong military and its connection of that stance to gun rights; this issue linkage is ideological in the sense that it ties support for gun rights to support for the military based on the notion that both stances protect liberty. Further, support for gun rights and support for a large, powerful military are not just issue stances but can also be the basis of identities. By linking these issue stances together through ideology, the NRA can also link together their associated identities.

In this case, the NRA does so by using support for the military to reinforce its portrayal of gun owners as patriotic defenders of freedom and the American tradition—gun owners are brave and heroic, just like soldiers.

This issue connection suggests that the gun owner identity is politically aligned with identification as a veteran or, more broadly, as a proud American. This sort of identity alignment—in which multiple identities held by individuals have the same political orientation— has been shown to strengthen each of the identities individually.[31] By creating an ideology that goes beyond just gun rights, then, the NRA is effectively able to link its gun owner identity to other politically relevant identities in a mutually reinforcing way.

This insight about linked identities helps explain some facets of gun ownership's place in American politics that are not entirely intuitive. When the NRA connects gun rights and crime, for example, it frequently does so in a way that connects gun ownership—and the identity associated with it—to white racial identity. One way it does this is by supporting harsh crime control policies that historically have been championed by racially regressive politicians and that have, in practice, been used to target and disproportionately harm racial minorities.[32] Mocking what it describes as "a catch-and-release criminal justice system," for example, the NRA has mobilized its members in support of state laws mandating that "if you commit three serious crimes you're put away for life."[33]

Moreover, the NRA's crime-related appeals seem designed to enhance the extent to which white people feel threatened by crime and suggest that gun ownership is a way to address this threat; it has warned, for example, of women "being terrorized and violated by thugs" while simultaneously noting, "we want everyone to realize that they have a constitutional and God-given right to protect themselves and their families" using guns.[34] By linking gun ownership and support for gun rights to both fear of crime and racially motivated crime policies, the NRA effectively links gun owner identity to white racial identity. This linkage helps makes sense of why—as other scholars have discovered—regressive views on race are statistically associated with opposition to gun control.[35] More broadly, this type of linkage also sheds light on the presence and role of gun owners at white nationalist gatherings like the August 2017 "Unite the Right" rally in Charlottesville, Virginia.

Ideology—and the NRA's active role in creating it—has been a crucial determinant of the organization's relationship with the Republican Party and its place in the conservative movement. The existence of a shared ideology decreases the number of political issues that NRA supporters disagree on. This broad political unification increases the group's attractiveness to activists and politicians; shared preferences across issues (not just gun rights) can lead to preference for the same candidates, and so to greater electoral impact than if members were pulled in different directions by competing issues.

Especially when combined with the political intensity associated with the identity described earlier, this unity makes gun owners a particularly valuable demographic to political parties and ideological activists. The NRA lacked a clear home in the party system for much of its existence and, in any case, had good reason to avoid partisan politics. When both party politics and the organization's internal incentives began to change in the 1960s and 1970s, however, it was well positioned to align with conservative activists and GOP politicians; the shared ideology and group identity that existed among many NRA supporters made them a clear fit in and attractive target of the insurgent New Right conservative movement and the Republican politicians associated with it.

The Alignment of Groups and Parties

In the summer of 2019, public pressure for new gun regulations soared following a string of deadly mass shootings, including two (in El Paso, Texas, and in Dayton, Ohio) that occurred only a few hours apart. Following the shootings, political leaders—including some Republicans—signaled that gun control might be on the table; Republican Senate Majority Leader Mitch McConnell, for example, acknowledged the public popularity of expanded background checks and said that they would be "front and center" during his chamber's next session.[36]

Even President Donald Trump seemed open to new regulations, telling reporters that "we have to have very meaningful background checks" in the wake of the shootings.[37] Yet less than two weeks later, his tone changed. Immediately after a thirty-minute phone call with NRA chief Wayne LaPierre, Trump used NRA talking points to make his support for gun rights clear. In so doing, he effectively closed the door on gun control, as new legislation wouldn't be possible if the president wouldn't sign it.[38] So, despite this momentum generated in the wake of the shootings, no new legislation was passed.

Trump's loyalty to the NRA was perhaps unsurprising given the important role the organization had played in electing him and other Republicans, providing key resources and infrastructure to support his generally disorganized 2016 campaign.[39] By the time Trump moved into the White House, the NRA's close relationship with the GOP was well known and understood. Yet for the first hundred-plus years of its existence, no such alliance existed. How and when did the NRA and Republicans become so close?

Many recent studies have argued that groups, formed together into coalitions, are central to political parties.[40] Although these accounts differ in the specifics, most share a general logic: groups have resources—voters, campaign volunteers, money, and so on—that are useful to politicians for winning elections. These groups care deeply about particular policy issues—such as gun rights—which they are eager for politicians to advance. Collective action is required; politicians need the support of numerous groups to win elections, and groups need the support of numerous politicians to advance their policy interests. Coalitions of politicians therefore form alliances with coalitions of policy-demanding groups; the groups provide the politicians with resources that help them gain and maintain office, and the politicians advance the groups' policy goals. These alliances are central to contemporary political parties.

This group-centric view of parties—which pushes back on a politician-centric view that focuses more on elections (the central interest of politicians) than policymaking (the central interest of organized groups)[41]—helps us understand, on a general level, why alliances between groups like the NRA and parties like the GOP

exist, as well as the functions they serve. It also helps us understand why parties sometimes advance the more extreme policy preferences of groups like the NRA—which demand policy results in exchange for the resources they provide—rather than the more moderate preferences of most voters (which politician-centric views would expect parties to prioritize).[42] But it also raises lots of important—and largely unanswered—questions.

Why and how do particular groups choose to enter the realm of ideological and partisan politics rather than maintaining independence? Would groups not be better served by having each party *compete* for their support? And assuming that they *do* want to join a party coalition, what factors make particular groups ripe for incorporation into one party or the other? Finally, what determines the timing of groups' entry into party coalitions?[43]

In order to explain how parties and groups align, we need to better understand the characteristics of groups' mass-level supporters (which shape a group's attractiveness to and fit within a party coalition), the broader political environment (which structures groups' incentives and opportunities), and the motivations of group leaders (which determine how groups respond to changing environments).

THE REPUBLICAN PARTY AND THE NRA

Party-group alignment[44] describes the set of conditions that together lead to a durable, ongoing alliance between a group and a party—for instance, the alignment that exists between the Republican Party and the NRA. Party-group alignment in this case involved the confluence of (1) the NRA's gun-centric worldview, which made gun owners a politically attractive demographic group well positioned to join a party coalition; (2) shifting institutional conditions, which provided the NRA with both an incentive and an opportunity to join such a coalition; and (3) entrepreneurial action by a group of NRA leaders, which enabled the organization to shift directions and enter a new partisan phase of its history.

Although not sufficient to cause its alignment with the GOP on their own, the NRA's ideational resources—its identity and ideology—were crucial to this process. These resources can be described as *mass-level inputs*—or to put it more simply, as ingredients central to the first condition listed above, which requires resonance between supporters of a group and of a party. Because of their shared worldview, gun owners are unusually politically unified and active in politics, and have long held an ideology that makes them neatly fit in contemporary conservatism. These characteristics facilitated their entry into the Republican Party.

Despite this long-held political worldview, however, the NRA has not always been a partisan group, in large part due to institutional conditions that rendered it both unable to form an alliance with a party and uninterested in doing so. For much of the twentieth century, gun control was a crosscutting issue and, as a result, the NRA—while politically active—was not a clear fit in either party. Nor was it interested in joining a party coalition; the substantial financial support it received from the federal government—support that might have been in jeopardy if it became aligned with one party—discouraged taking sides.

But as the NRA's efforts to defeat gun control became more controversial and federal support dried up, the organization no longer had an incentive to remain independent. As the group was moving out of its quasi-governmental phase, other institutional conditions also encouraged a partisan shift. An insurgent conservative movement called the New Right rose to prominence, gaining substantial influence within the Republican Party while advancing a platform that—by uniting conservative stances on social issues with support for small government, hawkish foreign policy, and harsh crime control policies—aligned very well with the gun-centric worldview the NRA had been advancing for several decades. Gun owners were very attractive to Republican politicians and the New Right as a result of both their political intensity and their ideological fit with the movement.

An entrepreneurial group of NRA members with ties to the New Right saw the opportunity this fit provided. In the 1977 "Revolt at Cincinnati," they seized control of the organization, overpowering the NRA's leading officials who hoped to maintain the organization's long-standing nonpartisan approach to politics. With this, the NRA entered its partisan phase.

The group's relationship with the New Right and the Republican Party quickly deepened, with the NRA formally embracing partisan politics in 1980 by endorsing Ronald Reagan for president. The NRA and the GOP have continually grown closer in the decades since; the NRA now almost exclusively supports Republican candidates, and its members have become increasingly reliable Republican voters. Moreover, the Republican Party strongly supports both gun rights and the NRA's view of the Second Amendment. Finally, Republican voters—regardless of their gun ownership status—are increasingly opposed to gun control. In this sense, the alignment of the NRA and the GOP has given the NRA access to an even greater base of people, enabling it to further strengthen its ideational resources; in other words, identity, ideology, and party alignment have become mutually reinforcing.

HOW PARTY ALIGNMENT ENHANCES THE NRA'S POWER

To what extent is the party-group alignment of the NRA and the GOP *desirable* for the NRA? The experience of some groups—such as African Americans and unions, whose loyalty to the Democratic Party has not always been rewarded with policy achievements—suggests that groups may want to avoid ideological and/or partisan incorporation, lest they become "captured" by a party—that is, become so tied up with it that the competing party is uninterested in gaining their support. When this happens, the captured group cannot credibly threaten defection, which enables the leaders of its own party to deprioritize its policy preferences when they deem it in their interest to do so.

Despite African Americans' loyalty to the Democratic Party, for instance, Bill Clinton generally distanced himself from them on the campaign trail in the 1990s and—in an attempt to win over white moderates—advanced a policy agenda that, at best, largely ignored the interests of African American voters (and that, at worst, worked against their interests).[45] For some groups, the risk of this sort of capture may outweigh the benefits of being incorporated into a party coalition; AARP (originally known as the American Association of Retired Persons), for example, advocates very effectively on behalf of older Americans and has historically been careful about remaining nonpartisan—a position that has likely magnified its influence. However, this does not seem—or, at least, has not so far seemed—to be the case for the NRA, which has been able to consistently use its alignment with the Republican Party to protect and advance its policy interests.

The NRA's avoidance of capture is likely a result of its maintenance of what political scientist Daniel Schlozman calls a high level of "independent movement capacity"—the ability to politically direct and mobilize its supporters into action independently of the party—which may enable it to maintain leverage over GOP politicians.[46] Further, the NRA prior to the late 2010s provided campaign support to a nonnegligible number of pro-gun Democrats. Although the bulk of its support goes to Republicans, its willingness to sometimes support Democrats—and to punish Republicans who fell out of line with its agenda[47]—likely also provided the NRA with leverage over the GOP.[48]

Regardless of why the NRA has avoided capture, it is clear that the organization's position in the GOP has consistently enabled it to advance its policy commitments, most notably by exerting substantial control over the legislative agenda. Before its alignment with the GOP, the NRA often defeated or weakened proposed gun regulations by launching massive mobilization campaigns against them. Following its alignment with the GOP, however, the NRA has not had to undertake such efforts very frequently; the widespread recognition that gun control proposals are likely dead on arrival if Republicans control either the White House or at least one branch of Congress has discouraged policymakers from even pursuing such proposals.

Beyond agenda control, the NRA's position in the Republican Party has also enabled it to influence politics in ways that are less visible during policy battles—for instance, favorable judicial and bureaucratic nominations that give it at least some amount of control over how existing gun laws are interpreted and enforced. The NRA, for example, began playing an active role in Supreme Court confirmation hearings in the 2000s, and Donald Trump's nominations of pro-gun Justices Brett Kavanaugh and Neil Gorsuch—whom the NRA publicly supported—were seen by many as rewards for the organization's efforts.[49] Outside of the court system, the NRA has also played an active role in undermining the Bureau of Alcohol, Tobacco, and Firearms (BATF), which enforces gun laws; it has pushed its allies in Congress to restrict the enforcement actions BATF is allowed to take and successfully blocked one of President Obama's nominees for BATF director. President Trump didn't even bother to nominate someone to lead BATF until several years into his presidency.[50] While I focus on legislative policy battles in this book, the NRA's influence—as these examples demonstrate—shows up in other contexts as well.

The NRA, Donald Trump, and the Nature of Political Parties

The alignment between the NRA and the GOP came into even greater focus with the 2016 election of Donald Trump, due in large part to the NRA's relationship with Trump and Trump's Republican Party. This relationship with Trump demonstrates how identity, ideology, and party-group alignment are interrelated, and how they help explain the NRA's place in contemporary politics.

The already close relationship of the NRA and GOP reached new heights during and after the 2016 election cycle. The NRA's 2016 endorsement of Trump came much earlier in the cycle than its endorsements of previous Republican presidential candidates,[51] and it spent more money in support of Trump than it ever has in support of a single candidate.[52] Trump, in turn, became the first sitting president since Ronald Reagan to speak at the NRA's annual meeting, doing so in 2017, 2018, and 2019.[53]

At first blush, the NRA's enthusiasm for Trump—an ostentatious billionaire from New York City who had previously supported gun control—may seem odd. Trump was in many ways more similar to individuals villainized by the NRA—like Michael Bloomberg and George Soros, whom it lambasted as globalist, big-city elitists— than to the prototypical gun owner depicted in the *American Rifleman*. Given these contradictions, what drew the NRA and Trump together?

One major factor was that Trump did not simply support gun rights, but instead advanced a political worldview remarkably similar to the long-held worldview of the NRA and its supporters. The bond between Trump and the NRA, in other words, went much deeper than a shared view on a single issue—it involved a unified set of first, guiding principles fundamental to their approach to politics. Trump's attacks on the media, his brand of nationalistic populism (in which he argued that America must be protected from globalist elites), his regressive views on race and gender, and his willingness to sometimes engage in antisystem rhetoric (implying that a deep state is working against the interests of real Americans) all aligned with themes associated with the NRA's contemporary worldview. In this sense, Trump's election did not just advance the NRA's gun rights policy agenda; it went much further than that, bringing its broader perspective on politics and society to one of the most powerful offices in the world. This made the NRA's relationship with Trump deeper and more expansive than its relationship with previous Republican leaders.

The NRA, in a sense, laid the foundation that enabled Trump's rise by disseminating a worldview remarkably similar to Trumpism prior to Trump entering politics. As a result, it is perhaps unsurprising that—despite his personal background and prior support for gun control—gun owners strongly supported Trump's 2016 campaign and continued to approve of his job performance at an unusually high rate after he took office. Put simply, one must take account of gun ownership's status as an important political identity in order to understand both Trump's rise and the NRA's status as a pillar of the contemporary Republican coalition.

The NRA's place in the Republican Party during the Trump years also has some broader lessons about how identity, ideology, and party-group alignment can come together to shape individuals' political outlooks. Beyond its linkage to support for Trump, gun ownership—along with NRA membership and adoption of the gun owner social identity—has also been statistically and symbolically linked to a number of other group memberships and social identities similarly associated with support for Trump and the GOP, including white racial identity, traditional masculine identity, Evangelical Christian identity, and rural identity.[54] Although these relationships are complex (and the nuances of them explored later in the book), the takeaway is that holding one identity associated with Trumpism and the GOP—like gun ownership—increases individuals' likelihood of holding other such identities. The gun owner identity, in other words, has been linked to—and interrelated with—a number of other politically relevant group identities as a result of their mutual inclusion in a party coalition.

This close alignment of the identities associated with gun ownership, Trumpism, and the GOP not only highlights the NRA's importance in contemporary politics, but also speaks to the nature of party coalitions. It suggests that such coalitions can consist of more than just shared issue positions and institutional alliances; just as ideologies, as discussed earlier, can link together and reinforce group identities, so too can party coalitions. Along these lines, the contemporary Republican coalition is more than an alliance between groups with individual policy demands; it is also a collection of aligned identities in which the social psychological attachments associated with each group are tied together in a way that defines what it means to belong to the party. The NRA's relationship with the GOP and other conservative groups, in other words, sheds light on how parties and ideologies may fuse together and reinforce otherwise distinct group identities into a broader political identity.[55]

Finally, the nature of the contemporary Republican coalition and the process through which the NRA came to be at its center highlight the importance of understanding mass-level behavior when attempting to explain subsequent institutional shifts.[56] The NRA's alignment with the GOP did involve the formation of alliances between political elites, but those alliances were made possible by the NRA's cultivation of a group identity and ideology. The NRA's control of these ideational resources was crucial to its transition into and rise within the Republican Party; they made gun owners a politically attractive demographic group that fit neatly into a broader conservative coalition and eventually enabled the NRA to alter the nature of that coalition. The NRA's route into the Republican Party therefore helps us understand how party coalitions evolve over time, suggesting that mass-level, ideational developments can play a crucially important role.

The "Third Face" of Power

I noted in the previous chapter the difficulty political scientists have had identifying and explaining political power. One way they disentangle the complexities of power is to imagine it having three different dimensions, or "faces." The first face relates to which groups prevail in open, visible political conflict; in the context of gun politics, for instance, this first face of power is relevant when the NRA is able to defeat gun control proposals that are actively debated in Congress.[57] The second face relates to which groups influence the policy agenda; this dimension is relevant when the NRA, for example, is able to keep gun control off the legislative agenda altogether, thus advancing its agenda without actually engaging in open conflict.[58] Finally, the third face of power—which is much more difficult to observe and measure—relates to the ability to shape the political opinions, identities, and preferences of others.[59] Due in part to the challenge of studying it, scholars have given this third dimension of power far less attention than others.[60]

The NRA's development and use of ideational resources—that is, its creation of a worldview that informs the political attitudes and actions of its supporters—is an example of the third face of power in action. And as the case of the NRA demonstrates, manipulating the behavior of mass-level supporters—that is, using the third face of power—can produce significant influence.

Often, these three dimensions of power intersect. When the NRA mobilizes its supporters against legislative proposals by portraying their identities as under threat (the third face of power), it contributes to the demise of proposed gun regulations (the first face of power). Similarly, when policymakers avoid gun control altogether in anticipation of the blowback from gun owners that could shape subsequent elections, the NRA's influence shows up on the second face of power, but is an indirect product of the third. Finally, the NRA's ability to shape its supporters' behavior has been key to its influence within the Republican Party—influence that has further enhanced its ability to exercise all three faces of power, including agenda control, influence over nominations, and guidance of the ideological direction of the party.

The NRA's advancement of its pro-gun agenda across all three faces of power demonstrates the usefulness of the framework described in this chapter for understanding the nature and consequences of the group's influence; attention to its identity, ideology, and alignment with the Republican Party sheds light on the interrelated factors that have enabled the group to build tremendous political power. Each part of the framework must now be filled in. Chapter 3 begins this task by demonstrating how the NRA has politically weaponized gun owners through its cultivation of a group identity.

3

The Political Weaponization of Gun Owners

THE NRA AND GUN OWNERSHIP AS SOCIAL IDENTITY

> You would get a far better understanding if you approached us as if you were approaching one of the great religions of the world.
>
> —FORMER NRA EXECUTIVE VICE PRESIDENT WARREN CASSIDY
> DESCRIBING THE DEVOTION OF THE NRA AND ITS MEMBERS
> TO THE GUN RIGHTS CAUSE, 2001[1]

The hostility of most leftists in regard to the very notion that their fellow citizens might have a right to own firearms or to engage in the shooting sports is difficult for many of us to understand, until we realize it's not just about guns. It's about freedom and traditional American values. . . . What they really object to goes far beyond our ownership of firearms. They believe the traditional American individualist values that drove the nation's founders to limit the power of government and protect our right to defend ourselves must give way to a new

set of values that cedes governance to the state. In a very real
sense, their hostility to firearms and the Second Amendment
isn't about guns or violence or crime; it's about values.
—FORMER NRA PRESIDENT DAVID KEENE WRITING IN
THE *AMERICAN RIFLEMAN*, 2012[2]

For many American gun owners, firearms are not merely tools for
recreation and self-defense. Owning them is a powerful symbol that
represents who they are and what they value—including their political views. But why is this the case? And what role, exactly, has the
NRA played in establishing gun ownership as an identity?

This chapter answers these questions, detailing the process
through which the NRA has built a group identity and used it to
spur action on behalf of its agenda; as discussed in the last chapter,
this gun owner identity is one part of the political worldview the
NRA has developed among its supporters, working in conjunction
with the group's ideology (discussed in the next chapter).

Identity fuels the NRA's power. Shared identity is a key source of
the dedication and intense political activity of the NRA's pro-gun
constituency—activity that has enabled the NRA to launch effective
mass-mobilization campaigns on behalf of gun rights and pro-gun
candidates. (I will take a closer look at the campaigns themselves in
chapters 5 and 7.) Further, by shaping gun owners into an unusually
politically dedicated and active group, identity eventually made the
NRA's constituency a valuable demographic to conservative politicians and served as a key mass-level input that helped cause the
organization's alignment with the GOP.

The first few pages of the chapter discuss how I've gone about
studying the NRA's cultivation of an identity. I then present my
findings in two separate sections. The first provides a summary of
the chapter's main takeaways and the evidence that supports them;
this section provides general readers with sufficient detail to move
forward to subsequent chapters. The second—geared more toward
social scientists—goes "under the hood," covering similar material
but providing much more detail about the methods I use and the
mechanisms that are at play.

Measuring Identity Cultivation

To examine the NRA's cultivation of an identity, I first needed to develop a way to measure what it says to its supporters—what ideas does it convey to them about what it means to be a gun owner? I also needed a way to measure how those supporters feel about gun ownership and politics more broadly—how do their views fit with the ideas conveyed by the NRA?

To get at the first measure—the NRA's messages to its members—I turned to the group's flagship publication, the *American Rifleman* magazine. This publication—the NRA's original "official journal"—is very useful for understanding its communication with members. For one thing, a subscription is included with NRA membership, which means that it reaches a very large proportion of the group's members. Moreover, the magazine—published under its current name since 1923—has existed throughout my entire period of study; as a result, it provides me with a consistent, comparable measure of what the NRA has said to its members over a very long stretch of time.[3] In short, the *American Rifleman*'s long, continuous existence and widespread distribution make it an ideal data source for an over-time analysis of the NRA's political ideas and messaging. Over the course of a summer, with the help of a small team of librarians, I obtained a full run of the magazine covering the years 1930 to 2008. I scanned each issue to create a digital corpus that contains over nine hundred issues in total.

I was particularly interested in the *American Rifleman*'s editorials, which are typically written by the NRA's top official and are one of the primary ways through which NRA leadership directly addresses members. Their content is a very strong indicator of the NRA's priorities. But not all editorials are focused on gun control—some discuss competitive shooting, membership programs, and other less relevant matters. To identify the subset of relevant editorials, I used a machine learning technique called automated topic modeling.[4] The details of this process are described in the appendix, but the general idea is to identify what each of the editorials talks about— the topics they cover—based on patterns in the words they use. The model pulls together a set of topics—automatically categorizing the editorials—and provides a list of words that are most closely associated with each topic. It also provides a measure of the extent to which each editorial "belongs" to each topic.

Rather than assigning each editorial to one and only one topic, the model instead provides a measure of the proportion of each editorial that is associated with each of the topics. This is a useful feature given that editorials can—and typically do—discuss more than just one topic; a single editorial, for example, can discuss the Second Amendment *and* self-defense using guns *and* highlight new programs that the NRA is offering for its members. Moreover, the technique enables me to examine the relative prominence of each topic over time; the next chapter highlights the usefulness of this feature, exploring how the topics emphasized by the NRA have shifted in accordance with broader social and political changes.

The results of the topic modeling process are presented in table 3.1 (which lists the topics in no particular order); gun control-related topics are shaded. The table contains words that are common within each topic ("high probability"), as well as words that both frequently appear within a topic *and* are relatively uncommon in other topics ("FREX"—FRequent and EXclusive). The model doesn't automatically name the topics; I've labeled and described each of them based on both these words and a close reading of numerous editorials that, according to the model, best exemplify them. The analyses that follow include all editorials that are mostly focused on any combination of the four gun control-related topics.

The *American Rifleman* provides a useful measure of the ideas the NRA communicates to its supporters—but how can we tell whether those supporters are listening? This task is more difficult than it may initially seem. Although surveys of gun owners can be helpful, they don't exist for large portions of the long period I am interested in. Moreover, those that do exist are ill-equipped to answer many central questions regarding identity and ideology.

Given this lack of historical survey data, I instead use the *words* of gun owners to measure how they feel about guns and how their feelings have changed over time. More specifically, I collected all

TABLE 3.1. Summary of Topic Model of *American Rifleman* Editorials

Topic Label	Words	Brief Description
Shooting Sports and Military Preparedness	FREX: rifl, train, marksmanship, war, program, shooter, match, game, civilian, fire High Prob: nation, rifl, associ, shoot, program, train, will, war, time, servic	Focuses on the NRA's role in shooting sports and its original mission of developing the American public's marksmanship skills as a form of military preparedness. Peaks around World War II, reflecting the environment of the time and the NRA's postwar recruitment of veterans. Declines following the postwar period and does not pick back up during later wars, likely because by those wars the organization had expanded its mission beyond marksmanship and its formal government ties had weakened.
Membership Programs and Benefits	FREX: nra, member, membership, futur, generat, perri, editori, hold, help, nras High Prob: nra, member, year, can, one, take, now, will, million, come	Highlights the array of programs and benefits available to NRA members in order to encourage membership renewal and recruitment. Rises during the postwar period, when the NRA launched recruitment campaigns focused on WWII veterans, and in the mid-1980s and early 1990s when it sought to generate revenue via membership growth amidst financial struggles.
Gun Regulation	FREX: citizen, registr, propos, possess, weapon, regist, purchas, honest, author, govern High Prob: firearm, citizen, state, arm, gun, use, govern, person, nation, weapon	Addresses gun legislation in more general terms than other topics. Is also more stable over time than other topics, perhaps also due to its generality. Peaks during the 1960s, when gun regulation was debated and eventually enacted following several high-profile assassinations.

Topic	Words	Description
Crime, Self-Defense, and Guns	FREX: law, feder, control, crime, handgun, crimin, bill, owner, legisl, court High Prob: gun, law, feder, legisl, control, polic, crimin, crime, bill, firearm	Argues that guns are a solution to crime rather than a cause, that gun control makes crime easier, and advocates for harsh sentencing in lieu of restricting access to guns. Peaks during debates over gun regulation aimed at gangsters in the 1930s, the rise of "law and order" politics in the 1960s and early 1970s, and during the Clinton years, when both crime control and gun regulation were salient issues.
Second Amendment	FREX: citi, amend, vote, liberti, hous, presid, second, ban, magazin, declar High Prob: right, american, will, power, amend, peopl, citi, polit, constitut, bear	Advocates for an individual rights interpretation of the Second Amendment, which is said to be critical to freedom because it enables the people to defend themselves against an abusive state. Argues that the right to bear arms is the freedom that makes all other freedoms possible. Portrays the Second Amendment as a cornerstone of the American tradition. Has gradually increased in prominence since around 1960, and is now the most prominent topic overall.
Americanism and Guns	FREX: hunt, men, safeti, board, respons, hunter, educ, cours, recreat, accid High Prob: america, will, men, hunt, american, safeti, peopl, hunter, respons, one	Emphasizes the centrality of guns throughout US history. Was used to frame opposition to 1930s gun regulation attempts and to rally support for war preparation measures involving firearms training. Advocates limited government and hawkish foreign policy, and highlights the connection between guns and the outdoors. Like the Second Amendment topic, depicts guns as central to the American tradition and the protection of liberty, but emphasizes foreign threats rather than the threat of domestic tyranny. Peaks earliest; was the most prominent topic in early years but has declined since.

Note: Topics are named based on a close reading of example documents and each topic's "highest probability" and "FREX" words. These words are stemmed. "Highest probability" words are those most likely to appear within a topic. "FREX" words are those which are both common and exclusive to each topic; these words are very useful for labeling topics because they not only frequently appear in a topic but also are relatively distinct to that topic. See the appendix for more details.

the letters to the editor pertaining to gun control that were published from 1930 to 2008 in four major US newspapers (the *New York Times*, *Arizona Republic*, *Atlanta Journal-Constitution*, and *Chicago Tribune*), including letters written both in opposition to and in support of gun control (around 3,200 in total). Pro-gun letters to the editor are useful for examining the political discussions of those who oppose gun control because they are written by regular people—typically not elites or paid activists—who are nonetheless engaged enough to participate in politics in forms that go beyond voting. The things they say about gun control therefore likely represent the views of the group I am most interested in—gun owners who participate in politics on behalf of the gun rights cause.[5]

I examine the extent to which the contents of the pro-gun letters resemble the contents of *American Rifleman* editorials described above in a number of different ways. Do they show evidence of an identity? Do they associate gun ownership with the same personal characteristics and qualities? Do they discuss gun control regulations in similar ways? Do the pro-gun letters seem to adopt ideas from the NRA? Along the way, I also compare the *American Rifleman* editorials and pro-gun letters to the letters written in *support* of gun control, which provides a useful point of reference.[6]

How the NRA Builds and Uses Identity: Major Takeaways

First, I find evidence that the NRA has systematically used its membership communications and programs to advance an identity built around gun ownership. Eighty percent of *American Rifleman* editorials contain what I describe as "identity-forming language"—positive characteristics to describe gun owners and/or negative characteristics to describe those who support gun control. The NRA's consistent use of this sort of language (portraying gun owners as courageous, law-abiding, patriotic citizens who love freedom) suggests that its editorials systematically advance a particular notion of what it means to be a gun owner. In other words, they promote an identity. The NRA reinforces the notion that gun owners are a noble class of courageous, ordinary American citizens by juxtaposing them with gun control supporters, who are depicted in the *American Rifleman* as, among other things, phony, big-city elitists.

Moreover, I find that this identity—originating with the NRA— has been adopted by gun rights supporters and impacts how they view politics. A similarly high rate (64 percent) of pro-gun letters to newspaper editors use identity-forming language, which suggests that many gun rights supporters, following the NRA's lead, associate gun ownership with an identity and are motivated by that identity. This finding is bolstered by the results of public opinion polls from recent years that also demonstrate the existence of a meaningful identity associated with owning guns.

As a point of reference, I also compared the use of identity-forming language in the pro-gun letters to the use of such language in letters written by gun control supporters; I find scant evidence of a shared identity among gun control supporters.

Further, the specific language gun rights supporters use to describe themselves (and, to a slightly lesser extent, the language they use to describe gun control supporters) mirrors the language used by the NRA, and does so in delayed fashion. Particular words and phrases originate in NRA materials and then later appear in pro-gun letters. Moreover, the NRA's use of these words and phrases statistically predicts their future use in pro-gun letters. Together, this evidence strongly suggests that the NRA hasn't merely tapped into an existing gun owner identity—it has, in fact, created and shaped that identity.

Second, I find that the NRA explicitly connects the gun owner identity to politics by using it as the centerpiece of its discussion of gun control policies. When the NRA discusses gun regulations, it focuses on how such regulations would impact the identities, lifestyles, and values of gun owners rather than, for example, on evidence about whether the regulations would (or would not) be effective at reducing the misuse of firearms. About three quarters of NRA editorials that discuss gun control policies frame them this way, portraying them as an affront to who gun owners are rather than as merely unlikely to achieve particular policy objectives. In doing this, the NRA suggests that the identity is politically salient—that it's a useful lens through which gun owners can and should view political conflicts.

Here too I find evidence that the NRA's ideas have influenced the views of gun rights supporters. More than half of the pro-gun letters I analyzed use identity frames when they discuss gun control policies. The gun owner identity has become highly relevant to how they think about gun control. Rather than focusing on why gun control policies are flawed, letter writers are motivated by a sense that such policies are an affront to who they are as people.

There's strong evidence that these identity frames—particular arguments about how gun control relates to the gun owner identity— originated with the NRA and were later adopted by gun rights supporters. The first way I measure this is through a novel adaptation of a statistical technique often used in software designed to detect plagiarism. Specifically, I look at the extent to which pro-gun letters to the editor (particularly those that contain identity frames) systematically adopt the language of—or "plagiarize"—NRA editorials. I find that gun rights supporters, in pro-gun letters, do indeed statistically adopt the NRA's identity-framing language over time.

I also measure the relationship between the NRA's identity frames and its supporters' identity frames in a qualitative fashion, tracing specific arguments back to their origins. I again find evidence of particular frames having been introduced by the NRA and later adopted by pro-gun letters. The NRA, for example, has closely associated the gun owner identity with a particular view of the Second Amendment (more on this in the next chapter); in this view, the Second Amendment symbolizes many of the virtues of gun owners, including patriotism, self-sufficiency, and respect for the American tradition. Gun control proposals, framed by the NRA as attacks on the Second Amendment, are thus seen as an affront to gun owners themselves. These ideas about the Second Amendment—which were first introduced by the NRA—are now commonly evoked by gun rights supporters when they explain their opposition to gun control laws.[7]

Third, I find evidence that the NRA actively disseminates this identity not just through its publications but also through its firearms-related programs—marksmanship courses, gun safety instruction for children and adults, concealed carry training, and more—which draw large numbers of participants and which have historically enabled the organization to expand its ranks. The *American Rifleman*, in other words, isn't the only way through which gun owners might be exposed to the NRA's identity-building efforts; instead, the organization uses its training programs—most of which are not explicitly political—as a way to introduce more people to American gun culture and further spread its identity. Indeed, while the NRA's courses provide participants with valuable skills and knowledge, the organization also sees them as a way to further enhance its political power by spreading politically charged notions about what it means to be a gun owner. (And to the extent that they help the NRA attract new members, they *also* increase the number of people exposed to the identity appeals in the *American Rifleman*, since it is included with membership.)

Lastly, I find evidence that the NRA has used identity to mobilize its supporters into politics by portraying gun owners' way of life as under threat from gun control proposals and imploring its members to take action in its defense. The NRA, for example, described a gun control proposal introduced by the Clinton Administration in response to the 1999 massacre at Columbine High School as amounting to a "hateful and bigoted war . . . against American firearms owners." It said that President Clinton was pursuing "what can only be called a 'cultural cleansing'—specifically targeting the bedrock Second Amendment beliefs of firearms owners for extinction." And it then told it members, "Every one of us has to act. Urge your Congressman and Senators to oppose and vote against the Clinton gun control package."[8]

These sorts of appeals are common; around two-thirds of *American Rifleman* editorials portray gun ownership as under threat, and more than one-third explicitly ask NRA members to take political action on behalf of gun rights. Moreover, I find that these two features are systematically linked together; editorials that portray gun rights as threatened are statistically more likely than others to also contain calls to action.

These appeals are effective at rallying gun owners. Using evidence I collected from numerous presidential archives, I find that the number of letters sent to politicians in opposition to gun control (many of which contain themes from *American Rifleman* editorials and clearly demonstrate feelings of threat) spikes immediately after identity-based mobilization appeals from the NRA—a pattern that suggests that the organization's tactics are effective at rallying action.

This, in broad stokes, is how we can see that the NRA has not only tried but also succeeded in cultivating a group identity among its supporters. Below, I provide much greater detail on how I came to these conclusions; the next chapter dives into the second part of the NRA's worldview—ideology.

Going into Greater Detail about the NRA's Cultivation of Identity

The remainder of the chapter tests a series of expectations about how groups like the NRA can cultivate identities; in so doing, I provide the details that support the conclusions that are summarized above. These expectations are derived from the four-step identity-building process I discussed last chapter, which was illustrated using an editorial by NRA chief Wayne LaPierre. In this chapter, I treat each step of that process as an expectation about what we would observe from the NRA if it has, in fact, cultivated an identity among its members. I then systematically test those expectations by analyzing the words and actions of both the NRA and its supporters.

As a reminder, the four steps I described last chapter are (1) cultivation, (2) politicization, (3) dissemination, and (4) identity-based mobilization. To be clear, these steps are both recurring—in the sense that the NRA consistently recruits new members and seeks to reinforce the identity among current members—and can be overlapping—in the sense that individual appeals to members can simultaneously achieve more than one of the steps. Nonetheless, breaking the process into multiple steps is helpful for specifying and measuring each of its components. A number of narrower expectations—which, as noted last chapter, are derived from social psychology—can be applied to this framework and are tested below.

First, to *create* a collective group identity and make that identity psychologically *accessible*,[9] I expect the NRA's communications to members to frequently emphasize a set of positive characteristics that apply to gun owners (the in-group) and a set of perceived negative qualities that apply to those who support gun control (the out-group). I expect the political discussions of gun rights supporters to use the same set of characteristics to describe the in-group and out-group.

Second, to *politicize* the gun owner identity—to make it psychologically *fit* in political contexts—I expect the NRA to portray the gun debate as a battle between competing identities and the values associated with them. I expect gun rights supporters to use similar identity frames when discussing gun regulation, describing it in terms of its impacts on their lives and identities rather than in terms of its likelihood of achieving particular policy goals.

Third, to more widely *disseminate* the identity, I expect the NRA to strategically grow its membership programs in order to expand the number of people connected to its social group and to directly include politically charged identity appeals in these programs.

Fourth, to *mobilize* political participation, I expect the NRA to portray the gun owner identity as under threat and to connect depictions of threat to explicit calls to action on its behalf. And I expect gun owners to be highly responsive to such calls.

Identity Cultivation

To assess my **first** expectation—that the NRA uses its membership communications to cultivate a group identity—I coded (i.e., categorized) each *American Rifleman* editorial in the gun control subset based on whether it uses *identity-forming language*; such language consists of (1) positive characteristics to describe gun owners and/or (2) negative characteristics to describe individuals or groups who are perceived as opponents of gun rights.[10]

TABLE 3.2. Identity-Forming Language in Gun Control Editorials and Letters to the Editor

Document Type	Identity-Forming Language	In-Group Positive	Out-Group Negative
NRA Editorials	80%	55%	66%
	(338/422)	(232/422)	(280/422)
Pro-Gun Letters	64%	43%	38%
	(1366/2135)	(909/2135)	(813/2135)
Anti-Gun Letters	39%	7%	36%
	(401/1018)	(71/1018)	(362/1018)

Note: The "Identity-Forming Language" column depicts the portion of editorials or letters that discuss either in-group positive or out-group negative characteristics, or both. The "In-Group Positive" and "Out-Group Negative" are more specific and depict the extent to which each type of identity-forming language is used.

Table 3.2 shows that 80 percent of editorials contain identity-forming language of some sort, indicating that the NRA very frequently uses language that we would expect from a group engaged in identity building.

I coded the newspaper letters to the editor in the same fashion in order to assess the extent to which gun rights supporters seem to share a collective identity. As table 3.2 shows, a substantial 64 percent of pro-gun letters use identity language—a rate consistent with the existence of a shared gun owner identity. It's no surprise that this rate of usage is lower than in the NRA editorials; the average letter to the editor—at 168 words—is much shorter than the average editorial—754 words—so the latter format allows more space for writers to exhibit particular characteristics. Moreover, given my theory that the NRA is the source of this identity, it would make sense for its appeals to exhibit particular characteristics at a greater rate than the appeals of its supporters—the targets of its identity cultivation efforts.

I also examined the letters written in *favor* of gun control in order to compare them to the letters written by gun rights supporters; I expect gun control supporters, who presumably do not share a collective identity, to use identity-based language much less frequently.[11] As table 3.2 shows, "pro-gun" writers do indeed use identity language at a substantially greater rate than "anti-gun"[12] writers—64 percent versus 39 percent. This difference is statistically significant.

Revealingly, the second and third columns of table 3.2 show that pro-gun and anti-gun letters use negative out-group language— language describing those on the other side of the gun debate in negative terms—at similar rates, but that pro-gun letters use in-group positive language—which describes those on one's own side of the debate in positive terms—far more frequently than anti-gun letters. Closer inspection reveals that the primary reason for the relatively high rates of out-group negative language in the anti-gun letters is the shared perception of a pro-gun villain: the NRA.

Although perhaps unsurprising, this pattern provides important additional evidence of a gun owner identity. Existing research indicates that positive feelings toward an in-group are a more prominent aspect of group attachment than negative feelings toward out-groups.[13] Along these lines, whereas pro-gun writers perceive both an "us"—an in-group—and a "them"—one or more out-groups—anti-gun writers do not have a common identity—they lack an "us" and, therefore, a shared sense of identity.

Recent public opinion polls support this general finding. Half of gun owners, as of 2017, say that owning a gun is either very or somewhat important to their overall identity, with even higher numbers among NRA members.[14] Other research identifies a very strong "issue identity" associated with opposition to gun control, especially among pro-gun Republicans, and—in a separate paper I coauthored Adam Howat and Jacob Rothschild—we find strong evidence of a shared identity among gun owning survey respondents.[15] This makes sense given additional evidence that gun ownership is strongly tied to one's social network, with ownership rates statistically significantly higher among those who are part of a "social gun culture."[16]

However, the NRA's use of identity-forming language, combined with the existence of a group identity among gun owners, does not by itself demonstrate that the NRA has actually played an active role in cultivating the identity. If the NRA is responsible for building the identity that exists among gun owners, then the identity language used by pro-gun letter writers should closely align with the language used in NRA editorials. To assess this, I examined the *content* of the editorials and letters that contain identity-based language—do the characteristics used by gun owners to describe themselves and their opponents mirror the characteristics used by the NRA?

Editorials in the *American Rifleman* describe gun owners as average citizens who obey the law and love America. The ten most frequently used descriptors are law-abiding, peaceable, patriotic, courageous, honest, average citizen(s), ordinary citizen(s), brave, freedom-loving, and reputable. At least one of these words or phrases appears in 80 percent of editorials that use in-group positive language.

As expected, the pro-gun letters to the editor use very similar characteristics to describe gun owners. One or more of the words in the set described above appear in 79 percent of pro-gun letters that use in-group positive language, nearly identical to the 80 percent in the *American Rifleman*. As a point of reference, only 13 percent of anti-gun letters with identity-forming language use at least one of these words, and often do so only when referencing the ways that gun owners describe themselves. Given that most of the in-group words defined above are not inherently related to gun ownership, the close alignment between use in NRA editorials and pro-gun—but not anti-gun—letters is strong evidence of a connection between NRA appeals and the appeals of gun rights supporters.

The NRA editorials describing out-groups in negative terms vary more than those describing the in-group. The perceived opponents of gun rights consist of several distinct groups, the three most prominent of which are politicians, the media, and lawyers. Politicians are frequently described as bureaucrat(ic), reformer(s), big city, urban, elitist, special interests, tyrannical, and "F" troop (which refers to politicians who have received "F" ratings from the NRA). At least one of those words, and/or politician(s), appears in 48 percent of editorials that use out-group negative language. The media is frequently described as lying, cowardly, elitist, phony, cynical, devious, shameless, and propagandist. At least one of those words, and/or the word "media," appears in 65 percent of editorials that use out-group negative language. Lawyers are described as greedy, fat-cat, opportunistic, big city, urban, elitist, phony, cynical, and lying. At least one of those words, and/or the word "lawyer(s)," appears in 42 percent of editorials that use out-group negative language. A set of more general characteristics is used to portray gun regulation proponents as un-American, including fanatic, extremist, radical, hysterical, anti-liberty, communist, tyrannical, globalist, and internationalist. Finally, gun control supporters are described as "antigunners" and "the gun ban crowd." At least one of the characteristics described here appears in 84 percent of editorials that use out-group negative language.

There is again a clear—although smaller—relationship between the *American Rifleman*'s out-group descriptors and pro-gun writers' descriptors. At least one of the words described above appears in 35 percent of pro-gun letters that use out-group negative language (versus 23 percent in anti-gun letters with identity-based language). The politician subset appears in 12 percent, the media subset in 19 percent, and the lawyer subset in 6 percent. This outcome is not surprising given the previously mentioned findings that in-group favoritism is more crucial to identity attachment than out-group derogation.

Of course, if the NRA is the source of the identity, we would also expect particular themes used in both the NRA editorials and the pro-gun letters to first appear in NRA materials and then later be adopted by gun rights supporters in the letters. In other words, if the NRA has indeed *created* the identity (and not simply tapped into a preexisting, independently developed identity), the words and ideas it uses should predict the subsequent words and ideas of its supporters.

I examined this in two different ways. First, I identified a set of phrases that are used in both NRA editorials and pro-gun letters, and then determined which set of documents they first appeared in. These phrases consist of the five most *distinctive* descriptors used by both the NRA and its supporters to describe either gun rights advocates or gun control advocates; by "distinctive," I mean those descriptors that are most uncommon in broader discourse.[17]

Why focus on the most distinctive descriptors? These phrases are analytically useful for testing my claim that the NRA is the primary *source* of the gun owner social identity. Whereas both the NRA and letter writers might borrow common in-group or out-group descriptors such as "brave" or "radical" from general social discourse, their shared use of words that are relatively unique to the firearms community (e.g., "anti-gunner")—and the origination of such terms in NRA materials—would much more clearly demonstrate that the NRA is responsible for creating the identity held by its supporters. As table 3.3 shows, of the five most distinctive identity phrases used by the NRA and its supporters, four originated in *American Rifleman* editorials and then later appeared in letters to the editor.

Second, I also estimated a series of statistical models that examine whether the NRA's use of each phrase in one year predicts its use by pro-gun letter writers in any of the following three years; in other words, I assessed whether there's a statistically significant relationship between the NRA's use of each descriptor and its supporters' *later* use of it (which is referred to as a "lagged" model, because the measure of the NRA's use of a phrase is lagged back to a prior year).[18] The results—shown in table 3.3—indicate that the NRA's use of three of the five phrases predicts their subsequent use by pro-gun letter writers (even when statistically accounting for each phrase's past use by letter writers themselves, which is likely a determinant of their future use of it).[19] These results are clear evidence that gun rights supporters have adopted an identity created by the NRA; indeed, when considered together, the likelihood of three of five statistical models (including four of fifteen total coefficients they produced) being statistically significant in the absence of responsiveness is very low.

TABLE 3.3. Relationship between NRA's Use of Distinctive In-Group/Out-Group Phrases and Their Use in Pro-Gun Letters to the Editor

Phrase	First appearance in an identity-framing document	Significant Effect in a Lagged Year	American Rifleman 1-Year Lag Coefficient (p-value)	American Rifleman 2-Year Lag Coefficient (p-value)	American Rifleman 3-Year Lag Coefficient (p-value)
Anti-gunners	American Rifleman (December 1975)	✓	–	–	0.219 (0.020)
Average citizens	American Rifleman (February 1936)	✗	–	–	–
Freedom-loving	American Rifleman (May 1944)	✗	–	–	–
Ordinary citizens	American Rifleman (March 1948)	✓	–	0.303 (0.083)	–
Law-abiding	New York Times (September 1931)	✓	0.203 (0.050)	0.249 (0.020)	–

Note: Table depicts the origin of the most distinctive in-group/out-group phrases and the results of lagged linear probability models predicting the presence of each phrase in pro-gun letters to the editor. Dependent variables are binary variables indicating whether a phrase appeared in a pro-gun letter to the editor in a given year for each year in the dataset (1930–2008). Separate models were estimated for each phrase. The independent variables presented in the table for each model are lagged binary variables indicating whether the phrase appeared in an *American Rifleman* editorial in each of the three previous years. Also included in each model, as controls, were a binary variable indicating whether a phrase appeared in the *American Rifleman* in the same year, as well as lagged binary variables indicating whether the phrase appeared in a pro-gun letter to the editor in each of the three previous years. All coefficients for variables included in the table that are significant at the p < 0.1 level are included.

Identity Politicization

To assess my **second** expectation—that the NRA has *politicized* the identity described above—I first examined the extent to which the NRA has made identity frames a centerpiece of its discussion of gun regulations.[20] The second column of table 3.4 lists the proportion of editorials, pro-, and anti-gun letters that explicitly discuss gun control policies. The third column depicts the extent to which those documents frame policy in identity terms; that is, the extent to which gun regulation is discussed in terms of its impact on the lifestyles and values of gun owners or, in the case of anti-gun letters, on the lifestyles and values of the letter writers and groups to

TABLE 3.4. Identity and Policy Appeals in Gun Control Editorials and Letters to the Editor

Document Type	Policy Discussion	Identity Frame
NRA Editorials	90%	74%
	(380/422)	(283/380)
Pro-Gun Letters	96%	54%
	(2054/2135)	(1110/2054)
Anti-Gun Letters	95%	23%
	(967/1018)	(224/967)

Note: The denominators in the "Policy Discussion" column are all documents within each category. The denominators in the "Identity Frame" column—which captures the proportion of policy-discussing documents that use identity frames—are all documents that discuss policy within each category.

which they belong. The overwhelming majority of NRA editorials (90 percent) discuss policy and, as expected, a large proportion of them (74 percent) frame policy in identity terms.

Similarly, pro-gun letter writers also frequently frame policies in identity terms; as table 3.4 shows, 54 percent of such letters that discuss policy do so using identity frames. This proportion is, as before, smaller than the corresponding proportion in the *American Rifleman* (74 percent), which is again to be expected, yet still substantively large on its own terms and large relative to anti-gun letters: as shown in the third column of table 3.4, the latter frame policy discussion in identity terms less than half as often. Whereas pro-gun letters tend to focus on the impacts that gun regulations have on the lives of gun owners, anti-gun letters more frequently focus on potential crime reduction and typically do so in abstract (as opposed to personal) terms.

Again, however, the use of identity frames in both NRA editorials and pro-gun letters does not by itself demonstrate that the NRA is responsible for politicizing the identity. If the NRA is responsible for connecting the identity to politics, gun rights supporters should use identity frames that are very similar to those used by the NRA. Moreover, particular frames should originate in NRA editorials and appear in pro-gun letters later on.

To ascertain the similarity and responsiveness of gun rights supporters' identity frames to the NRA's, I created an original measurement technique that uses a method—called cosine similarity[21]—that is common in plagiarism detection software. This somewhat complicated method ultimately produces a simple measure of the similarity of two documents; the higher the score (which ranges from 0 to 1), the greater the extent to which one document has replicated the contents of the other. The technique I created uses these cosine similarity scores in an over-time fashion, measuring the extent to which documents from one period of time are similar to documents from a subsequent period of time. In short, the technique—called cosine similarity responsiveness—is a systematic way to measure whether the NRA's ideas in one period of time are then adopted by its supporters in the next period of time.

To go about producing this measure, I first broke the NRA editorials and pro-gun letters to the editor into separate time buckets of various lengths based on the year in which they were published—I grouped them into 8 buckets of ~10 years of documents, 6 buckets of ~13 years, 5 buckets of ~16 years, and 5 buckets of uneven lengths with break points based on important, theoretically driven moments in the history of the NRA.[22] I then measured the cosine similarity—the common word usage—of all NRA editorials from one time period and all pro-gun letters from the next. In other words, I aggregated all of the editorials from each period and measured their similarity with all of the pro-gun letters from each of the subsequent periods (e.g., the similarity of *American Rifleman* editorials from the 1930s and pro-gun letters from the 1940s, then the similarity of editorials from the 1940s and letters from the 1950s, and so on). I call these "lagged *American Rifleman* scores" because they refer to the cosine similarity scores of pro-gun letters from one point in time and *American Rifleman* editorials lagged back to the prior period. I then reversed this procedure, measuring the similarity of pro-gun letters from one period and NRA editorials from the next period; I call these "lagged letter scores."

To single out the impact of NRA editorials on pro-gun letters, I first subtracted the lagged letter scores from the lagged *American Rifleman* scores for each period; this identified the net impact of the NRA editorials on the pro-gun letters by period, above and beyond any reverse impact that the letters have on the editorials. I then calculated the average net difference across periods and used another statistical technique[23] to produce confidence intervals, which provide a measure of statistical significance.

Identifying the "net" impact that the NRA editorials have on the pro-gun letters is crucial for several reasons. First, because both sets of documents discuss the same topic (gun control), they would be expected to use some common words at relatively high rates[24]—and therefore produce high cosine similarity scores—even in the absence of any true responsiveness; identifying the net responsiveness of one set of documents to the other effectively cancels out these effects. Second, the procedure enables me to identify the influence that the NRA has on its supporters above and beyond any reverse effects that its supporters might have on it; such reverse effects are plausible, as one can imagine the NRA potentially picking up on and borrowing useful arguments it notices its members making.

To be clear, a positive average difference that is statistically significant (i.e., distinguishable from zero) would indicate that the contents of pro-gun letters systematically respond over time to the contents of *American Rifleman* editorials (whereas a difference that is not different from zero would indicate that there is no systematic directional relationship between the content of NRA editorials and pro-gun letters). In other words, if the confidence intervals in the figure below do not overlap with zero, then we have evidence that gun owners adopt the NRA's ideas.

As figure 3.1 shows, the average difference between the lagged *American Rifleman* scores and the lagged letter scores is indeed positive and statistically significant for every time grouping, both within the subset of documents that use identity frames and across all of the documents. Further methodological refinement of the cosine similarity responsiveness technique is needed in order to substantively interpret the size of the contrast score depicted on the y-axis (i.e., the "amount" of responsiveness, as measured using cosine similarity). Nonetheless, the statistically significant difference for each grouping indicates that gun rights supporters systematically adopt the language of the NRA over time, providing

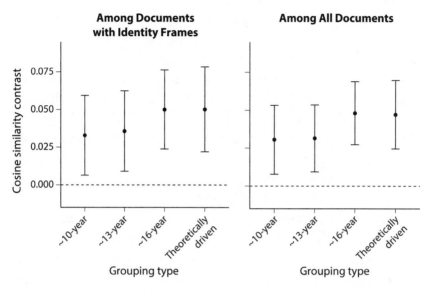

FIGURE 3.1. Responsiveness of Pro-Gun Letters to the Editor to NRA Editorials. Figure depicts the average cosine similarity responsiveness of pro-gun letters to NRA editorials from the *American Rifleman*. Cosine similarity contrast is the cosine similarity score of the *American Rifleman* at t_i and pro-gun letters at t_{i+1} minus the cosine similarity score of the letters at t_i and *American Rifleman* at t_{i+1}. Grouping type describes the approximate size and nature of the time buckets compared for analyses. The theoretically driven grouping uses time breaks that correspond to important moments in the history of the gun debate: 1930–1945, 1946–1962, 1963–1976, 1977–1991, and 1992–2008. The average cosine similarity contrast for each grouping was calculated by averaging the cosine similarity differences described above across periods. The depicted 95 percent confidence intervals are 1,000 iteration bootstrap estimates.

strong evidence that the NRA is indeed the *source* of the identity described in this chapter.

In order to validate these findings—and also provide examples of what they look like in practice—I conducted careful qualitative analyses, which reveal further evidence of pro-gun letters responding to NRA editorials. In early decades—when the NRA was in its quasi-governmental phase and maintained strong ties to the military—the organization often linked gun control with communism. Proposed laws were framed as existential threats both to gun owners—since gun confiscation and the imprisonment of gun owners, it was said, is the ultimate goal of communist-based gun control schemes—and to America itself. The April 1948 editorial, for example, declares, "The pattern of Communist action is now well established," noting that "[i]n Hungary . . . all shooting clubs were closed by legal decree. . . . In Czechoslovakia all patriotic citizens had been disarmed when the arms registration lists were seized by Hitler's Fifth Column. In both countries Communists infiltrated the army and the police departments." It then asks readers, "How can anyone, squarely facing the contemporary record, seek or support laws which would require American citizens to register their privately owned firearms with any [government] agency? . . . Who will guarantee that the registration lists of arms owned by reputable, loyal Americans will not, now or in the future, fall into the hands of disreputable, disloyal persons?"[25]

As expected, letters to the editor during this period echoed—in delayed fashion—these concerns. A February 1955 letter printed in the *Chicago Tribune*, for example, specifically cites the NRA while opposing gun legislation that the Chicago city council was considering. The writer argues, "This law, of course, would hurt no one except the honest citizen, sportsman, and target shooter. It would have, no effect upon the criminal," before noting, "The National Rifle association [*sic*] has traced these laws back to their source on a great many occasions and found a very large percentage of them inspired by the Communist party. All are vigorously supported by the Communists, as such disarming of private, honest citizens is a major aim of any organization which advocates the overthrow of a government by force."[26]

Use of these themes continued throughout the Cold War era, with numerous letters to President Johnson invoking comparisons to communism to oppose gun control. The writer of a June 1968 letter sent to the White House, for example, said that they were "inclined to believe reports being circulated in various quarters that those who now clamor for anti-gun laws applicable to everyone in the USA are wittingly, or unwittingly, seeking to disarm the American people, which is one of Communism's major objectives." According to the letter writer, communists seek disarmament because with guns "Americans could resist being hauled before firing squads or being dragged from their homes at nite [*sic*] as is done in Russia, by Communist agents, & as they want to do here." Based on this view, they then instructed the president to "veto anti-gun legislation" and "[k]eep America free."[27] This view of public disarmament as the first move made by those interested in overthrowing the government lingers among gun rights supporters even today. When interviewed, some NRA members bring it up unprompted, commenting, for instance, "If you look throughout history, people who have taken over government, that's their first concern is to disarm the population."[28]

Other editorials, particularly during the high crime rates of the late 1960s to 1970s and the crime control debates of the Clinton years, focused heavily on the impact of gun control on the ability of gun owners to use guns for defense. The January 1971 editorial, for example, argues strongly against the Gun Control Act of 1968 for, in its words, depriving law-abiding citizens of their ability to protect themselves. Referring to defensive gun use, it notes that "[l]ast year *The American Rifleman* published in its 'Armed Citizen' columns 112 actual instances in which the mere presence of a firearm in the hands of a resolute citizen prevented crime without bloodshed." It then asks, "Can anyone show us where 112 crimes have been averted by the Federal Gun Control Act of 1968?" before arguing for the law's repeal:

> Those who uphold this act and would further disarm law-abiding American citizens owe it to the American public to explain themselves. . . . There is reason to believe and hope that the next Congress will . . . repeal the 1968 Act, at least insofar as it places burdens and restrictions on individual law-abiding gun owners. That, coupled with the mandatory penalty laws that the NRA has long advocated for criminal misuse of guns, will do more to curb crime than the senseless provisions of the 1968 act which tend to stamp out legitimate gun ownership while criminals run riot and thumb their noses at all laws.[29]

Around this time, pro-gun letter writers expressed similar thoughts. For example, an August 1971 letter printed in the *New York Times* (which echoes thoughts from numerous letters around this time) argues that gun control laws simply disarm law-abiding citizens, rendering them unable to defend themselves. It also advocates stricter punishments for crime in lieu of restricting access to guns. The letter writer notes that "it is not the law-abiding citizen who uses firearms in a lawless manner. It is those with crime in mind who make lawless use of firearms, usually as against the law-abiding citizen who usually is defenseless because of gun laws which infringe his right to keep and bear arms." Therefore, according to the writer, "it seems logical that in the public interest all law-abiding citizens be trained in the use of firearms" and "[t]hose who use firearms for the commission of crimes should be imprisoned for life" because then "law-abiding citizens would not be 'sitting ducks' for those with crime in mind." Reemphasizing their point, the writer concludes, "The only 'effective gun laws' Congress can make are those which are designed to protect the law-abiding citizen from the lawlessness now so rampant in this nation."[30]

Similar examples can also be found, again, in letters sent to President Johnson. The following June 1968 letter argues that gun laws only affect law-abiding citizens, whose ownership of guns actually prevents crime. It calls for stricter enforcement of existing laws (and also connects gun control to communism):

> I feel it is my duty to speak out on the currently proposed Gun Legislation. . . . The law would only deprive <u>law abiding citizens</u> of one of their freedoms guaranteed by the Constitution. Each year hundreds of potential rapes, robberies, and murders are prevented by armed citizens or the fear that a citizen might be armed. There are enough laws on the books, if properly enforced, to control firearms. . . . [Firearms registration] is a removal of a safeguard against the Communist takeover of the country.[31]

Later, in the 1990s, when the NRA was frequently framing gun control as harmful to self-defense, it ran a book review—which reads more like an advertisement—of John R. Lott Jr.'s controversial book, *More Guns, Less Crime: Understanding Crime and Gun Control Laws*.[32] Although numerous academics have argued that Lott's analysis is misleading (while commentators have accused him of being bought by the NRA),[33] the NRA, perhaps unsurprisingly, embraced his main finding that liberalization of concealed carry laws causes decreased crime rates. Following the NRA's promotion of the book, several pro-gun letters were written citing Lott's book and framing gun control in terms of its impact on gun owners' abilities to defend themselves with firearms. An August 1999 letter in the *Atlanta Journal-Constitution*, for example, criticized an editorial the paper had run for diagnosing "millions of law-abiding citizens with 'criminal lunacy' for believing that they have the right to the means to defend themselves from violent predators" and then argued that "[o]bjective, scholarly studies, such as 'More Guns, Less Crime' by John R. Lott Jr., have demonstrated that every time law-abiding American citizens are given the opportunity to legally carry guns for self-defense, rates of violent crime drop. Not just occasionally— every time." The letter concludes, "Real lunacy is to advocate laws mandating that citizens surrender the means for self-defense."[34]

Gun rights supporters also echo these sentiments while discussing the relationship between guns and crime more generally. While discussing "gun-free zones"—signposted areas in which even individuals licensed to carry concealed firearms are prohibited from doing so—gun owners told sociologist Angela Stroud that these areas restrict their ability to defend themselves and invite criminals because "bad guys don't read signs." Another gun owner commented that gun-free zones "don't realize the message they're sending to the bad guys. They're telling the good guys, 'We don't want your business,' and they're telling the bad guys 'Come on in and rob us cause it's easy pickings.'"[35]

Most recently—with the NRA well into its partisan phase—identity frames have become increasingly tied to the Second Amendment as the prominence of the NRA's focus on—as it often calls it—"2A" has grown (a trend discussed in depth next chapter). A close reading of editorials from the topic model's *Second Amendment* topic indicates that the NRA associates an individual rights view of the Second Amendment with a number of positive values and characteristics, including patriotism, self-sufficiency, and the American tradition. Second Amendment defenders are reputable, law-abiding, average citizens who love freedom and are skeptical of the urban elite. Conversely, Second Amendment opponents are associated with a set of negative values and characteristics: they are radicals who rely on others (including government) to provide for themselves and their families, and who disrespect the long-standing traditions—dating back to the Revolutionary War—that make America exceptional. They are elitists who believe bureaucrats should implement the collectivist policies associated with other countries and political systems. The association of the gun owner social identity with the Second Amendment makes the politicization of that identity straightforward since the Second Amendment is inherently at least somewhat political.

As expected, more recent letters to the editor—written following the NRA's emphasis on the Second Amendment—emphasize similar themes. The following letter, for example, printed in the *Arizona Republic* in February 2000 and written by a self-identified NRA member, invokes the Second Amendment as the basis for the letter writer's opposition to gun control. The letter writer notes that they were "very disappointed in your editorial" in support of gun control and then explains, "I am a member of the National Rifle Association, not because I am a 'gun lover' any more than I support the First Amendment because I am a 'newspaper and magazine lover.' I am an NRA member because I believe strongly in the rights of law-abiding citizens to arm and defend themselves against dangerous criminals and governments, just as I believe in a free press." The writer, defending the NRA, continues, "Why don't you quit trying to vilify the NRA and its members? The NRA is a grass-roots, 3 million member organization that is overwhelmingly funded by individual contributions. Please accept the fact that we cherish Second Amendment freedoms for the same good reasons that we cherish First Amendment freedoms."[36]

Examples can also be found in more recent letters sent to the president. A letter sent to President George H. W. Bush just prior to his inauguration, for example, encourages the president to make sure that any potential Supreme Court appointees support an individual rights view of the Second Amendment. The letter writer tells Bush, "I voted for you because your campaign promises were true American. The one that influenced me the most was your stand on the Second Amendment rights. Now I am . . . asking that you stick by those promises and if you appoint any judges to the Supreme Court, please make sure he is in total support of our individual Second Amendment rights!" Underscoring this point, the letter goes on to say, "We pro gun people came through for you in November, so please come thru for us by keeping your promises."[37]

Outside of letters to the editor and to politicians, gun owners also often invoke the Second Amendment in conversations about their views on gun control and the NRA. One NRA member, for instance, told an interviewer, "We are not a special interest group . . . we are a constitutional rights issue group,"[38] with another gun owner commenting that "we take our 2A rights very seriously. If you don't think the government's coming for your guns, you need to reread your history."[39]

In summary, citizens' letters not only mimicked the frames circulated by the NRA, but did so *after* the NRA had first articulated those frames in its magazine, thus lending support to the notion that the NRA was instrumental in both the creation and subsequent use of those frames by activist gun owners.

Identity Dissemination

To assess my **third** expectation—that the NRA has used its firearms programs to *disseminate* the gun owner identity discussed above— I closely examined both the history and the content of these programs. What strategic considerations affected the NRA's development of them? Are they mostly apolitical and focused solely on providing participants with firearms-related skills and knowledge? Or do they simultaneously push politically charged, NRA-crafted ideas of what it *means* to be a gun owner?

First, and as discussed in chapter 1, it should be noted that NRA programs are currently very popular and have been for a long time. Collectively, these programs draw over a million participants annually.[40] And across the more than century-long history of its programs, the NRA has demonstrated a consistent ability to develop service offerings that address social needs and then to lock themselves

in—often legally—as the primary or sole provider of those programs. In the case of concealed carry courses, the NRA's role was
even broader; rather than simply tapping into external demand for
concealed carry training, it actually played a major role in *creating*
that demand by aggressively pushing the spread of concealed carry
laws.[41] Moreover, NRA programs bring lots of children into contact with the organization, thereby including them in the firearms
community early on in their lives, while they are still forming their
social and political views. The Eddie Eagle gun safety program, for
example, reached thirty million children by 2017,[42] and the NRA's
juniors offerings include shooting camps, competitions, education
programs, marksmanship courses, and scholarship opportunities.[43]

As a result of its long-standing prominence within the realm of
firearms, the NRA is—and long has been—very well positioned to
drive the cultivation of an identity among gun owners that it uses
to its political advantage. And, as it turns out, it has indeed consistently used its widely popular programs and services to spread a
politically charged group identity. The NRA has often taken these
actions strategically and self-consciously, recognizing that they carry
numerous advantages for the organization. It recognized early on the
importance of the Civilian Marksmanship Program to its membership base and funding, and aggressively fought to maintain funding
for programs associated with this cause throughout the twentieth
century. It recognized later that safety courses of various kinds could
similarly grow the organization. Additionally, it clearly recognized
that its service offerings—particularly related to safety—can preempt restrictive firearms legislation by cutting down on accidents.[44]
More closely related to the topic of this chapter, it recognized that its
programs are an entry point into "all else that the NRA stands for"—
or, as a social scientist might describe it, into a community with a
shared collective identity. And finally, it has long recognized the
political advantages of a mobilized gun owner community, noting
repeatedly that such a community is the key to its political success.[45]

Indeed, as the NRA's offerings expanded and participation in
them spread, membership in the organization ballooned: from just
3,500 in 1921 to (following the expansion of the surplus firearms

program) 10,700 in 1925 and 54,000 in 1940,[46] to (following its post-WWII growth) 267,000 in 1955 and 325,000 in 1960,[47] to (following continued growth) 1 million in the 1970s,[48] to (following further expansion of its offerings) 3.5 million in 1995,[49] to its current self-reported membership of approximately 5 million.[50] Since joining the NRA as a result of its programming has always meant also receiving a subscription to the *American Rifleman*, all of these new members have been exposed—at least to some extent—to the NRA's identity appeals.

But aside from exposure to the NRA's written communications, the NRA injects politically charged identity appeals into the service programs themselves. Its oldest programs—which focused on marksmanship and were offered during the NRA's quasi-governmental phase—associated gun ownership and use with patriotism, citizenship, courage, and personal responsibility.[51] Its junior marksmanship programs, in particular, were used to both incorporate new members into its social group and advertised based on the positive personal qualities with which they endow children. It closely associated participation in its shooting matches—which, again, were the preeminent and official US matches due to its relationship with the government—with several key identity characteristics. Take, for example, the August 1932 editorial's description of match participation:

> Riflemen of America, you are pointing the way for cowards and for weaklings as you have always done. By your attendance at those regional shoots which you can afford to reach; by your fighting support of your National Association, finding, as you are, men who can afford to support it even though your own purse is empty; by your very mental attitude, you are showing the nation as you have shown it often in the past that you are its most courageous sons. That from your ranks spring leaders, not followers![52]

Shortly after, in 1934, the NRA for the first time mobilized the clubs who participated in these matches into political action to oppose restrictive legislation.[53] These politicized shooting clubs—which were strongly encouraged to come under the NRA umbrella due to the NRA's government funding—took their guidance in the form of information and strategy from NRA headquarters.[54] The *American Rifleman* also explicitly connected these programs to opposition to gun regulation.[55]

By 1960, following its post-WWII growth and facing changing social conditions, the NRA sought continued expansion and anticipated a renewed push for gun legislation after a couple of quiet decades. It recognized that continued growth could help cultivate favorable attitudes toward guns, which would help preempt restrictive legislation. The May 1960 *American Rifleman* editorial, entitled "The Future of Firearms in America," summarizes these themes well; it makes clear that the NRA saw its programs as means to grow its membership and, as a result, spread both its identity and its positions on firearms regulations. It describes its "Centennial Plan" (which outlined its goals for the last decade of its first century), focusing in large part on addressing "more and more efforts . . . to deny reputable citizens the right to keep and bear arms" by drawing more participants to its programming. The editorial ultimately argues, "The future of firearms in America depends to a large degree upon the willingness of gun owners to establish and promote educational programs for the use of firearms in the home, on the range, and in the field."[56]

More recently—with the NRA in its partisan phase—the organization has spread its identity through its concealed carry training courses. These courses begin with a focus on gun culture itself rather than simply focusing on technical firearms skills, while often also using scare tactics in which crime is repeatedly described as "out of control"—even during periods when crime is down.[57] Sociologist Jennifer Carlson, who studied NRA concealed carry courses by embedding herself in them (going so far as to become a credentialed NRA instructor), argues that that "NRA gun training reshapes gun culture from the ground up."[58] Carlson notes, "Rather than prioritize hands-on defensive training, these courses teach gun carriers that they are a particular kind of person—a law-abiding person willing to use lethal force to protect innocent life if faced with a violent threat."[59] These courses—which are in many cases mandatory for anyone hoping to get a concealed carry license—promote the same politically charged identity revealed in the *American Rifleman*: they tie gun ownership to personal responsibility, good citizenship, and civic virtue and promote a vision of gun owners as "'responsible, law-abiding citizens' capable of self-governance."[60] The materials for these courses refer to the Second Amendment as "America's First Freedom," and the courses, in various ways, tie gun ownership to the NRA's conception of good citizenship.[61] Crucially, Carlson's study reveals how concealed carry can increase the *accessibility* of the NRA identity—individuals who constantly carry firearms are constantly reminded of the identity that goes along with those firearms.

The NRA's attempts to disseminate the gun owner identity through its programs appear to have been successful. In the previously mentioned paper I coauthored with Adam Howat and Jake Rothschild, we find that contact with the NRA and participation in firearms-related activities are statistically significant predictors of the extent to which individuals socially identify as gun owners, with both factors increasing the strength of gun owner identification.[62] Elsewhere, sociologist Scott Melzer, in interviews with NRA members, finds evidence that at least some members join exclusively to participate in NRA programming and then later become politically awakened. One member, for example, said that he joined the NRA to compete in shooting competitions, but now understands that gun rights are threatened and feels like he is part of the NRA's power base. He told Melzer, "So, that's [competitive shooting] really what motivated me to join, because [back then] I wasn't as politically active or as politically knowledgeable that there was even a threat to the Second Amendment. I was just oblivious to it. I never thought that the Constitution was in jeopardy in any way."[63]

Identity, Threat, and Political Mobilization

To assess my **fourth** expectation—that the NRA uses the gun owner identity to *mobilize* political action on its behalf—I first examine the extent to which it (a) depicts the identity (not just particular aspects of gun ownership) as threatened and (b) connects depictions of the threat to explicit calls to action. By portraying the group's identity as under constant threat, the NRA could both motivate members to take action and maintain the identity's salience.

The NRA, as it turns out, does indeed frequently use threat—about two-thirds (66 percent) of its editorials portray gun rights as under siege. It also frequently asks its members to defend gun rights, with 36 percent of the editorials containing explicit calls to action. Moreover, the NRA systematically *links* depictions of threat with calls to action; using a statistical model, I find that the NRA's depictions of threat are a significant and important predictor of whether it asks its members to take action on behalf of gun rights.[64] The NRA, in other words, strategically uses threat to mobilize its members, simultaneously portraying their identity as under attack while also asking them to actively defend gun rights.

Notably, this approach to mobilization is seen throughout my entire period of study, indicating that the NRA has engaged in threat-based mobilization for a very long time. The December 1940 editorial, which discusses efforts to pass gun regulation as a national security measure aimed at subversive groups, is an early example of this strategy. Using militaristic language that fits well with the NRA's mission during its quasi-governmental phase, it warns, "Sportsman of America, the 'zero hour' has come." It then casts those who support gun control in a negative light and calls for vigilance, noting, "An unscrupulous, well-organized enemy is on the march. Stand to your arms! Break up this attack, and counter-charge with all the power of which you are capable." The editorial then implores readers to persuade others: "Make your position known to your City Councilmen and State Legislators before they have these bills presented. Tell the true story of this misleading propaganda to your friends. Reply by letter to the editor to every newspaper editorial supporting this dangerous theory."[65]

The April 1997 editorial is a more recent example. It discusses several legislative proposals in vague terms and then includes the following, telling readers that they are the government's targets—a common refrain in the NRA's partisan phase—and that protecting themselves requires political action:

> If a combination of these proposals becomes law, people who are now peaceable and innocent gun owners surely could become victims of a kind of political purge not seen before in America. . . . In all of them, we—you and I—are the target. . . . But thank goodness these are merely proposals—draft legislation that will have to clear the Second Amendment majority you elected to Congress. Can this really happen? Yes. It can if we fail to fight. . . . You fight by using your voices, by writing Congress. I will let you know when these proposals surface, and when and how you must respond. . . . We still are the most powerful grassroots lobby in the nation but only if we believe and respond, only if we keep democracy working.[66]

Notably, although the specific arguments the NRA uses shift in response to the political context, its portrayal of gun rights as under threat has been present even during periods in which no reasonable threat existed. There was little chance of strong gun regulation passing, for example, during the George W. Bush Administration, particularly during the stretch of unified Republican government from 2003 to 2007. The NRA, however, frequently portrayed a dire situation and called for constant vigilance, arguing that things like United Nations treaties and questionable judicial appointments posed immediate threats to gun rights. On numerous occasions, the editorials even claimed that gun regulation proponents were intentionally creating a false sense of security among gun owners in order to defeat them later.

In moments when the NRA does face a legitimate threat—for example, following a prominent mass shooting—it argues that passing measures like universal background checks will create a slippery slope and lead to outright gun confiscation (while often portraying gun control supporters as either opportunistic or emotional). For example, in the July 1968 editorial following Robert Kennedy's assassination, the NRA informed its readers, "Some Congressmen and anti-gun extremists now demand that all private ownership of firearms be stamped out" and then commented, "Sane Americans outside the unreal atmosphere of Washington meanwhile are unnerved at the spectacle of a national leadership, befogged by natural grief and upset by unrestrained public emotionalism, taking action that may someday stand against the stark background of history as unwarranted and excessive."[67]

Similarly, following the Columbine High School massacre in 1999, it told its supporters that a "hateful and bigoted war has been declared against American firearms owners in the aftermath of [Columbine]." After noting that "President Clinton charged that the mass murders stemmed from 'the culture of hunting and sport shooting in America,'" it warned readers, "With those words, he began what can only be called a 'cultural cleansing'—specifically targeting the bedrock Second Amendment beliefs of firearms owners for extinction." The editorial then called gun owners into action, arguing, "Every one of us has to act. Urge your Congressman and Senators to oppose and vote against the Clinton gun control package. Don't buy into the idea that anything proposed today will be the end of it."[68]

These threat-based calls to action appear to be successful. All available data indicates that gun rights supporters participate frequently and intensely, particularly relative to gun control supporters. Moreover, their participation appears to often be in response to NRA appeals.

As chapter 5 will explore, intense participation on behalf of gun rights first occurred in 1934, during the heart of the NRA's quasi-governmental phase. As hearings began on what would eventually become (in substantially weakened form) the National Firearms Act, NRA members—following instructions from the NRA—inundated members of Congress with letters and telegrams opposing the legislation. The February 1934 *American Rifleman* editorial contained an explicit, identity-laden call to action. It read,

UNDER date of January 11th there was introduced in the Senate of the United States a bill . . . designed to bring the strong arm

of the Federal Government into play in the direction of disarming the average American citizen. . . . [T]he expressed intention
of [the bill] is to make it more difficult for criminals to obtain
firearms and to make it easier to apprehend such criminals after
they have used firearms . . . but, the expressed intent of the bill
and the results which it would actually accomplish are radically
different things. . . . While Senator Copeland [says] this bill is
not intended to inconvenience sportsmen, he nevertheless suc-
ceeds in so drafting his law that it actually will affect 98% of all
the sportsmen in this country. . . . [It would] make it next to
impossible for the man of average means to purchase a pistol
or revolver, or to do much shooting with any kind of gun, and
[would] place the criminal in a position of absolute dominance
over our citizens. . . . Senate Bill #2258 . . . must be killed. Your
United States Senator in Washington must be advised of your
views on the matter without delay.[69]

The next month, in the March editorial, entitled, "Keep Those Letters and Telegrams Coming," the NRA wrote yet another editorial
imploring members to take action. The National Firearms Act of
1934 still passed, but only after the NRA substantially weakened it,
as discussed in chapter 5.[70] These appeals, which clearly worked,
drew the attention of members of Congress, who were furious with
the NRA for mobilizing its members.[71]

A similar pattern of events occurred in the 1960s, which witnessed
a number of proposed gun regulations following the assassination of
John F. Kennedy (which are also explored in chapter 5's case studies). The NRA again mobilized its members, using identity-based
appeals on numerous occasions to implore them to contact their
representatives in Congress. It sent a special legislative bulletin to
the entire membership in April 1965, encouraging them to tell their
friends and family to join them in writing, along with instructions
on how to write effective letters. It warned members, "If the battle is
lost, it will be your loss and that of all who follow you." The membership responded dramatically. In the month prior to this bulletin—
and the NRA's general campaign against the bill, which extended

into the *American Rifleman*—President Johnson received only fifty letters, many of which were in support. The following month, he received around twelve thousand letters, nearly all of which were in opposition.[72] Similarly, a member of Congress received three thousand letters, only three of which were supportive of the legislation.[73]

These trends have continued during the NRA's partisan phase. One such episode occurred following President Bush's decision, in March 1989, to halt the import of assault weapons in response to the schoolyard shooting in Stockton, California. The April 1989 issue of the *American Rifleman* included—along with an editorial focused on the topic—a special cover insert that began, "Last year anti-gunners said criminals use handguns. So they conspired to ban handguns. This year they say criminals use semi-autos. So they're conspiring to ban semi-autos." It then argued, "What they really want is a ban on *all* guns. Long guns. Handguns. Your guns," before calling readers into action: "if we don't act now, they'll have their way. . . . 70 million law-abiding gun owners should say, 'Enough is enough! Leave our rights alone!'"[74]

That month, following the NRA's appeal, the Bush Administration was contacted 143 times in support of the ban—and 4,000 times in opposition. Two years later, in 1991, a similar cover insert was placed in the May issue of the *American Rifleman* pertaining to the version of the Brady Bill that was being discussed at the time. During the last two weeks of April of that year—presumably right after members had received the May issue—the Bush Administration was contacted 5,242 times in opposition to the bill and only 92 times in favor of it.[75]

More recent participation rates are captured in public polling. Evidence from as long ago as 1978 and as recently as 2017 indicates that gun rights supporters are much more likely to engage in nonvoting political participation—including letter writing, phone calls, and donations—than gun control supporters. Notably, NRA members are even more likely than other gun owners to contact public officials, suggesting that the NRA's mobilization efforts are an important driver of gun owner participation.[76] Further, as noted in chapter 1, an astonishing 71 percent of people who favor weaker gun regulations are unwilling to ever vote for candidates who support gun control (compared to only 34 percent of gun control supporters who refuse to vote for candidates who do not share their gun preferences).[77]

Moreover, this participation among gun owners seems to be driven by feelings of both threat and identity. In the previously mentioned paper with Howat and Rothschild, we examined the extent to which social identification as a gun owner predicts both (a) individuals' gun control preferences and (b) their propensity to take political action in regard to gun control. Even when holding constant a wide range of factors—including partisanship, ideology, geographic region, and even objective gun ownership[78]—gun owner identity is a statistically significant and very substantively important predictor of a number of outcomes of interest. Those who more strongly identify with gun ownership are more likely to oppose gun control, more likely to consider gun control an important political issue, and more likely to take action against proposed gun regulations.[79]

These findings are also supported by others' research. In Melzer's previously mentioned interviews with NRA members, for instance, many told him that they believe gun rights are deeply threatened and indicated that the information with which the NRA provides them affects their political behavior.[80] And another recent study found that those who score higher on identity measures pertaining to gun ownership demonstrate a much greater intention to engage in non-voting political participation than others.[81]

Perceived identity threat can also be seen in the appeals written by the NRA's mass-level supporters. The following *Chicago Tribune* letter writer, for instance, opposes post-Columbine gun control proposals by connecting gun rights to the defense of his family, while using lots of in-group and out-group identity language. The writer even explicitly states that he is an NRA member because he perceives gun rights to be threatened (emphasis added):

Unfortunately [Columbine] has . . . produced . . . mindless anti-gun owner diatribe from the editorial staff of the *Chicago Tribune*. . . . An editorial demanded that all legitimate gun owners and their guns be registered and their guns incarcerated in police stations, to be withdrawn only for such "lawful" purposes as hunting. Evidently the defense of my home and four young daughters from criminal gun-users is not considered to be "lawful" in the eyes of *Tribune* editorial zealots. . . . *Inflammatory attacks on us and our lawful pursuits are exactly what drive us into the arms of the National Rifle Association, the only group that adamantly stands up for a legitimate defense of our rights as law-abiding citizens.* Until the power of the media is harnessed to an objective, thoughtfully developed, overall approach to these complicated aberrations, we'll keep supporting the NRA and making our voices heard, before media zealots seize on future tragedies to completely disarm us all. And because tens of millions of guns are legitimately owned and used in the United States, with but a tiny fraction of 1 percent ever used in a crime, our representatives know there are millions of these rational voices to be heard.[82]

Notably—although, as a result of spotty archival records, it is not always clear how *intentional* the NRA's historical use of identity was—contemporary NRA leaders openly acknowledge that the organization's power is intimately tied to its members' actions, and, further, they recognize that the NRA's ability to mobilize those members into action is tied to the deep personal meaning associated with gun ownership. David Keene, a former NRA president, said in an interview that the NRA's power is not a product of its money but instead of the votes it delivers. Keene—who describes the NRA as a "family"—then said, "The difference between the NRA and other groups is that we've developed a community [and] when they see Second Amendment rights threatened they vote. They do whatever they need to do. They get out." Kayne Robinson, a former president and executive director of the NRA, emphasizes the importance of threat, saying, "The most important thing motivating the members is the threat. Understanding the gravity of the threat is what produces action."[83] These claims are reiterated by the candid account of former NRA lobbyist Richard Feldman. Feldman—whose departure from the NRA was acrimonious, indicating that he has no incentive to sugarcoat the NRA's tactics—makes clear that grassroots action, and the single-minded devotion to gun rights driving it, is key to the NRA's influence.[84] Feldman notes, "To millions of Americans, a gun is a symbol of all sorts of positive, traditional values of independence and freedom. When the government which can't protect its citizens wants to restrict the rights of citizens who have never misused their guns, those citizens get fearful."[85]

———

This chapter brings together diverse evidence to demonstrate that the NRA has used its firearms programs and membership communications to strategically cultivate an identity among gun owners. Gun owners, in this view, are patriotic, law-abiding citizens who defend American freedom against threats posed by elitist bureaucrats, greedy lawyers, and a dishonest media. The NRA has connected this identity to politics by portraying gun control not just as ill-conceived, but as an existential threat to both the gun owning community and the United States more broadly.

This identity is clearly an important factor that shapes how the NRA's supporters think about—and act against—proposed gun control regulations. When gun owners discuss gun regulation, they do so in ways that mirror the NRA's discussions. Moreover, when the NRA asks gun owners to take action to defend gun rights—and especially when it pairs these requests with claims that such rights are under threat—they frequently listen. As the case studies in chapters 5 and 7 will demonstrate, this widespread mobilization has often been successful.

Of course, compellingly demonstrating causal relationships is very challenging; I can't necessarily claim that the NRA has been the *sole* driving force behind the cultivation, politicization, and activation of a gun owner identity. Moreover, the NRA's identity certainly taps into other identities—co-opting, expanding, and connecting its gun owner identity to the values and characteristics associated with a number of other politically relevant group memberships— including those related to rural life, military service, masculinity, and whiteness. The objective of this chapter is not to discount such connections—which are explored in chapters 4 and 6—but instead to identify and specify the NRA's clear role in interrelating, expanding, and disseminating these otherwise distinct themes and using them to cultivate a devoted, politically active membership. And indeed, the evidence presented here—which links the NRA to the views of its mass-level supporters in a number of distinct ways—leaves one hard-pressed to construct an alternative account that does *not* place the NRA at the center of the action.

The NRA's cultivation of a collective group identity is one example of an ideational resource that it uses to influence politics. This identity comprises one half of the political worldview the NRA has built around guns. The next chapter discusses another ideational resource—ideology—which builds on the identity discussed in this chapter and comprises the second half of the NRA's worldview.

4

"America's First Freedom"

THE NRA'S GUN-CENTRIC POLITICAL IDEOLOGY

As I've stood in the crosshairs of those who target Second Amendment freedoms, I've realized that firearms are not the only issue. No, it's much bigger than that.

—THEN-NRA PRESIDENT CHARLTON HESTON SPEAKING ABOUT GUN RIGHTS—AND MORE—AT HARVARD LAW SCHOOL, 1999[1]

The Second Amendment is not just words on parchment. It's not some frivolous suggestion from our Founding Fathers to be interpreted by whim. It lies at the heart of what this country was founded upon. Our Founding Fathers knew that without Second Amendment freedom, all of our freedoms could be in jeopardy. . . . Our individual liberty is the very essence of America. It is what makes America unique. If you aren't free to protect yourself—when government puts its thumb on that freedom—then you aren't free at all.

—WAYNE LAPIERRE AT THE CONSERVATIVE POLITICAL ACTION CONFERENCE, 2013[2]

The NRA is often thought of as a single-issue interest group focused solely on the advancement of a pro-gun political agenda. But for many gun owners, gun rights stand at the center of a broader political ideology that embraces liberty, nationalism, limited government, and law and order. Where did this ideology come from? And how is it related to the gun owner identity discussed last chapter?

In this chapter, I address these questions by examining the NRA's decades-long efforts to build an ideology around gun rights. Working in conjunction with its group identity, the NRA's ideology comprises the second stream of the gun-centric worldview it has used to advance gun rights. This group ideology increases the political unity of gun rights supporters—they are similar not just in their shared support for gun rights, but also along a broader range of issue positions and values. In connecting gun rights to other issues, ideology also links the gun owner identity to other politically relevant identities, strengthening each.

In conjunction, the unity of NRA supporters (a product of a shared ideology) and their political intensity (a product of a shared identity) explain why the NRA is such a politically valuable demographic group to politicians. Indeed, the political attractiveness of the group—along with its shared support for what in contemporary politics are considered conservative issue positions—helps explain why, when the time was right, gun owners fit neatly into the contemporary Republican Party (a topic that is explored in detail in chapter 6).

As with the last chapter, I will start with a section—written with general readers in mind—that reviews the chapter's major takeaways and the evidence supporting them. The rest of the chapter—written with social scientists in mind—goes into greater detail about these findings and the methods I used to come to them.

How the NRA Cultivates Ideology: Major Takeaways

I explore the NRA's efforts to cultivate an ideology using the same *American Rifleman* editorials and gun control-related letters to newspaper editors that show the emergence of a gun owner identity.

Ideologies—as you might recall from chapter 2—can be thought of as sets of interrelated issue stances, along with the broader beliefs and values associated with those stances.[3] Following from this definition, one of the primary ways I measure ideology is by focusing on issue connections contained in the *American Rifleman* and letters to the editor. Does each editorial or letter portray gun rights as a stand-alone issue? Or does it suggest that the gun debate is wrapped up with other issues and that support for gun rights is part of a broader, coherent view of politics?

I find evidence that the NRA has frequently sought to advance an ideology in which gun rights play a central role; more than half (54 percent) of *American Rifleman* editorials connect gun rights to at least one other issue stance. This is mirrored by NRA supporters: a similar rate (49 percent) of pro-gun letters to the editor also connect the gun debate to other political issues. In comparison, support for gun control is generally not portrayed as a part of a broader political outlook: only 6 percent of letters written in support of gun control connect that stance to other issues.

Examining these connections demonstrates how support-ers took their ideological cues from the NRA. During its quasi-governmental phase, for instance, the NRA often focused on the importance of guns for protecting American liberty against for-eign threats and (particularly when crime rates were high during the 1930s) from crime. One *American Rifleman* editorial in this vein argued that gun control had rendered England unprepared for World War II and in grave danger. "England," it warned, "dis-armed and gun-ignorant by reason of the same type of gun law that is now proposed for America, is forced to turn to American arms plants and to American gun-owners for guns and ammuni-tion for defense against invaders from without and criminals from within."[4] A month later, a *New York Times* letter to the editor said that gun regulations would "place us in the unfortunate predica-ment of England. Strict arms regulations in the past left the rank and file of the English people gun-ignorant and gun-shy." It then went on to note that existing gun laws have "backfired, doubly arming the crook by disarming the honest citizen."[5]

Tracking these sources also reveals an ideology that has been consistent over time but has shifted in how key values are framed. Most notable is the NRA's embrace of the Second Amendment as its dominant ideological lens.

The topic models that I introduced in the previous chapter illumine the emergence of the Second Amendment as a focal point. Throughout its governmental phase, the NRA's ideological appeals were anchored in the themes associated with *Americanism and Guns*, emphasizing the importance of firearms throughout US history, their place in the American tradition, and their role in the defense of liberty against foreign threats. But as the NRA entered its partisan phase, its ideology increasingly became grounded in the *Second Amendment* topic. Although similar to *Americanism and Guns* in terms of portraying firearms as crucial to both patriotic citizenship and the history of the United States, *Second Amendment* differed in one crucial way: rather than focusing on the importance of gun rights for national defense—for protecting liberty from foreign threats—it emphasizes the importance of guns for protecting against domestic tyranny.

The issue connections the NRA made shifted accordingly. When linking gun rights to liberty, for example, it began referring to the Second Amendment as "America's First Freedom"—the freedom that is necessary for the protection of all others. "Without the ability to physically defend the other provisions of our Constitution from encroachment, the remainder of the Bill of Rights become privileges granted by the government and subject to restrictions at the whim of government."[6] With this came more frequent connections between gun control and big government,[7] and the portrayal of self-defense against criminals as a matter of individual rights.

These appeals reinforce the gun owner identity and align it with other politically relevant identities. In linking gun rights to liberty and limited government, for example, the NRA suggests that gun owners are self-sufficient individuals who don't need to rely on the government, even for protection. Moreover, the ways in which the NRA has linked gun rights and crime have also aligned the gun owner identity with white racial identity; by warning of instances, for example, in which women have been "savagely raped, sodomized and beaten in their home" while unable to defend themselves due to gun control laws, the NRA establishes a connection between gun ownership and racialized fears of violence.[8]

The shift in emphasis associated with the NRA's transition into its partisan phase is also apparent in the pro-gun letters, which continue to echo the NRA's ideas. Using further topic modeling and the same adaptation of plagiarism detection software discussed last chapter, I find evidence that the ideology discussed in this chapter originated with the NRA and was later adopted by its supporters.

The similarity of this ideology to contemporary conservatism was an important factor in the NRA's developing relationship with the Republican Party. And once the NRA became a key player in GOP politics, it continued to advance an ideological perspective not only aligned with Republican politics but even began to lead the party in new directions. Starting in the early 2000s, for example, the NRA began to promote a nationalistic brand of right-wing populism, in which gun rights were necessary to protect the American tradition against the threat posed by globalist elites, like George Soros and Michael Bloomberg, along with their allies in the media and government. This view aligns closely with the outlook that Donald Trump eventually used to gain political prominence. As the next chapter explores, the NRA's early adoption of this brand of populism is one reason why its relationship with the GOP grew even stronger when Donald Trump won the presidency.

Measuring Ideological Cultivation Using Topic Models

Having highlighted the chapter's main takeaways, the remainder of the chapter goes into much greater detail about the evidence I use to draw the conclusions described above. I use the same data discussed last chapter—NRA editorials from the *American Rifleman* and gun-related letters to newspaper editors—and analyze it in similar ways, as noted throughout the following pages. However, this chapter also directly incorporates topic models—which were discussed last chapter—in order to measure the ideological commitments of the NRA and its supporters over time; rather than using topic modeling solely to select relevant documents for closer analysis, this chapter directly uses them as evidence. As noted last chapter and discussed further in the appendix, topic models use machine learning to group documents—in this case, editorials and letters to newspaper editors—into computer-generated topics based on patterns in the words that they contain.

The specific topic modeling technique I use—the Structural Topic Model[9]—enables me to examine the relative prominence of each topic over time; in other words, I can examine the relative attention that the NRA and its supporters pay to particular topics, as well as the extent to which the topics they discuss change over time. As demonstrated in the following sections, this is one helpful way to measure the existence, contents, and over-time development of a group ideology.

This chapter uses two different topic models. One—which was presented last chapter—includes only the NRA editorials from the *American Rifleman* and covers 1930 through 2008. The other—not discussed last chapter—combines both those editorials and letters to newspaper editors written in opposition of gun control; due to the data demands of topic modeling and a relatively low number of gun-related letters to the editor in early decades of the study, this second model only covers 1963 through 2008. Table 3.1—contained in the previous chapter—summarized the *American Rifleman*-only model, and table 4.1 similarly summarizes the *American Rifleman* + letters model. In general, the topics in this second model—which are discussed throughout the chapter—are rather similar to the topics in the first model.

Ideology across Time

Before tracing the over-time development of the NRA's ideology, it is useful to first take a more comprehensive, cross-time look at it. What is the full set of issues to which the NRA has connected gun rights and that, as a result, comprise its ideology? How frequently do the NRA and its mass-level supporters connect gun rights to other

TABLE 4.1. Summary of Topic Model of *American Rifleman* Editorials and Pro-Gun Letters to the Editor

Topic Label	Words	Brief Description
Crime, Self-Defense, and Guns	*FREX*: crime, handgun, murder, purchas, prevent, possess, licens, illeg, check, requir *High Prob*: gun, law, crimin, crime, firearm, control, handgun, citizen, law-abid, weapon	Very similar to identically named topic from the *American Rifleman*-only model. Argues that gun control laws are unlikely to reduce crime and that gun ownership is a solution to crime rather than a cause. Advocates harsh criminal sentencing in lieu of new regulations. Prominent throughout the period covered by the model, with a peak during the crime-focused gun control debate of the 1960s and 1970s that resulted from high-profile political assassinations and high rates of gun violence. Generally rises and falls in correspondence with gun violence rates.
Children and Guns	*FREX*: respons, hunt, children, letter, school, percent, conceal, find, illinoi, kid *High Prob*: gun, peopl, respons, mani, need, shoot, one, think, dont, problem	Discusses gun control in the context of school shootings and home firearms accidents that harm children. Argues that gun-related accidents should be addressed through gun safety education, including in schools. Blames school shootings on factors other than access to guns, including poor parenting and a breakdown in society's moral fiber. Advocates for arming teachers and providing more armed security as a way to stop school shootings. Peaks around the time of the school shooting at Columbine High School.
Gun Regulation	*FREX*: feder, violent, street, disarm, buy, convict, bradi, happen, congress, manufactur *High Prob*: gun, firearm, will, feder, one, bill, make, state, violent, use	Very similar to the identically named topic from the *American Rifleman*-only model. Discusses gun control in more general terms than the other topics. As such, it varies less over time than the other topics.
Second Amendment	*FREX*: right, amend, arm, constitut, second, bear, freedom, defend, tribun, advoc *High Prob*: right, arm, will, amend, peopl, protect, constitut, second, keep, citizen	Very similar to the *American Rifleman*-only model's identically named topic. Advocates for an individual rights interpretation of the Second Amendment. Gun rights are portrayed as crucial to freedom because they enable citizens to defend themselves against government tyranny. Gun rights, portrayed as the freedom that enables the protection of all other freedoms, are depicted as a centerpiece of liberty and the American tradition. The topic has dramatically increased in prominence since the 1960s, eventually becoming the most prominent topic overall.

Continued on next page

TABLE 4.1. (*continued*)

Topic Label	Words	Brief Description
NRA Membership Programs and Benefits	*FREX*: nra, nation, rifl, associ, member, million, year, support, will, must	Very similar to the *Membership Programs and Benefits* topic from the *American Rifleman*-only model. Consists mostly of NRA editorials, which promote new offerings designed to increase membership. Prominent at the beginning of the 1960s, when the NRA planned a large membership drive. Peaks again during the 1980s and early 1990s when the NRA addressed its financial struggles by heavily promoting new revenue-generating programs and benefits.
	High Prob: nra, associ, million, nation, member, vote, parent, organ, posit, hunter	

Note: Topics are named based on a close reading of example documents and each topic's "highest probability" and "FREX" words. These words are stemmed. "Highest probability" words are those most likely to appear within a topic. "FREX" words are those which are both common and exclusive to each topic; these words are very useful for labeling topics because they not only frequently appear in a topic but also are relatively distinct to that topic. See the appendix for more details.

issues; in other words, just how ideological are they? And how do they compare to gun control supporters—are gun control supporters more or less ideological than gun rights supporters?

Beyond enabling me to address these questions, a high-level discussion of the NRA's ideological commitments also helps inform the more detailed, over-time discussion of these commitments contained in the next section. Moreover, although there have been important over-time changes to the *relative* emphasis the NRA has placed on various issue connections, the major issue sets to which it has connected gun rights have remained constant throughout my period of study. It is therefore not misleading to aggregate these issue connections together over time; indeed, doing so enables me to paint a complete picture of the NRA's ideological commitments.

On a basic level, cultivating an ideology involves connecting distinct political issues to one another, implying that such issues "go together" and collectively form a cohesive and comprehensive perspective on politics. For example, in the case of the NRA, this might consist of identifying similarities between gun rights and other issues (e.g., crime control), or framing gun rights as one part of a broader issue set (e.g., limited government). The NRA may even argue that gun rights are the defining—or most important—issue within a given

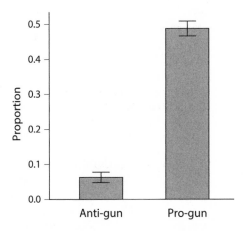

FIGURE 4.1. Proportion of Letters Containing Issue
Connections

issue set. If the NRA is successful at ideological cultivation, then gun
rights supporters would be expected to also frequently connect gun
rights to other political issues, particularly those to which the NRA
connects them.

Along these lines, I first examined the *American Rifleman* editorials and the gun control letters to the editor on a high level, coding
them based on whether they connect gun rights to one or more
political issues. A solid majority—54 percent—of *American Rifleman*
editorials link gun rights to other political issues. And a very similar
proportion of pro-gun letters to the editor—49 percent—also connect gun rights to other issues.

Like I did last chapter, I can compare pro-gun letters to anti-gun
letters in order to contextualize the rates at which gun rights supporters exhibit particular characteristics. As figure 4.1 indicates, there
is a very substantial and statistically significant difference between
pro- and anti-gun letters to the editor—just 6 percent of the anti-gun
letters connected gun control to one or more political issues.[10] This
strongly suggests that the NRA and gun rights supporters see guns
as a more ideological issue than their anti-gun counterparts—support for gun rights is much more integrated into a broader political
outlook than support for gun control is.

But what do these issue connections consist of? And do the NRA
and its supporters connect gun rights to the same sets of issues? To

TABLE 4.2. Issue Sets Connected to Gun Rights by the NRA

Issue Set	Brief Description
Crime	Gun rights are a solution to crime because the personal ownership of firearms is the best defense against criminals. Harsh sentencing and, in general, incarceration are preferable to what the NRA refers to as "prior restraint"—limiting access to guns prior to misuse of them. (Not included here are editorials that discuss crime but argue exclusively that gun control measures aimed at it are unlikely to work.)
Liberty	Gun rights are crucial to social and political freedom, broadly conceived; they are necessary as a means to prevent government tyranny and are also a fundamental end of freedom. The Second Amendment is America's "first freedom" because it is necessary to protect all other freedoms.
Limited Government	Infringement on gun rights is one example of government interference in individuals' lives, among others. Gun control is a form of "big government." (This topic focuses more on specific policy issues than it does on the inherent rights of free societies, which is the focus of the "Liberty" category.)

address these questions and get a clearer picture of the relationship between the issue connections contained in NRA editorials and those in pro-gun letters to the editor, I examined the ideological *content* of both the *American Rifleman* editorials and the pro-gun letters. Both sets of documents primarily focus on three distinct issue sets, as described in table 4.2.[11]

Figure 4.2 depicts the proportion of *American Rifleman* editorials and pro-gun letters *within each topic* from the topic models discussed earlier that make issue connections. Before discussing the specifics of the figure, it is worth noting the similarity of the topics across the *American Rifleman* and *American Rifleman* + pro-gun letter to the editor models, which itself demonstrates a common way of discussing guns. Aside from the similarity of the topics themselves, there are also similar issue connections drawn. When aggregated across time, the *American Rifleman*'s *Second Amendment, Gun Regulation,* and *Crime* topics all make issue connections a majority of the time. In the letters to the editor, the *Second Amendment* topic leads the way, with 77 percent of letters connecting gun rights to other issues. All

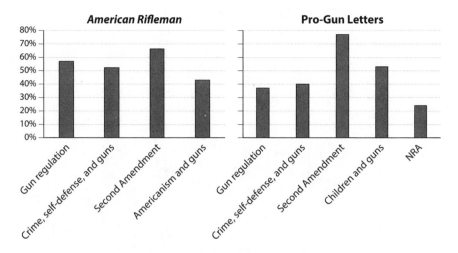

FIGURE 4.2. Proportion of *American Rifleman* Editorials and Pro-Gun Letters with Issue Connections by Topic

other topics aside from the NRA topic, however, make issue connections at solid rates, especially given—as discussed last chapter—the relatively short average length of letters to the editor.

Figure 4.3—focusing on the subset of documents that make at least one issue connection—depicts the types of issue connections made across topics; the top chart depicts connections in *American Rifleman* editorials and the bottom in pro-gun letters to the editor. The horizontal axis within each chart lists the topics, and the bars depict the proportion of documents within each of them that connect guns rights to each issue set (labeled *Crime, Liberty, Limited Government,* or *Other*). These bars give a sense of what the spread of issue connections within each topic looks like. In general, similar issue connection patterns exist across the editorials and letters: crime is the most prominent issue in both *Crime* topics, liberty is the most prominent in both *Gun Regulation* and *Second Amendment* topics, and both *Second Amendment* topics are connected to other issues most frequently in each dataset.

Figure 4.4 depicts the relative prominence of each type of issue connection in *American Rifleman* editorials and pro-gun letters to the editor, regardless of topic. It shows that the most prominent overall issue connection in the *American Rifleman* is liberty—at

American Rifleman Editorials

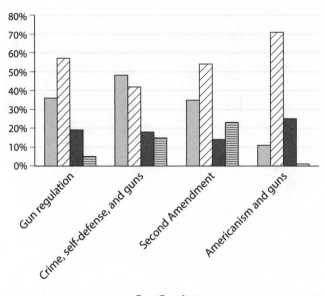

Pro-Gun Letters

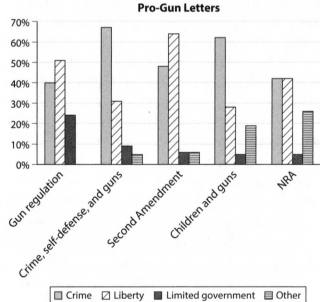

Crime ☐ Liberty ☐ Limited government ■ Other ☐

FIGURE 4.3. Issue Connections in *American Rifleman* Editorials and Pro-Gun Letters by Topic (among Documents with Issue Connections)

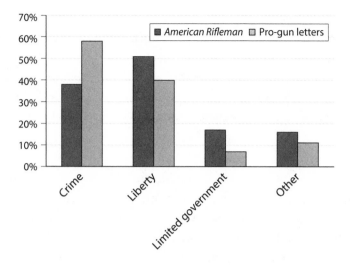

FIGURE 4.4. Issue Connections in *American Rifleman* and Pro-Gun Letters by Issue Type (among Documents with Issue Connections)

51 percent—whereas the most prominent connection overall in the pro-gun letters to the editor is crime. This is likely driven by the overall prominence of the *Crime* topic—which is, unsurprisingly, very likely to connect gun rights to crime[12]—in the letters to the editor. This prominence may be a product of the nature of letters to editors, which typically respond to events in society and/or earlier letters. Since the gun control debate often becomes more salient as a result of crime, it makes sense that crime would be the most prominent letter topic.

Aside from outright issue connections, both the *American Rifleman* editorials and pro-gun letters very frequently argue that current gun laws would be sufficient if only the government more strictly enforced them and handed out harsher punishments to those who violate them. The *American Rifleman* editorials (26 percent) and the pro-gun letters (25 percent) use this argument at nearly identical rates. Although not an explicit limited government argument (and not coded as one), it is related to limited government arguments in the sense that it opposes creating new laws when those currently on the books are (it is claimed) not being enforced. Moreover—and as discussed later—the use of this argument is ideological in the sense that it closely aligns with relatively recent conservative support for harsh sentencing as a way to control crime.

Overall, the positions taken by the NRA and by pro-gun letter writers are very similar. When aggregated, the positions to which gun rights are connected form a set of positions that closely resembles what is now considered conservative ideology in the United States. If an individual adopted all of them, he or she would oppose "big government" (and, contained in the "Other" categories, tight restrictions on campaign finance), support crime control approaches focused on harsh sentencing and personal self-defense using firearms, advocate for a large military apparatus and independence from international organizations (also contained in the "Other" category), and argue that together these positions comprise a pro-liberty agenda—the protection of which requires a constitutionally protected individual right to own firearms.

This high-level picture—given the similarity of both the topics themselves and the issues to which they are connected—demonstrates substantial congruence between the ideological content of the NRA's political appeals to its members and the public political appeals of gun rights supporters. Gun rights supporters' appeals mimic the political discussion of the NRA, and, in the aggregate, both sources espouse a set of issue positions—an ideology—that closely resembles contemporary US conservatism.

Ideology over Time

Having examined the NRA's gun-centric ideology on a high level, the remainder of the chapter focuses on its over-time development. How, when, and in what ways has the NRA's ideology shifted over time? How have these shifts related to the NRA's transition from a quasi-governmental to a partisan phase? How has the ideology's over-time development interacted with the identity described in the last chapter? And, finally, to what extent have the ideological views of NRA supporters been historically *responsive* to the ideological contents of the NRA's editorials?

BUILDING AN IDEOLOGICAL FOUNDATION

During the first few decades of my period of study—when the organization was firmly in its quasi-governmental phase—both the NRA and pro-gun letter writers consistently connected gun rights to other prominent political issues of the time and did so in ways that reflected the organization's strong relationship with the government. Prior to World War II, the NRA voiced its opposition to 1930s efforts at gun control by connecting gun rights to both collective liberty—focused on defense against foreign threats—and individual liberty—namely, individuals' rights to protect themselves from crime. After World War II, emphasis was placed on the role of guns for national defense, focusing mostly on the protection of collective liberty.

1930s to Early 1940s

Early on, the NRA's approach to politics was largely embedded in the language associated with the *Americanism and Guns* topic, which—as noted in table 3.1 from last chapter—describes the centrality of guns throughout US history and their importance to the American tradition. This aligns well with the NRA's quasi-governmental role during this period and the related fact that its programming, as discussed in prior chapters, was closely associated with the US military through the National Board for the Promotion of Rifle Practice and the Civilian Marksmanship Program. These defense-related programs were used to build the identity described last chapter by associating gun ownership with patriotism, citizenship, and personal responsibility.

The issue connections drawn by the NRA during this period align with and reinforce these themes. As figure 4.5 depicts, the *Gun Regulation* and *Crime* topics both see upticks in the mid-1930s, which correspond to debates over the National Firearms Act of 1934 and the Federal Firearms Act of 1938. *Americanism and Guns* remains prominent throughout the decade. A closer look reveals that the NRA's appeals against these laws connected them to both an individual sense of liberty—through an emphasis on self-defense from crime (e.g., the rights of people to defend themselves and their homes)—and a collective sense of liberty—through an emphasis on

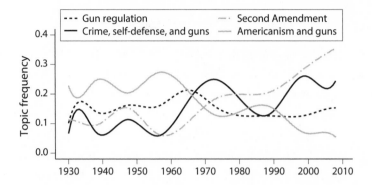

FIGURE 4.5. Frequency of Gun Control-Related *American Rifleman* Editorial Topics over Time

national defense, especially against the threat of communism (e.g., the importance of gun ownership for the defense of US freedom from external forces that threaten it).

Figure 4.6 depicts, over time, the proportion of documents containing issue connections that connect gun rights to the liberty and crime issue sets.[13] It demonstrates that connections to both crime and liberty are present in the 1930s and 1940s, with crime relatively more prominent in the '30s and liberty relatively more prominent in the '40s. The close association of each issue sets' time trends within the *American Rifleman* and the pro-gun letters to the editor throughout the period of study provides compelling evidence of a strong relationship between the ideology cultivated by the NRA and the mass-level pro-gun ideology revealed in the letters to the editor.

Qualitative examinations of both *American Rifleman* editorials and pro-gun letters complement these time trends. An example of the *American Rifleman*'s discussion of collective liberty and gun ownership comes from the September 1935 editorial, which focuses on the connection of gun ownership to the defense of freedom and the Constitution. It warns against altering the Constitution, arguing that "[t]ampering with the truly representative form of government typified by the American Constitution can have only one possible end in view: the breaking down of that representative government and the establishment of some different form of government. The only different form of government possible is some form of dictatorship."

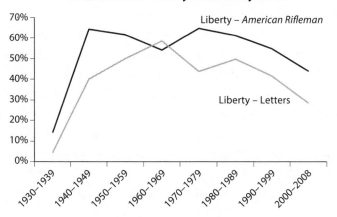

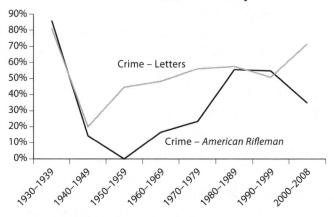

FIGURE 4.6. Issue Connections to Liberty and Crime over Time in *American Rifleman* and Pro-Gun Letters

It then connects this warning to gun ownership, noting, "Dictatorships throughout the history of the world have . . . resulted in the disarmament of the citizenry and the arming of a special few. It is on this ground that the civilian rifleman of America is directly and personally concerned with the Constitution."[14]

The January 1934 editorial addresses both collective and individual liberty in a way that shows how these distinct themes come together to form a broader outlook. It opposes the anti-gun stance of FDR's attorney general, Homer Cummings, by connecting guns to both individual protection from crime and the broader protection of democracy. Quoting Cummings's words from a recent speech, the editorial comments, "We respectfully call the attention of the Attorney General to the fact that the majority of the 'robbers of fact and fiction,' in this country at least, have been stamped out by an aroused armed citizenry" and "that the principal 'weapon of democracy' through the ages has been the ability of the individual citizen to possess and to use with skill arms which were the equal of those possessed by the criminal and by the political and financial masters of the period." The editorial goes on to argue that the "great democracies of the world have invariably been built upon this doctrine. The dictatorships of the world have been built upon the disarmament of the common people."[15]

Similarly, the April 1935 editorial discusses a report that describes a meeting at "Trotsky Headquarters" in which "one speaker boasted 'When we have weakened the country by suppressing its rifle bearers . . . we shall be in a position to go ahead with our plan for setting up a government based on the theories of Karl Marx, Lenin and Stalin,'" and then connects gun ownership to freedom from both crime and government tyranny—again using gun rights to link these two distinct themes:

> Can such a collection of incidents be reviewed without raising a question in any sane man's mind as to how deep-rooted and far-flung may be the sinister influence behind the continuing agitation for that type of firearms regulation which would place the honest citizen at the mercy of the armed criminal, the crooked politician, and the petty bureaucrat? We are convinced that the majority of anti-gun laws are proposed by honest, well-meaning persons, but the continued cropping-up of the sinister influence leads to the belief that these well-meaning persons have been hoodwinked more often than they realize, and are supported more often than they would like to believe by those forces within and without the United States which are concerned not at all with the welfare of the American home and American institutions, but rather are bent upon the pilfering and destruction of both.[16]

There are not enough letters to the editor from early periods to use topic modeling, but a close reading of letters reveals that pro-gun writers at this time echoed the issue connections and general themes of the NRA. A February 1932 letter printed in the *New York Times*, for example, emphasizes an individual's right to self-defense, arguing that the "[p]rotection of the home is an inherent right of every citizen. When the community has shown that it cannot afford him adequate protection, there can be no excuse for a law that penalizes his efforts to protect himself by the most efficient means he can devise." The writer goes on to say that "[i]t is time that all fanatical laws that experience has shown fall short of their purpose and operate to the detriment of the law-abiding citizen should be repealed or suitably modified. . . . There is no way to keep pistols out of the hands of criminals. Why make it unlawful for people to have them who want them only for defense?"[17] And a February 1935 letter printed in the *Chicago Tribune* actually cites NRA programming and connects gun ownership to military preparedness and the defense of collective liberty while supporting training programs and opposing gun regulation:

> The National Rifle association [*sic*] encourages civilian training in the [use of firearms]. . . . Such training leads to what Woodrow Wilson said at the entry of the United States into the world war was the chief reliance of our country, "a citizenry trained and accustomed to arms." . . . Inimical to such training is the current idea . . . that prohibiting the possession of firearms by citizens of good character will suppress crime. . . . [Gun control] would prevent the adequate protection of life and property and threaten the peace and safety of California, in that it was in accord with communistic activities . . . by breaking down national and state defenses. That anti-firearms laws have secret subversive support is not new to the military Intelligence. A Sportsman's Reserve corps would promote safety and foster patriotism.[18]

Beyond just connecting gun rights to collective liberty and crime control, the appeals of both the NRA and its supporters also emphasize characteristics associated with the gun owner identity described in the last chapter. In connecting gun rights to collective liberty, they imply that gun owners are patriotic defenders of American democracy whose strong citizenship prevents dictatorship from occurring in the United States. Such appeals connect gun ownership to themes associated with military service, which may serve to align gun owner and military identities—a connection that fit well with the NRA's mission during its quasi-governmental phase. The NRA's appeals also imply that gun owners are "common people" who can protect the country from an out-of-touch and potentially overbearing elite. Finally, in connecting gun rights and individual liberty through a focus on self-defense, they imply that gun owners have a strong sense of personal responsibility and can take care of themselves. Sociologist Scott Melzer argues that appeals like these—in which gun ownership is connected to "rugged individualism, hard work, protecting and providing for families, and self-reliance"—promote "frontier masculinity," an identity that shapes the worldview of many white men.[19] Melzer's work helps demonstrate how the NRA's connection of gun rights to individual liberty and self-sufficiency also likely aligns the gun owner identity with a certain type of masculine gender identity. In sum, the NRA appeals identified in this section show how the organization's efforts at ideological cultivation and identity building are not distinct endeavors but instead are mutually reinforcing.

Finally, both the NRA and several pro-gun letter writers—including one of those quoted above—explicitly connect the ideological linkage between gun ownership and liberty to NRA programming.[20] In so doing, they provide evidence that the identity-laden, politicized programming discussed in the last chapter also served to advance the NRA's political ideology. Further evidence that the NRA used its programs during this period to advance its ideological commitments comes from the *American Rifleman*, in which the NRA connected participation in its civilian rifle and Junior Rifle Corps programs with the protection of American freedom and explicitly connected such freedom to opposition to gun control.[21] The NRA also created a Police Division during this period, in which it held firearms training classes for police in an attempt "to sell the NRA idea to police chiefs and subordinates throughout the United States"; it seems that the NRA sought to combat the notion that gun control should be used to fight crime by convincing police officers of the worthiness of its cause.[22]

Early 1940s to 1950s

Throughout the 1940s and into the 1950s—before, during, and after World War II—the NRA continued to connect gun ownership to liberty. However, during this period, the NRA's appeals focused largely on gun ownership's impact on collective rather individual liberty. The drop in the prominence of the crime issue set (seen in figure 4.6)—which tended to be tied to an individual sense of liberty—is evidence of this. These developments—occurring in conjunction with WWII, the Korean War, and the beginning of the Cold War—demonstrate that the NRA's ideological framing of gun ownership was responsive to external sociopolitical changes. They also fit well with both the NRA's mission during its quasi-governmental phase and its post-WWII recruitment of veterans by connecting gun rights to a political perspective that likely appealed to many service members. Finally, and relatedly, the NRA's ideological appeals during this period continued to reinforce themes associated with the gun owner identity, most notably (and appropriately given the nature of the period's ideological appeals) by associating gun ownership with patriotism and the American tradition, and continuing to connect it to military service.

The February 1943 *American Rifleman* editorial exemplifies the NRA's focus during this period. This editorial argues strongly against gun registration by connecting it to disarmament and connecting guns to the defense of freedom, insisting that "[w]e need to clearly understand that registration, with the resultant possibility of confiscation of privately owned arms, is . . . essential to successful invasion of our democratic rights . . . [and] our native soil." Preempting a counterargument, the editorial continues, "It is meaningless to say that no one has such a result in mind when they propose registration of firearms. We are not concerned with present intentions. . . . We face the facts of history. The registration of privately owned arms has always been a prerequisite to conquest by foreign or domestic dictators. Whether the dictator's intentions are benign or oppressive is beside the point." It then ends, "Freedom shackled soon starves."[23]

An August 1952 letter printed in the *New York Times*, which appears to have been inspired by the *American Rifleman*, similarly connects gun ownership to collective liberty and war preparation while opposing gun regulations. The writer states, "The National Rifle Association of America . . . through its official journal, *The American Rifleman*, has been endorsing the fight by sportsmen against these various bills for many years. . . . The reason? In Norway and Denmark a national firearms registration act was in force prior to the Second World War." It then further explains this logic, arguing that "[w]hen these countries were occupied by the Germans it was a simple matter for the Nazis to obtain the complete registration lists of guns of all types owned by the populace and confiscate them" before warning, "that this same situation could happen here should be apparent to all of us." Finally, it connects gun ownership to war preparation and the Constitution, contending that "a citizenry well versed in the use of small arms is an enormous advantage in time of mobilization, and it should be remembered that the right of the people to keep and bear arms guaranteed under the Second Article of the Bill of Rights carries with it the obligation to be prepared to use them for the security of the state."[24]

As part of this theme, the NRA—in both its editorials and other sections of the *American Rifleman*—repeatedly emphasized throughout the 1940s how gun regulations left England unprepared for WWII and thus susceptible to hostile takeover.[25] The December 1940 editorial, for example, discusses proposed state level gun regulations and connects them to England's lack of war munitions. It uses this discussion as part of a call to action—and actually instructs members to cite England's experience in letters to newspaper editors (emphasis added):

Make your position known to your City Councilmen and State Legislators before they have these bills presented. . . . *Reply by letter to the editor to every newspaper editorial supporting this dangerous theory.* Point to England's experience. An England, disarmed and gun-ignorant by reason of the same type of gun law that is now proposed for America, is forced to turn to American arms plants and to American gun-owners for guns and ammunition for defense against invaders from without and criminals from within![26]

It appears that this instruction was followed. After the NRA began making this argument—but not before—letters to the editor from various regions of the country repeated the NRA's version of England's experience.[27] The following March 1941 *New York Times* letter to the editor, for example, specifically cites the NRA's argument about England while opposing a gun law, and connects gun ownership to liberty while doing so:

The proposed legislation to restrict or to regulate possession of private arms, if adopted in any form, would ... constitute a menace to civil liberty and place us in the unfortunate predicament of England. Strict arms regulations in the past left the rank and file of the English people gun-ignorant and gun-shy, hence their urgent call on American sportsmen and householders for spare arms for home defense in this crisis. We believe the Sullivan Law should be repealed because it has backfired, doubly arming the crook by disarming the honest citizen. We believe that private arms regulations would eventually deprive us of one of our cherished birthrights and be a violation of our Constitution, which reads in part, "The right of the people to keep and bear arms shall not be infringed."[28]

Notably, this argument continued to show up even years later, including in a 1966 letter sent to then-member of the House of Representatives Bob Dole.[29]

As before, there is evidence that during this period the NRA used the programming discussed in the last chapter to not only spread a social identity but to also advance its ideological commitments. The September 1958 *American Rifleman* editorial, for example, argues that support for gun legislation is a result of ignorance about the benefits of gun ownership; it notes that "[t]here is a growing prejudice against firearms. More excuses constantly are being found to propose legislation which denies the right to use firearms for protection, for marksmanship training for national defense, or for the recreational pleasures of shooting and hunting. . . . The time has come to make a positive nation-wide effort to overcome the ignorance." It then implores members to educate others about gun ownership and the NRA's safety programming in order to change their minds: "Let's educate public officials and people in general . . . about the positive values of shooting and hunting; about the hunter safety and marksmanship programs of the National Rifle Association of America which has conducted safe and worthwhile rifle and pistol activities for millions of people." And, finally, it connects all of this to the protection of collective liberty in the United States, asserting that the "right of the people to keep and bear arms, as well as all other individual rights, is effective only to the degree that the people are willing to meet the obligations of freedom. Only by eternal vigilance can those rights be protected and our nation remain free."[30]

Similarly, a September 1949 letter printed in the *New York Times* opposes gun regulation by connecting gun ownership with military preparedness and the protection of collective liberty, arguing that "laws seeking to disarm the entire population are not only contrary to our Constitution but prove most dangerous . . . in providing hostile invaders with ownership lists of small arms." It then connects both of those things to NRA training and safety programs (and does so while framing gun control in personalized identity terms):

> Real sportsmen using guns in either hunting or target shooting have a minimum of accidents, due to careful training in the use of firearms. Ask the National Rifle Association in Washington, headquarters for 6,500 shooting clubs with hundreds of thousands of members. . . . Should all these sportsmen who are spending many millions of dollars yearly for their sport be deprived of it? Ask rifle instructors who trained recruits during the last war how many were already familiar with the rudiments of handling firearms. . . . Anti-firearms legislation is not the solution, and clubs

and sportsmen from Coast to Coast will fight for the preservation of their constitutional rights vigorously.[31]

THE ENEMIES WITHIN: GUNS AS A DEFENSE AGAINST ONE'S OWN GOVERNMENT

The NRA's ideological cultivation continued during the 1960s and 1970s, but the content of the ideology evolved in response to both changing sociopolitical conditions and the organization's shift from its quasi-governmental to its partisan phase. As crime rates in the United States soared, the NRA's emphasis on both the usefulness of guns for self-defense and the rights of individuals to defend themselves using firearms increased. Further, as the NRA's formal ties to the government weakened—as its quasi-governmental phase began to end—it shifted away from its prior emphasis on the importance of guns for the protection of US liberty from foreign threats. Instead, the NRA, as it moved into its partisan phase, began to emphasize the importance of an individual right to own firearms in order to protect against the threat of domestic government tyranny. Finally, gun regulation was connected to issues of limited government by framing gun control as one form of "big government."

1960s and 1970s

Following its postwar emphasis on the relationship between gun ownership and collective liberty, the NRA's approach began to change during the 1960s in response to various external developments. One such development was a dramatic increase in crime, especially gun violence, beginning in the early 1960s.[32] The period also witnessed numerous high-profile shootings, including the 1963 assassination of President Kennedy, a prominent mass shooting at the University of Texas in 1966, and the 1968 assassinations of both Martin Luther King Jr. and Robert F. Kennedy. These media-generating events, combined with increased overall crime rates, led to renewed calls for gun regulation following a relatively quiet postwar period.

The NRA's response to these trends is seen in figures 4.5 and 4.7, which depicts the *American Rifleman* + pro-gun letters to the

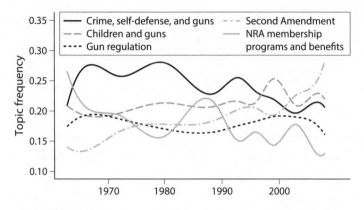

FIGURE 4.7. Frequency of *American Rifleman* and Pro-Gun Letter to the Editor Topics over Time

editor topic model mentioned earlier. Both of these figures show an increased emphasis on crime during this period. Additionally, in figure 4.6, we see a return to prominence of issue connections between gun ownership and crime (with issue connections to liberty remaining high throughout). The NRA's crime issue connections during this period, like in earlier periods, emphasized the right of individuals to use firearms for self-defense. In a new development, however, the NRA argued with much greater frequency that existing gun laws would be sufficient to curtail crime if only the criminal justice system better enforced them and handed out harsher punishments to offenders. Whereas only 15 percent of NRA editorials made this argument during the gun control debates of the 1930s, 31 percent and 29 percent did so, respectively, in the 1960s and 1970s.

In a separate development, the NRA's formal relationship with the military began to weaken considerably at this time. As discussed in greater detail in chapter 6, this was due in part to the NRA's increasingly controversial public image, which led to scrutiny of its support from the federal government. This scrutiny, along with a shift away from a post-WWII social climate that better aligned with the NRA's mission, led to the elimination or reduction of government support for numerous NRA activities.[33] Figure 4.8 captures the NRA's response to this trend, depicting a steady and dramatic decline in the prominence of the *Americanism and Guns* topic—which typically

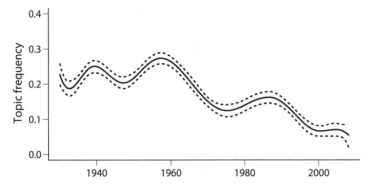

FIGURE 4.8. Frequency of Americanism and Guns Topic (*American Rifleman*-only) over Time

emphasized the NRA's relationship with the military—beginning during this period. The steep decline of this topic vividly illustrates the end of the NRA's quasi-governmental phase.

At almost the exact point at which the prominence of the *Americanism and Guns* topic began to decrease, the prominence of the *Second Amendment* topic began to increase. As the sociopolitical salience of war preparedness declined (particularly as it pertained to individual marksmanship in an age of nuclear weapons) and the NRA's military ties weakened, the organization increasingly began to connect its political appeals to the Second Amendment—or, more specifically, the *meaning* it associated with the Second Amendment.

The *Second Amendment* topic is, in some ways, similar to the *Americanism and Guns* topic: each generally emphasizes both collective and individual liberty, connects gun ownership to patriotism and citizenship, and emphasizes the historical role of guns in US society. The topics differ substantially, however, in that the *Second Amendment* topic associates the protection of gun rights with defense against tyranny from one's own government rather than as protection against tyranny that might be imposed by foreign invaders or domestic subversives. Guns continued to be depicted as crucial to freedom, but their role was increasingly framed in terms of protecting liberty from government rather than from foreign dictators.

As the NRA moved into its new partisan phase, the Second Amendment quickly became the anchor of its ideological perspective.

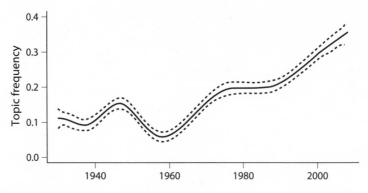

FIGURE 4.9. Frequency of Second Amendment Topic (*American Rifleman*-only) over Time

Notably, however, this increased emphasis on the Second Amendment occurred despite the conclusion of an internal 1955 study—requested by NRA chief Merritt Edson and now contained in his papers—that there is minimal evidence the amendment protects an individual right to own guns.[34] The NRA clearly ignored this finding, perhaps as a result of a belief that an individual rights reading of "2A" could be politically useful. This trend is captured in figure 4.9, which is from the *American Rifleman* topic model, and in the *Second Amendment* topic in figure 4.7, which depicts the topic model of both pro-gun letters and *American Rifleman* editorials.

An example of this new frame comes from the July 1963 *American Rifleman* editorial's celebration of Independence Day, which ties an individual right to own firearms to the spirit of the Declaration of Independence and the Constitution, and connects this right to all others in the Constitution. Consistently emphasizing the rights of individuals, it argues that the essence of America is individual liberty from government:

> [The] Declaration of Independence is an assertion of the principles of a form of government in which the individual is recognized as the source of authority. . . . The Constitution of the United States confers certain powers upon the national government but reserves to the people large areas of freedom. . . . These rights which the people kept for themselves became the first ten Amendments to the Constitution. . . . They were intended to

safeguard cherished individual liberties from invasion by . . . our government. . . . The Second Amendment asserts that "the right of the people to keep and bear arms shall not be infringed." . . . One of the most sacred and meaningful liberties of the individual American is the right to possess firearms and to use them for lawful purposes. . . . We who are citizens of the United States of America today have been given the precious heritage of freedom. . . . Let us take a deep look at our freedoms as they exist on this Independence Day and then silently, but determinedly, resolve under God that we are going to preserve and pass on to future generations those basic individual rights for which our forefathers fought, bled, and died.[35]

The following January 1964 letter printed in the *New York Times* echoes this sort of argument. It connects gun rights to other constitutional freedoms and argues that protecting the Bill of Rights is necessary to safeguard individual liberty against tyranny from the Federal government; it contends that "[t]o question any one of the amendments is to throw open the door to tyranny. The Bill of Rights was designed to protect the individual citizen against possible acts of tyranny on the part of Federal (or any other) authorities. . . . The inclusion of the Second Amendment at that time was almost superfluous in a country the greater part of whose people were almost totally dependent on arms for livelihood and protection." Further, it associates these views with aspects of the gun owner identity described in the last chapter, connecting them to the American tradition: "Without the indomitable spirit of our pioneer and his rifle our country would not be the great nation it is. Ownership of a rifle is part of our national heritage. Let's keep it that way."[36]

It was also during this period that gun rights became increasingly connected to limited government positions, with gun control portrayed as a form of "big government." The NRA laid the foundation for this argument in earlier periods, framing gun control as a form of "big government" beginning in the late 1940s and early 1950s.[37] Pro-gun letters began to use this argument in the 1960s.[38] As figure 4.3 shows, limited government issue connections are common in the

Gun Regulation topic, which, as figures 4.5 and 4.7 show, were prominent in both the *American Rifleman* and the *American Rifleman* + letters to the editor datasets during this period.

Letters to President Johnson also tended to echo these themes. Some opponents of new gun control laws noted that they would "require a gigantic and costly bureaucracy to establish and operate." Others argued against gun control by noting that the security it hoped to achieve came at the cost of constitutional freedoms; a letter from June 1968, for example, noted that "security can never be the possession of a free democratic people. The people must always guard their freedom, and fight for it. . . . We must not permit anyone, no matter what their reason, to remove any freedom given to us by our constitution." Another letter from that same month opposed gun control because of the power it gives the government over individuals, noting, "Our most important argument against [gun] registration is that it gives the government too much power over the people. It is too easy for such laws to go further than just finding out who owns the guns. After the arms are registered, we could easily be taxed and then who knows—perhaps even confiscation of arms altogether. . . . It is every American's duty to do all he can to prevent a gun law, for once we lose our right to bear arms, we lose our freedom."[39]

Gun rights supporters used these arguments in other forums as well. During committee hearings on gun control legislation in the 1960s, for instance, a gun owner who had traveled from Arizona to testify invoked a constitutional right to own guns while connecting gun control to a loss of freedom and the rise of communism. He told the Senate's Commerce Committee, "The gun is the standard of freedom in the United States of America. When there are restrictions placed on the right of the American citizen to keep and bear arms, then it is only a matter of time before the Communist take-over."[40]

As it did in prior years, the NRA continued to depict its programming as key to advancing its ideological perspective. The NRA's so-called Centennial Plan—which, as discussed last chapter, laid out the organization's goals for the last decade of its first century of existence—called for the use and expansion of NRA programs to "create a more favorable public opinion for guns" in order to stem renewed interest in gun control.[41] The NRA also revamped its Police Training Program during this period and included a police division in its target shooting competitions; the NRA, during a period of intensifying crimes, explicitly tied these new programs to its belief that "[e]ffective enforcement of our laws is essential to the protection of individual rights."[42]

GUNS AND MAINSTREAM CONSERVATISM

The NRA's ideological commitments remained fairly constant during the 1980s and 1990s, even as it moved further into its partisan phase and its place in the political system continued to change. The NRA and pro-gun letter writers continued to emphasize individual liberty by focusing on both self-defense from crime and protection from government tyranny. They also continued to frame gun control as a form of "big government" while increasingly emphasizing the importance of the Second Amendment to their political worldview. In a new addition to this worldview, the NRA began advancing a right-wing brand of nationalistic populism beginning in the early 2000s, which focuses on the threat posed to both guns and American liberty by so-called globalist elites—a seeming preview of the future of conservative politics.

1980 to Early 1990s

The issue connections made by both the NRA and gun rights supporters during the 1980s and into the 1990s were mostly the same as those made in previous eras, although they were now generally more closely aligned with official Republican Party positions—a reflection of the organization having moved into a new phase of its history. As figure 4.6 demonstrates, connections to liberty remained high, and the upward trend of crime issue connections continued (as did, not depicted, connections to limited government). The prominence of the topic models' *Second Amendment* topics (see figures 4.5, 4.7, and 4.9) continued to grow, becoming the most prominent topic during this decade in the NRA-only model and rising in prominence in the combined *American Rifleman*-letter model.

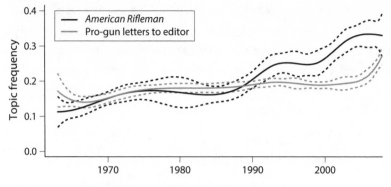

FIGURE 4.10. Second Amendment Topic by Source

Figure 4.10 (which includes confidence intervals around each of the topic estimates) depicts the *Second Amendment* topic from the letters to the editor + *American Rifleman* model split by source, with separate lines for NRA editorials and pro-gun letters to the editor. It demonstrates that the prominence of this topic within each source grows together and, importantly, suggests that letter writers followed the NRA's lead in emphasizing the Second Amendment. Editorials and pro-gun letters from this period, in general, demonstrate a continuation of the pattern that began in the previous period, in which emphasis is placed on the relationship between guns and individual liberty. This trend makes sense given the NRA's alignment during this period with a political party that emphasized small government and personal responsibility.

An example of the increasing prominence of the *Second Amendment* topic within editorials connecting gun rights to liberty and crime comes from the August 1989 editorial, which is an excerpt of a speech given by then-NRA Executive Vice President J. Warren Cassidy. Cassidy places gun rights at the center of a broad ideology focused on individual rights and limited government. He argues that without a constitutionally protected individual right to own guns, all other constitutional freedoms, along with the right to personal self-defense, would be threatened. The NRA now uses the phrase "America's first freedom" to refer to this line of reasoning; the Second Amendment, the argument goes, is America's first freedom because without it no other freedoms would be safe. Cassidy also connects this view to the gun owner identity described in the last chapter by depicting gun owners as the defenders of the American tradition—associated with rugged individualism and self-sufficiency—and their opponents as "collectivists" who hope to destroy that tradition. The editorial is a very useful example of how the themes associated with the NRA's ideological perspective come together with its identity to form a cohesive political worldview:

> The right to own and use firearms is the preeminent individual right. Without the ability to physically defend the other provisions of our Constitution . . . , the remainder of the Bill of Rights become privileges granted by the government. . . . Does the government trust the people enough to recognize the rights and allow the power? . . . [C]an the people trust the government with a monopoly on firepower? Our Declaration of Independence and Second Amendment unhesitatingly answered "yes" to the first and "no" to the second. . . . Until the middle of the 19th century, the American dream was of an individualistic society, with individual rights and responsibilities, and a deep distrust of government interference. . . . Here and abroad, the dream of individual rights took a collectivist twist. . . . Our traditional abhorrence of government meddling has been reversed. . . . We are told we must give up essential liberty for some temporary safety. . . . Whereas the Framers dreamed of a strong citizenry who could remove any threatening government, modern collectivists attempt to reduce the Second Amendment to a measure of the "sporting use" of firearms. . . . The American dream of individual rights and responsibilities, a beacon to the world even in its diminished form, may well see a renaissance. Self-defense, defense of country, and resistance to tyranny (the Second Amendment's triune) are not abstract principles. The right of the people to keep and bear arms guarantees the rest of our freedoms.[43]

The April 1987 editorial, also written by Cassidy, gives a clearer picture of specifically how Second Amendment rights are connected to crime. Cassidy argues that the right to own firearms for self-defense is a matter of individual freedom, stating that "[t]he fundamental human instinct is self-preservation. And a fundamental freedom is the right to choose to keep and bear a firearm for that purpose." Reemphasizing his point and connecting it the Constitution, Cassidy continued, "Human beings must be allowed the freedom to defend themselves in the face of clear and present danger and to choose the means to do so. One of those choices may be a firearm. I believe in the precise wording of the Second Amendment, that there shall be no infringement of the inalienable 'right of the people to keep and bear arms.'"[44]

Pro-gun letters to the editor during this period adopted these same frames. An April 1989 letter printed in the *Atlanta Journal-Constitution*, for example, argues that Second Amendment rights are needed as protection against government tyranny, stating that "[f]irearms . . . have been a valuable and necessary part of our tradition because our Founding Fathers understood that people need personal protection not only from each other, but from the threat of oppressive government." It then opposes gun control by connecting widespread gun ownership to reduced crime rates, arguing that "[r]ather than scheming to eliminate guns, politicians and media moguls would better serve our country by examining evidence that suggests we would be safer if citizens were required to possess guns. . . . If all law-abiding citizens of age were armed, the nuts who decide to rob banks, kidnap children and shoot dozens of people in crowded places would either change their minds or they would die." Throughout, the letter reinforces the gun owner identity described in the last chapter, depicting gun owners as average, law-abiding citizens and gun control supporters as out-of-touch media and political elites. Indeed, it goes on to claim that "[m]ost Washington politicians simply do not have time, between fund-raisers and tropical vacations, to bother learning facts such as these. They probably get most of their education on the evening news, which would explain the worsening leftist tilt of governmental policies over the last few decades."[45]

Similarly, a May 1991 letter, also from the *Atlanta Journal-Constitution*, connects the Second Amendment to both personal self-defense and the prevention of government tyranny. It first points out that the "police cannot protect all of the people all of the time," which means that "[p]ersonal defense of self, family, and property is a legitimate justification for the Second Amendment." It then shifts, noting that "[a]ccording to Thomas Jefferson, though, the principal idea of this amendment is to guard against governmental tyranny. If as individuals we cannot be entrusted with personal firearms, then what evil indeed shall we devise upon our disarmed brethren as we organize ourselves into legislatures, police forces and standing armies?"[46]

NRA members also consistently espouse these views in other forums, often telling interviewers, for instance, that "my Second Amendment protects your First" and that it is "by far the most important of all the amendments" because, as another member comments, it serves as "the armed guard of the rest."[47] Connecting this view to individual liberty and limited government, another NRA member says that the Second Amendment is crucial because "the right to bear arms is a serious thorn in the side of those who desire greater government control over our society and our individual lives."[48] Some gun owners explicitly relate their support for gun rights to opposition of what they perceive as big government liberalism; one commented, "*Why* do liberals hate guns? They don't believe in personal responsibility, that's why, and think the government should take care of everything!"[49]

Similar comments from others make especially clear how this view—in which guns are a symbol of self-sufficiency and as such align with opposition to government programs—connects to the gun owner identity discussed last chapter. One gun owner told an interviewer, for instance, "I think you . . . either adopt an attitude of, 'I'm gonna depend on society, I'm gonna depend on government to make sure I'm cool' or 'I'm gonna take responsibility for my own safety.'"[50] Another said that people believe that "government and someone else is responsible for everything that they do. And the more I see that view, the more I don't want to be that person. Ever."[51] Finally, a different gun owner said, "There's a big divide of people who want to be taken care of and people who don't want to be taken

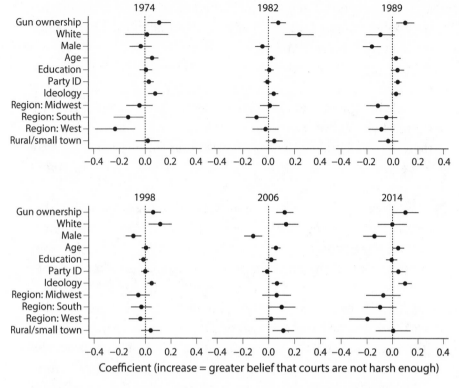

FIGURE 4.11. Relationship between Gun Ownership and Views on the Court System. The figure depicts original analyses of the General Social Survey. The depicted OLS models use standardized independent variables that are weighted to be nationally representative. The bars represent 95 percent confidence intervals. Separate models were estimated for each year. Years were selected based on proximity to presidential elections and variable availability. Gun ownership in the depicted models is based on whether a respondent lives in a household with a gun (which is the only gun ownership variable available in the 1974 data); the results are substantively the same when personal gun ownership is used for 1982 and forward. The dependent variable asks, "In general, do you think the courts in this area deal too harshly or not harshly enough with criminals?" with responses including "too harsh," "about right," and "not harsh enough."

care of. And the people who don't want to be taken care of are the same people who want to keep their guns."[52]

The NRA also continued to advocate for "Law and Order" style crime policies, with 45 percent of editorials in the 1980s and 41 percent in the 1990s arguing that existing gun laws would be sufficient if they were more strictly enforced and if offenders were given harsher sentences. Moreover, this view took hold among gun owners. Figure 4.11 depicts the results of statistical models that—while holding other important factors constant—measure the extent to which gun ownership has, at different points in time, been related to whether individuals think the courts need to be harder on criminals.[53] As the figure demonstrates, gun ownership has consistently been a statistically significant predictor of individuals' views on the court system since as early as 1974, with gun owners more likely than others to say that courts are not harsh enough when doling out punishments.

The NRA's support for harsh "Law and Order" crime policies also connects gun ownership and the gun owner identity to white racial identity. These policies have historically been favored by candidates with racially regressive views, are associated with rhetoric that increases fear of crime among whites, and have been shown to disproportionately impact African Americans and other racial minorities.[54] Although it is difficult to measure the relationship between gun ownership and white racial identity that existed during this period, the contemporary relationship between the two is well documented.[55] Moreover, NRA appeals that advocate for harsh sentencing demonstrate how the organization connected gun ownership with white racial identity. The following November 1993 editorial written by Wayne LaPierre, for example, discusses the murder of two police officers in North Carolina by a Black man in a way that is clearly designed to stoke fear of urban crime among the NRA's mostly white members:

The suspect in the slayings . . . ? Alden Jerome Harden. On probation for a 1992 armed robbery—plea-bargained down to robbery. Arrested 19 times . . . —convicted only nine times. Sentenced to seven years in 1992—sentence suspended. And when he violated parole last spring, when he could have been sent straight to prison, a . . . judge sent him to the streets. This is the face of crime in America: assault, arrest, release. . . . The latest cop killer may be behind bars, but his accomplice—a runaway criminal justice system—is still on the loose. . . . It's time to scrap a system designed for pranksters who stole hub caps and replace it with one for gangsters who rape and kill. . . . "3 Strikes, You're Out!" . . . There is no reason that violent predators have to be housed any better than law-abiding poor people. . . . The families of these officers know too well the brutal face of crime. One day soon, they will recognize the face of law and order. Its initials: NRA.[56]

As in prior periods, the NRA continued to use its programs to advance its ideological commitments. In addition to growing programs developed earlier, the NRA created a new handgun program, the "Voluntary Practical Firearms Program," in 1983. The program aimed to "provide law-abiding citizens with basic instruction in the safe-handling and use of handguns for personal and family protection." Wrapped up in this program was a strong claim that individuals have a right to own and use handguns, and that such a right is an important crime-fighting tool.[57] The course—which was marketed to both women and men—drew 250,000 participants by 1986, more than half of whom were women.[58]

NRA leaders were explicit about the importance of these programs to the organization. Harlon Carter, who oversaw a large membership drive in the early 1980s, discussed the significance of cultivating participation in firearms programs for advancing the NRA's political agenda, noting that, in democracies, "the numbers count," and he connected the NRA's general ideological views to the number of people using firearms.[59] Warren Cassidy was even more explicit, writing in January 1987 that "[t]he potential for unprecedented growth is enormous for it is through basic firearms courses that many individuals are introduced to guns and shooting—and the [NRA]. . . . In this respect, the educational process that NRA instructors provide is of vital importance to the NRA cause and is the cornerstone of our Association, its purposes and objectives." Further clarifying his point, Cassidy wrote, "NRA instructors not only educate new shooters, they introduce them to the NRA and what it stands for: the protection and use of their constitutional rights." Although the "NRA is highly respected for its tremendous commitment to and effectiveness in legislative action," Cassidy went on, "successful legislative action must be accompanied by effective educational programs. It is through education and training programs that we ensure that the right to keep and bear arms is exercised."[60]

Early 1990s to Present

As the relationship between the NRA and the Republican Party has deepened in the most recent decades—as the organization has moved further into its partisan phase—the NRA has continued to push conservative ideological positions favored by Republicans. It has also continued to adapt its positions to respond to external events. As figure 4.5 demonstrates, the *American Rifleman*-only model's *Second Amendment* topic has continued to grow and has been the most prominent topic in NRA editorials since the 1980s. The *Crime* topic also saw an additional uptick during this period, particularly during and after the point at which the Clinton Administration pursued crime legislation proposals that often included gun control. As figure 4.6 demonstrates, NRA editorials continued to connect gun rights to liberty at high levels, and—unsurprisingly given the *Crime* topic's increase in the 1990s—issue connections to crime remained high (trailing off somewhat within the *American Rifleman* in recent years). The substantive content of these issue connections is very similar to prior periods.

Notably, toward the end of my period of study but well before Donald Trump's political ascendance, the NRA began advocating the conservative brand of populism and nationalism associated with Trump's successful 2016 presidential campaign. In this line of reasoning, gun rights are seen as part and parcel of the United States' authority over its laws and culture. UN treaties containing internationally written and enforced gun control laws, for example, are seen as a threat that must be defeated. And gun control advocates are seen as globalist elites who want US policy to reflect international norms; opposition to gun control thus protects traditional American culture. These appeals—like Trump's—are notable for the vitriol and conspiratorial thinking they contain. The September 2004 editorial written by Wayne LaPierre, for example, implores gun owners to vote for George W. Bush over John Kerry in order to avoid the advancement of the globalist agenda of George Soros and Michael Moore:

If President George W. Bush is driven out of office—or if the Senate and House change hands next year—two men will claim the credit. And they will stand firmly in position to change the cultural destiny of America and . . . [declare] war against those of us who believe in the Second Amendment. If you think those two figures are Senators John Kerry and John Edwards, you're wrong. . . . Don't look at Kerry and Edwards; look through them—and you will see political manipulators: globalist billionaire George Soros and agitprop filmmaker Michael Moore. . . . Among Soros' goals is a global U.N. gun ban, which fits in with his larger plan to diminish, weaken and subjugate the United States as a world player, to erode our sovereignty, and to domestically erase the dominant traditional values of the American people. . . . And Soros most likely won't stop there; he will buy himself a U.S. Supreme Court, stacked with anti-gun justices who can rule against our rights for a lifetime. The Soros nationwide voter registration targets Michael Moore's angry, undiscerning, fan club. Moore, who tells foreign audiences that Americans are "the dumbest people on the planet," is inciting a hate-America . . . mob. . . . There is only one force in America strong enough to stop them—the membership of the NRA and our supporters. . . . We must vote. And we must get our friends and neighbors to register and vote. Make yourself responsible for getting five or 10 voters to the polls. We can reelect George W. Bush and we can elect a Second Amendment-safe Senate and House. But only if we mobilize, right now, today.[61]

The NRA's relatively early advancement of this type of nationalistic populism suggests that—despite its increasingly close relationship with the Republican Party—the organization has maintained ideological independence and the ability to drive (rather than be driven by) change in the party. Additionally—and as discussed in greater depth in chapter 6—the NRA's advancement of this worldview has tied the gun owner social identity to numerous other politically relevant identities and attitudes held by many supporters of right-wing politics, including those related to race, gender, religion, and region.

Pro-gun letter writers continued to echo the NRA's arguments during this period. As figure 4.7 demonstrates, the *Second Amendment* topic in the letters + *American Rifleman* model continued to increase, eventually becoming the model's most prominent topic. The *Crime* topic remained prominent, but declined a bit; this trend is likely due to the rise of a more specific crime-oriented topic— *Children and Guns*—which spiked following the Columbine High School massacre in 1999. Issue connections to crime and liberty both remained high, as did the substantive content of connections to these issue sets. Pro-gun letters, as of 2008, had not yet adopted the specifically nationalistic form of populism from the *American Rifleman* that is described above, but in more recent interviews NRA members have mentioned the threat of UN gun bans and the importance of gun rights to American sovereignty.[62] And based on gun owner—and general Republican—support for Donald Trump in 2016, it seems likely that this ideological perspective did eventually take hold among the NRA's constituency.

The NRA's new programmatic offerings during this period—particularly its concealed carry courses—advanced its ideological commitments in the same ways that its programs had in prior eras. NRA concealed carry courses explicitly link gun rights to crime issues, depicting guns as a solution to crime rather than a cause of it.[63] Jennifer Carlson's work, as discussed last chapter, closely examines these courses and finds that they are heavily political. Moreover, Carlson argues that these programs connect gun rights to masculinity by emphasizing the usefulness of guns for taking care of one's family; they are thus an additional example of how the NRA's efforts at ideological cultivation also connect the gun owner identity to other politically salient social identities.[64]

Further Quantifying the NRA's Causal Role

Throughout this chapter, I have presented evidence suggesting that the NRA has been an important source of the ideological perspective that has been adopted by its supporters. As was the case with the identity described last chapter, the issue connections drawn by the

NRA and pro-gun letters are strikingly similar, clearly demonstrating a shared ideology that is advanced by the NRA and held by gun owners. Further, the NRA's status as the preeminent group in the US firearms community—combined with its positioning vis-à-vis the identity discussed last chapter—puts it in a strong position to lead this community ideologically—a position that its leaders have consistently recognized and sought to use strategically. Further evidence comes from the over-time responsiveness of pro-gun letter writers to issue and topic connections contained in NRA editorials. Figures 4.6 and 4.10—and qualitative examples from throughout the chapter—suggest that the NRA's supporters have indeed taken cues from it.

But to get at this further—to provide an additional and more systematic quantitative test—I can again use the cosine similarity responsiveness procedure described last chapter. In this instance, I restrict the analysis only to documents that make issues connections; in other words, I exclusively examine editorials and pro-gun letters that exhibit ideological reasoning. As a reminder, this measurement technique uses cosine similarity scores—which are commonly deployed by plagiarism detection software—in an over-time fashion to examine the extent to which the contents of two sets of documents respond to each other systematically. In short, they enable me to examine whether pro-gun letters to the editor from one time period systematically adopt NRA ideas—in this case, an ideology—from the prior period.

I again broke the NRA editorials and pro-gun letters to the editor into separate time buckets of various lengths based on the year in which they were published; as I did in the last chapter, this consisted of 8 buckets of ~10 years of documents, 6 buckets of ~13 years, 5 buckets of ~16 years, and 5 buckets of uneven lengths with break points based on important moments in the history of the NRA.[65] I then repeated the same procedure as in the last chapter, but only used editorials and letters that contain issue connections.[66]

Figure 4.12 depicts the results.[67] As the figure shows, three of the four time groupings have statistically significant, positive average differences, and the fourth—the 10-year grouping—is positive and nearly significant; not depicted, the 16-year and theoretically driven

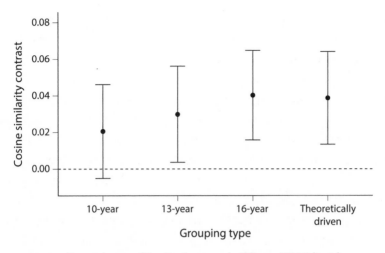

FIGURE 4.12. Responsiveness of Pro-Gun Letters to the Editor to NRA Editorials among Documents with Issue Connections. Figure depicts the average cosine similarity responsiveness of pro-gun letters to NRA editorials from the *American Rifleman* among the subset of documents that contain issue connections. Cosine similarity contrast is the cosine similarity score of the *American Rifleman* at t_i and pro-gun letters at t_{i+1} minus the cosine similarity score of the letters at t_i and *American Rifleman* at t_{i+1}. Grouping type describes the approximate size and nature of the time buckets compared for analyses. The theoretically driven grouping uses time breaks that correspond to important moments in the history of the gun debate: 1930–1945, 1946–1962, 1963–1976, 1977–1991, and 1992–2008. The average cosine similarity contrast for each grouping was calculated by averaging the cosine similarity differences described above across periods. The depicted 90 percent confidence intervals are 1,000 iteration bootstrap estimates.

groups are also significant at the 95 percent confidence level. By and large, these results indicate that, in the subset of editorials and letters that exhibit ideology, pro-gun letter writers do indeed systematically adopt the NRA's language. This adds further evidence supporting my claim that the NRA is indeed the source of the gun-centric ideology described throughout this chapter.

———

This chapter documents the NRA's efforts at ideological cultivation over the course of approximately eighty years. It demonstrates that the issue positions that the NRA and its supporters have taken, when aggregated, closely align with contemporary conservative ideology in the United States. This ideology opposes "big government" (of which gun control is one form), favors crime control efforts that focus on harsh sentencing and personal self-defense using firearms, advocates for a large military apparatus and independence from international organizations, and argues that these positions collectively amount to a pro-liberty agenda. Further, this chapter demonstrates that gun rights proponents are much more likely than gun control proponents to connect gun policy to other political issues. This indicates that the issue is much better integrated into the broader political ideologies of NRA supporters than it is into the ideological perspectives of the NRA's opponents. Finally, the chapter documents how the issues to which the NRA and its supporters have connected gun rights, as well as the nature and substantive content of those connections, have varied over time as the NRA has reacted to broader sociopolitical changes and as its place in the political system has changed—especially as it transitioned from its quasi-governmental phase into its partisan phase.

Building on last chapter's discussion of the gun owner social identity, the NRA's cultivation of a gun-centric ideology is another example of an ideational resource that interest groups can use as part of an effort to advance their policy agendas via mass channels of influence. As noted throughout this chapter, the NRA's framing of gun rights as part of a broader ideology has also reinforced the identity described in chapter 3 by both connecting it to other politically relevant social identities and tying its themes to broader political attitudes. Together, these two resources comprise the political worldview that informs the attitudes and actions of the NRA's supporters.

Chapter 6 shows how this worldview eventually played a crucial role in facilitating the NRA's entry into the Republican Party coalition—how it contributed to the NRA's transition into its partisan phase. But first, the next chapter—chapter 5—examines how the NRA used the worldview to influence gun policy outcomes during its initial quasi-governmental phase. It shows how the NRA harnessed this worldview to advance its political agenda during a period in which it abstained from partisan politics.

5

Gun Policy during the NRA's Quasi-Governmental Phase

> [T]he NRA is regarded as perhaps the most powerful lobby
> in America—even though its lobbyists are not registered.
> For years, at both the state and federal level, it has blocked
> the enactment of effective gun control laws by stimulating an
> avalanche of letters from gun enthusiasts decrying even the
> most minimal controls.
>
> —DEMOCRATIC STUDY GROUP RESEARCH MEMO DISCUSSING
>   THE POWER OF THE NRA, 1968[1]

The battles over what would eventually become the National Firearms Act of 1934 (NFA) and Federal Firearms Act of 1938 (FFA)
marked the first attempts at substantial federal level gun control legislation.[2] Raised in response to increasing crime rates—particularly
the violence associated with organized crime—these bills were an
initial test of the NRA's ability to mobilize its members into action.[3]
The rapidly growing organization had been working hard to cultivate a gun owner social identity and gun-centric ideology among its
supporters, which together formed a cohesive political worldview.

Would it be able to effectively rally those supporters on behalf of gun rights?

The answer, in short, is yes. While the NFA passed, it did so only after being substantially weakened—largely thanks to the tenacity of NRA members. And the NRA actually supported passage of the FFA as a way to preempt stronger legislation sought by the Justice Department; in fact, the NRA played a substantial role in developing the FFA and used its role to insert a provision that made the law virtually unenforceable.[4] Later, in the 1960s, during another federal push for gun control, the NRA was once again able first to block legislation and then to shape and weaken the laws that were actually passed.

With these early successes, the NRA demonstrated the power of its identity-based appeals, rallying gun owners into political action on its behalf and creating a blueprint it would follow in subsequent policy battles. As the group's mobilizational capabilities became clear, it established itself as a political force so formidable that policymakers were discouraged from pursuing the sorts of strict regulations on guns that they would have otherwise preferred (and that most Americans supported).

The NRA fought these early battles alone; still in its quasi-governmental phase, it did not work in conjunction with a major political party. Without party support, it wasn't able to keep gun control off the legislative agenda altogether, or get pro-gun legislation onto it. That would change during the group's partisan phase—as we will see in chapter 7.

The cases discussed here and in chapter 7 serve several functions. First, they enable me to examine how the nature and effects of the NRA's efforts to cultivate identity and ideology—and, relatedly, its political influence—have developed and grown over time. Second, they also enable me to compare the effectiveness of the NRA's efforts during several different debates over gun policy; by comparing the NRA's influence across different cases, these analyses provide leverage to identify the factors that explain the NRA's success or failure at defeating or weakening gun control laws at different points in

TABLE 5.1. Summary of Cases from the NRA's "Quasi-Governmental" Phase

Policy Debate	Years	Summary of NRA Influence
The National Firearms Act and the Federal Firearms Act	1934–1938	A mass-mobilization campaign led to a substantial reduction of the scope and severity of the 1934 law.
		Reputational effects were evident in 1938 as a result of the NRA's 1934 mobilization efforts; following its 1934 mobilization campaign, policymakers gave the NRA a role in drafting the 1938 legislation in the hope of avoiding a similar campaign. The NRA then inserted a clause that made the law extremely difficult to enforce, rendering it toothless. The Justice Department ultimately opposed the law, and the NRA—accurately viewing it as an opportunity to preempt more meaningful legislation—supported it.
The Gun Control Act	1963–1968	During the 1963–1964 period, a mass-mobilization campaign stalled momentum on a bill being debated in Congress, temporarily killing it before it came up for a vote.
		From 1965 to early 1968, mass mobilization nearly stalled a subsequent proposal being debated in Congress prior to a vote, but the proposal regained momentum following the assassinations of MLK and RFK. Following these assassinations, some gun control provisions were inserted into an existing crime bill and passed before the NRA had time to mobilize its supporters.
		During mid-to-late 1968, the NRA recognized the momentum behind additional gun control proposals, but was able to substantially weaken the law that eventually passed by launching another large mass-mobilization campaign.
		Reputational effects were present, with legislative proposals sometimes crafted in ways deemed more likely to avoid strong NRA opposition.

time. Finally, the cases also provide additional evidence for and detail about claims made in previous chapters—further exploring, for example, how the NRA mobilizes its members by portraying their identity as under threat.

In this chapter, I keep my focus on the NRA's efforts during its quasi-governmental phase. Looking at the NFA and FFA from the 1930s, as well as the Gun Control Act of 1968 (see table 5.1),[5] we can see not only how the ideational resources the NRA developed came into play in specific policy debates, but also how these were intertwined with—and often went beyond—other potential sources of power, such as the NRA's financial resources. My goal is not to *dismiss* alternative explanations of the NRA's clout, but to show that the NRA's ideational resources had independent impacts on key policy outcomes—that they mattered above and beyond any other advantages and resources that the NRA may have had.

The National Firearms Act and the Federal Firearms Act: 1934 to 1938

As noted above, the legislative effort that would ultimately lead to the NFA began in the early 1930s in response to increased crime rates and concerns about gangsterism. Pushed by Franklin Roosevelt's Attorney General Homer Cummings and Senator Royal Copeland of New York, the initial proposals associated with the NFA sought to require the registration of numerous classes of firearms (including many handguns), mandate licensing for anyone who made or sold such weapons, and substantially restrict interstate shipment and sales.[6]

The NRA opposed the NFA and began deploying identity-based appeals to mobilize its members in opposition to the bill. *American Rifleman* editorials from September, November, and December of 1933 as well as January, February, and May of 1934 contained calls to action on the NRA's behalf, often depicting gun rights—and the gun owner identity—as under threat. The NRA told its members that this legislation "must be killed," lest criminals gain "a position of absolute dominance over our citizens" when it became "next to impossible for the man of average means" to own guns.[7] These editorials connected the bill to its nascent, gun-centric ideology, bringing in concerns about crime, self-defense, and national security. "The issue is clear cut between the Attorney General and his undesirable law on the one side, and the sportsmen of American and all other law-abiding citizens of America on the other side, with the armed criminals of the country on the side lines, rooting for the Attorney General."[8]

In their discussions of the bill, gun rights supporters were clearly motivated by perceived identity threat, and their sentiments reflected the NRA's connection of gun rights to crime prevention. Numerous letters to the editor described gun control as helpful to criminals and harmful to law-abiding citizens, who would be unable to defend themselves.[9] One supporter wrote to the *New York Times* in May 1935, arguing that "[e]xperience demonstrates that rigorous anti-firearms legislation merely disarms the respectable, law-abiding citizen and does not prevent the possession and use of firearms by criminals" before concluding, "The most effective way, therefore, to prevent crimes of violence . . . is to enable law-abiding citizens to exercise their constitutional right to possess and carry firearms for purposes of self-defense."[10]

Similar letters were published in the *Chicago Tribune*. One from January 1937 argues, "A gun law is merely a joke to the fellow who is ready to rob or kill. Yet the decent citizen who has to be out late at night, the man who would protect his wife or daughter, the woman who has to make her way home alone in the darkness are all placed in the criminal class if they possess the only practical means of self-defense."[11]

Gun rights supporters flooded their representatives with mail in opposition to the bill; the size of the response alone indicates that the NRA succeeded in activating the gun owner identity. Indeed, members of Congress angrily accused the NRA of misrepresenting the bill as being much more intrusive than was actually the case in order to motivate its members.[12]

The NRA's efforts worked. During committee hearings, the bill's scope was substantially reduced. Unlike the relatively strong proposals described above—which targeted a wide range of weapons, including many handguns—the final bill eliminated reference to all firearms other than sawed-off shotguns and fully automatic "machine guns."[13] Although effective at tightly regulating the ownership, sale, and transfer of the classes of firearms to which it pertained, the NFA, as passed in summer 1934, focused only on guns associated with gangsterism.[14] A frustrated Joseph Keenan, then assistant attorney general, said publicly that the NRA had "emasculated" the bill prior to its passage.[15]

The NRA, on the other hand, seemed satisfied with the revised bill; reinforcing the relationship between gun rights, crime control, and national security, it told its members, "We are hopeful that an end has been reached in the efforts to place upon the Federal statute books that fanatical type of gun legislation which would not only make the armed criminal supreme in this country but would also emasculate our whole scheme of national defense." Nonetheless—continuing to portray the group's identity as threatened—the NRA warned its members to remain vigilant: "As Congressmen campaign for reelection this year, sportsmen should . . . seize every opportunity to discuss the problem with the men who are running for office. The anti-gun element will be active. The shooters must be no less active in making known their views."[16]

The weakened bill left gun control advocates—most notably Attorney General Cummings, Assistant Attorney General Joseph Keenan, and Senator Copeland—eager for additional legislation that would pertain to a wider range of firearms. While Copeland had been infuriated by the NRA's 1934 letter writing campaign,[17] he was also wary of having another attempt sidetracked. His solution was to engage the group early, asking for their input on a draft of the bill that would become the Federal Firearms Act; the bill slightly bolstered licensing requirements for firearms dealers (although licenses would only cost one dollar) and called for the prosecution of dealers who sold weapons to criminals.[18] As Robert Spitzer notes in his illuminating history of the gun debate, however, the NRA used the opportunity to insert a clause requiring prosecutors to demonstrate that gun sellers *knowingly* provided criminals with guns. This legal standard would prove so difficult to meet that the law was basically unenforceable.[19]

In cooperating with Copeland, the NRA saw a chance to preempt additional, stronger legislation favored by others, including the Attorney General; it explicitly told its members that passage of Copeland's FFA "would mean the death of the Attorney General's bills."[20] Indeed, while the NRA consistently voiced vague support for gun regulations, in practice it directed its members to oppose all regulations other than those it had written or influenced and worked hard to defeat or weaken all proposals put forth by Roosevelt's Justice Department—a contradiction that Roosevelt Administration officials themselves noted.[21] Attorney General Cummings's favored legislation—which was much stronger than Copeland's bill—never made it out of committee, due at least in part to a large number of letters sent to Congress in 1937 opposing it.[22] The FFA, which passed in 1938, was ultimately opposed by the Justice Department, which argued that it was far too weak and correctly predicted that its major provisions would be nearly impossible to enforce.[23]

These early examples show how effectively the NRA leveraged its ideational resources[24]—and how these resources dovetailed with more traditional forms of interest group influence. Behind-the-scenes influence over the policymaking process is often understood as a result of traditional lobbying efforts (typically fueled by financial resources); in the case of the FFA, Copeland sought to work with the NRA to preempt the NRA's use of ideational resources to mobilize its supporters.

This is a subtle—but important—form of NRA influence, in which policymakers write weaker bills in the hope of avoiding a pro-gun mail campaign while also often including NRA-favored provisions that actually *weaken* existing aspects of gun regulation. In other words, the NRA's ability to shape the political behavior of its supporters—influence on the third dimension of power—gives it the ability to shape the contents of the gun policy agenda—influence on the second dimension of power. (Later, as it gained partisan influence, the NRA would be able to keep gun control off the agenda entirely.) While data limitations make it difficult to precisely weigh the NRA's use of ideational resources against its use of money, the evidence available suggests that money did not play much of a part in its 1930s political efforts. The annual reports periodically printed in the *American Rifleman* do not contain any line items pertaining to politics, and the spending that conceivably could go to politics—such as membership communications—does not comprise a large part of its budget (and, in any case, would have consisted of mailings asking members to take action).[25]

The FFA debate established several patterns that would repeat themselves in future gun control battles (including those discussed later, in chapter 7). First, pro-control policymakers, thwarted by the NRA in an initial attempt to pass relatively strong regulations, went out of their way to gain its approval in a subsequent attempt. Second, the NRA—while generally using alarmist rhetoric about gun control in its communications with members—nonetheless "hedged its bets," working to make any new regulations that did pass as weak as possible. Finally, NRA leaders voiced vague support for gun control—claiming while testifying before Congress, for example, that the organization is "absolutely favorable to reasonable legislation"—while actively mobilizing gun owners against proposed laws and refusing to specify what legislation they would actually deem "reasonable."[26]

Contemporary accounts of the NRA's early legislative efforts often take words like these at face value, assuming that they indicate genuine support for gun control. These accounts also sometimes misinterpret the NRA's support for the FFA, seeing it as an indication of actual support for gun regulation when in reality it was an attempt to preempt stronger legislation.[27] That the NRA pushed for clauses that would make the law unenforceable further demonstrates that it did not genuinely support gun regulation.

Gun control was mostly off the national political agenda between the passage of the FFA and the early 1960s.[28] The NRA nonetheless continued to focus on politics, organizing its members to take state level action and to oppose a small number of proposed federal level measures. In the few instances that national gun policy did come up, the NRA appeared to be effective in its opposition. It was able to get guns excluded from the Property Requisition Act of 1941 (which allowed the government to acquire private property deemed useful for military purposes)[29] and contributed to the demise of a gun registration bill briefly debated in 1947.[30] In 1957, the NRA led a mass-mobilization campaign against proposed changes to the enforcement of FFA; the changes that went into effect were substantially watered down as a result.[31]

The Gun Control Act: 1963–1968

In the 1960s, increased rates of violent crime and a string of high-profile political assassinations put gun control back onto the national political agenda. There was broad public support for gun control, highly motivated members of Congress, and a president bullish on new legislation.[32] In light of these combined forces, strong new regulations on guns seemed poised to pass.

The 1960s gun debate actually began in August 1963—a few months *before* John F. Kennedy's assassination—when Thomas Dodd, a Democratic senator from Connecticut, introduced a bill that would have made it harder for individuals to obtain licenses to deal firearms; due in part to the FFA, these licenses were inexpensive and easy to get, which meant that many individuals who were not bona fide gun dealers had them. The bill stalled in the Commerce Committee, which was chaired by pro-gun Democrat Warren Magnuson (himself an NRA member).[33] After JFK's assassination, however, momentum for gun control began to build—a development that Dodd capitalized on by expanding his legislation to include a ban on mail-order sales of certain types of guns; this was how Lee Harvey Oswald—responding to an advertisement in the *American Rifleman*—obtained the gun he used to shoot Kennedy. Other members of Congress began to introduce similar proposals directed at mail-order firearms.[34] While the NRA had signaled a (perhaps disingenuous) willingness to accept Dodd's pre-assassination bill,[35] it changed its tune in late 1963 as the gun debate became more intense and the severity of proposed regulations increased.[36]

As it had during the debates of the 1930s, the NRA mobilized its supporters via the *American Rifleman* and depicted gun owners as being severely threatened in the current legislative environment. The January 1964 editorial noted, "Never before has there been such a wave of anti-firearm feeling or such a vocal and almost universal demand for tighter controls over the mail-order sales of guns" and asked members to take action. "The lawmakers must be enlightened on the views of reputable citizens who believe in the Second Amendment" and "the preservation of our heritage to keep and bear arms."[37]

The themes that the NRA used to frame its opposition to gun control had evolved since the 1930s. Not just the January but the February and March *American Rifleman* editorials invoked the Second Amendment. As I discussed in chapter 4, it was during the 1960s that the *Second Amendment* topic from the *American Rifleman* topic model began to increase in prominence while the *Americanism and Guns* topic declined—a trend apparent in the NRA's messaging in regard to the legislative proposals of this period. While we don't know the exact motivation for this shift, contemporary NRA officials have emphasized how the defense of a constitutional amendment furthers its identity and ideology-building project. As one official told author David Cole, members are motivated by the belief that the Second Amendment is "fundamental and uniquely American" and by their desire "to pass it down to the next generation intact." Another NRA official told Cole, "We have the constitutional right. No one else has that. The difference it makes in terms of your credibility is immense."[38]

The NRA linked its opposition to gun control with its ideology in other ways, too; it advocated, for instance, harsh enforcement of existing gun laws in lieu of new laws restricting access to them—an approach that fit well with the "law and order" crime policies advanced by insurgent conservatives at this time—while also connecting gun rights to support for limited government by portraying new gun laws as examples of federal overreach.[39] The NRA's allies in Congress picked up on these as well; in explaining his opposition to the bill, Commerce Committee Chairman Magnuson cited concerns that it infringed on states' rights.[40] Opposition to big government would become a central argument as the NRA entered the realm of partisan politics in the decades that followed.

A constant from prior periods was the effectiveness of the NRA's appeals to its supporters, which again led to the widespread political mobilization. Dodd's office reported that its mail was initially eight to one in favor of his bill; other members of Congress reported a similar trend. Once gun owners were alerted and asked to oppose it, however, the volume of mail Dodd received increased dramatically— "stacked knee-deep all around the subcommittee offices" according to staff—and nearly all of it opposed the bill. The Commerce Committee received approximately twenty-thousand pieces of mail over a two-week period in early 1964, only two of which were in support of the legislation.[41]

Some gun owners went so far as to actually attend committee hearings in Congress, which meant opponents of the legislation far outnumbered proponents at these hearings.[42] Many of those in attendance appeared to be unaware of—or unconcerned with—the actual contents of the proposals in Congress, using arguments very similar to those made by the NRA about the Second Amendment and the disarmament of honest, law-abiding citizens. These arguments made it into news coverage of the hearings, which may have further spread misperceptions that the bill would require gun registration or even disarmament.[43] This opposition—together with a shift of public attention toward civil rights and Vietnam—killed momentum for the legislation, which ultimately failed.[44] Dodd himself attributed this failure to NRA-led public protests—to what he described as "the blind, almost mindless, efforts of a segment of gun enthusiasts, with their shabby, time-worn slogans."[45]

The gun debate, however, did not stall for long. Lyndon Johnson, who had become president following JFK's assassination, won a strong victory in 1964 and—along with the liberal Congress elected that year—was eager to act in the face of increasing violent crime. In early 1965, a stronger version of Dodd's bill was introduced, along with an additional bill developed by the White House.[46] Although stronger than Dodd's earlier bill, these new proposals were nonetheless fairly modest; they called for greater limits on and federal control over who could ship guns across state lines, stronger restrictions on mail-order sales, increased firearms-related taxes and licensing fees, new limits on the importation of surplus military weapons, and expanded dealer registration requirements.[47]

Despite the relative modesty of the proposals, the NRA took immediate action against them, telling members in an ominous message in early April 1965[48] that they must "write now, or it may soon be too late" and to "not leave this to someone else" because "if the battle is lost, it will be your loss and that of all who follow you."[49] In the week prior to the mailing, 352 letters had been sent to the White House opposing the bill; in the four weeks that followed, 9,528 letters were sent, averaging 2,382 per week. The White House did not record any "pro" letters during any of these weeks.[50] Altogether, the White House received just over 18,000 letters on the Dodd Bill during 1965, all of which it categorized as opposing the proposed legislation—surpassing the combined amount of mail sent about the Voting Rights Act of 1965 and the enactment of Medicare.[51]

While there are not similar records kept of mail sent to members of Congress, by the NRA's account the volume was substantial. The December 1965 issue of the *American Rifleman* bragged that "probably no issue before the first session of the 89th Congress drew the volume of mail that poured in to the nation's lawmakers in opposition to S. 1592. Letters by the thousands were received by virtually all members of the Senate and House of Representatives." It then congratulated NRA members for their effort: "That these letters were effective in preventing the passage of S. 1592 is beyond any question. Each of you who played his part is entitled to be proud of his participation in the democratic process."[52] This general trend in mail to policymakers continued throughout the 1965–1967 period, with the only deviation coming after the August 1966 mass shooting at the University of Texas at Austin.[53]

The NRA was strategic in its deployment of ideational resources, instructing its members to write personalized rather than form letters so that policymakers would find it harder to dismiss their appeals.[54] Memos from inside the Johnson Administration attest to the effectiveness of this tactic. In one, an official from the Treasury Department—which, at the time, enforced gun laws and therefore also received public mail—wrote the White House for advice in dealing with pro-gun letters. The memo stated,

> I have received the attached report from IRS showing a total of 16,000 letters received as of June 8. . . . On April 9, the National Rifle Association wrote to its members (which I understand totals some 650,000) urging them to oppose the Dodd Bill. As you will see from the copy of the April 9 letter, they tell their members to write <u>personalized</u> communications. This, accordingly, makes it difficult for us to easily dismiss letters we are receiving as strictly campaign letters to which no reply would be reasonably expected. I attach a few copies of letters received. . . . As you

can see they clearly appear to be the result of the NRA campaign, but they reflect individualized interest on the part of the writer.[55]

The content of the letters sent to both President Johnson and newspaper editors indicates that many gun rights supporters who took political action during this period were motivated by perceived identity threat. Moreover, their appeals emphasized the personal impacts they (often inaccurately) believed the proposed laws would have on their lives while deemphasizing—or demonstrating outright ignorance of—the actual content of the bills. Many included hyperbolic statements about the full disarmament of citizens—something that was not proposed in any of the bills. One letter to the White House read, "All Hunters Will Lose A Part Of Themselves If Their Guns Are Taken Away . . . Take Away 'My Right To Bear Arms' And You Are Taking Away A Part Of America. Take Away My America And You Must Take Away My Life."[56] Another said, "As a gun collector and responsible citizen, I beg you to forestall this madness which is attempting to disarm this nation's private citizens. . . . Our American heritage is at stake."[57] Policymakers accused the NRA of intentionally exaggerating the bills' potential impacts.[58]

Although actively debated throughout 1965, 1966, and 1967, the bills never made it out of committee and, by early 1968, had stalled.[59] Senator Joseph Tydings of Maryland, a gun control supporter, attributed the stalemate to the NRA's misrepresentation of the Dodd bill to its members, complaining, "What the NRA has been able to do is instill in the minds of the people . . . that there is a conspiracy back here in Washington to take away a substantial part of the life they know. The NRA has convinced outdoor people—mainly people who mean to protect their way of life and what they consider their inalienable rights—that the gun bill would deprive them of their right to hunt, or to shoot a marauding coyote or a human predator." Continuing, Tydings then cast doubt on the likelihood of gun control passing in the future, noting that "[i]n their minds, this is only the first step in a conspiracy to disarm them altogether. The NRA's lies have a very great effect—so great that I don't know whether we can ever reverse it."[60]

One senator said that he would "rather be a deer in hunting season than a politician who has run afoul of the NRA crowd" because, despite coming from different sectors of society, they all "have one thing in common: they don't want *anyone* to tell them *anything* about what to do with their guns, and they *mean* it."[61] Another senator—Jacob Javits of New York—in a speech explaining the difficulty of passing gun control, attributed the power of the NRA to the behavior of its supporters and implied that such behavior caused policymakers to overestimate public opposition to gun control. Javits commented, "First of all, there is the power of the pen—in the hands of avid gun control opponents." He then mentioned how a "recent Gallup poll indicat[ing] that 83% of the American public favored gun registration and licensing . . . came as a surprise to many members of Congress, since for years, we had been bombarded by thousands of letters generated by the National Rifle Association." Javits later noted that, even when gun control supporters did mobilize in large numbers, their interest faded quickly and his mail again became overwhelmingly pro-gun.[62]

An internal memo on gun control produced by the Democratic Study Group in 1968 offers a revealing assessment of the NRA's power over the decade. The private memo described the NRA as "perhaps the most powerful lobby in America," saying it had "for years . . . blocked the enactment of effective gun control laws by stimulating an avalanche of letters from gun enthusiasts decrying even the most minimal controls."[63]

Just as it seemed the NRA had been victorious in quashing the legislation, the assassination of Martin Luther King Jr. in April 1968 and of Robert Kennedy in June put gun control back onto the agenda, with the pressure to pass new regulations now greater than ever. The day after MLK's assassination, the Senate Judiciary Committee voted to include some of the Dodd Bill's provisions—namely a prohibition on the interstate shipment of handguns between individuals—in a large crime bill Congress had been working on since the previous year. Congress—with the NRA's opposition in mind—refused to include stronger regulations, which angered President Johnson to the point that he almost vetoed the bill.[64] Congress nonetheless passed the bill the day after Robert Kennedy's assassination. Johnson—despite feeling that its weakness was a victory for the NRA—signed it into law while also calling for Congress to pass a separate, much stronger bill that would mandate the registration of all guns and require gun owners to have licenses.[65]

Dodd—working with New York Democrat Emanuel Celler in the House—took up this call and began pursuing legislation favored by the White House.[66] By this time, the NRA had formidable opposition in the form of the Emergency Committee for Gun Control, led by astronaut and future senator John Glenn. The group, founded in mid-1968, bolstered the pro-gun control efforts of the National Council for a Responsible Firearms Policy, which had formed a year prior. These organizations put both direct and indirect pressure on policymakers via advertising, letter-writing campaigns, marches, and protests.[67] Their efforts were successful; for the first time during his presidency, gun control-related mail to President Johnson during the summer of 1968 was often evenly split between letters on each side of the issue. During some weeks, letters in support of gun control even exceeded letters in opposition to it, sometimes by wide margins.[68] Accounts from 1968 describe similar trends in mail sent to members of Congress, who reported receiving vast quantities of anti-gun letters.[69] While the pro-control mobilization would prove short-lived, it put public pressure on policymakers at a crucial time.[70]

The NRA countermobilized its supporters.[71] It continued to use identity-based appeals in the *American Rifleman*, including a July editorial entitled "Can Three Assassins Kill a Civil Right?"[72] It also sent an emergency letter in mid-June, in which it told its nearly one million members that their opponents' goal "is complete abolition of civilian ownership of firearms" and said that the "situation demands immediate action by every law-abiding gun owner in the United States."[73] NRA President Harold Glassen told members of Congress, "I want Congress to know as it makes the final decision on gun control legislation that there are millions upon millions of American hunters and sportsmen and farmers and housewives and workers and businessmen who do not want their rights trampled and thrown aside." Portraying the media as an out-group while exaggerating the reach of the proposed law, he continued, "I want them to know that there are millions of Americans who won't stand by mutely while a few metropolitan newspapers shove an undesirable and restrictive law down their throats and lay the groundwork for the ultimate move to prohibit completely the ownership of arms in the United States."[74]

But even as it countermobilized its members, the NRA privately recognized that its position was much weaker than it had been over the previous five years of debate.[75] Its goal shifted from preventing a vote outright to weakening the legislation. Time was on the NRA's side; numerous hearings would be required to pass the sort of national licensing and registration bill desired by the president, and Congress's summer recesses were approaching, with an election to follow. NRA allies in Congress helped delay action until after the July Fourth recess and then again until after the August recess.[76]

The NRA capitalized on these delays by keeping up a steady stream of mail to policymakers, which further reduced momentum for a strong bill. With its identity-based appeals, it was able to sustain its mobilization well past the strong but fleeting showing from Americans who supported gun control. The NRA—through its mail campaign—put particularly intense pressure on members of Congress from southern and western states who were up for reelection, perhaps hoping that the intensity of supporters' appeals would send a message to legislators about the potential electoral consequences of their actions.[77]

With time running out, gun control proponents substantially reduced the scope of the proposed legislation, taking licensing and registration—the provisions most strongly opposed by the NRA—completely off the table. The NRA became much less active in its opposition following this change; while it never publicly *supported* the legislation, by the fall its discussion of the bill was pushed toward the back of the *American Rifleman*, and it used dry policy terms (rather than identity appeals) in describing its provisions. Mail sent to the president about the legislation slowed down dramatically.[78] By the time the November issue of the *American Rifleman* came out (the last to go to print before passage of the GCA), the NRA focused more on supplying its members with information about where their Congressional representatives stood on gun control than on motivating them to take further action against the pending legislation. After the law passed, NRA Executive Vice President Franklin Orth lamented some of its features but commented that the "measure as a whole appears to be one that the sportsmen of America can live with" and noted that its final form included several pro-gun provisions that had been recommended by the NRA, suggesting that the organization may have been satisfied once the licensing and registration components were removed.[79]

The bill that finally went through—the Gun Control Act of 1968 (GCA)—was the first piece of major gun control passed into law since the FFA in 1938. Yet it was nothing like Johnson had envisioned. It extended the ban on interstate shipment of handguns by individuals to also cover rifles and shotguns, and—in language filled with loopholes—banned gun sales to certain felons, minors, drug addicts, and the mentally ill.[80] Proponents of strong gun control laws attributed the weakness of the GCA to the NRA's actions—including President Johnson, whose tone upon eventually signing the bill in October sounded more like one of defeat than triumph.[81] Given the immense pressure to pass gun control in mid-1968 and deep public support for it, the weakness of the GCA meant that the law—far from being a dramatic defeat—in some ways constituted a victory for the NRA.

The NRA then gloated in its first post-election issue about the defeat of policymakers who supported the GCA and immediately began to use the new law—which it said was evidence that gun owners must continue to protect their interests—as fodder to further cultivate its identity.[82]

The NRA's use of ideational resources to influence the gun control debate in the 1960s was similar in many ways to its use of such resources in the 1930s. In both periods, the NRA's influence stemmed mostly from its ability to mobilize its supporters into action after gun control was thrust onto the legislative agenda. Moreover, the NRA again benefitted from its reputation, with legislators—aware of the organization's documented ability to mobilize gun owners—at times proposing more modest regulations than they likely would have otherwise pursued.[83]

Further, NRA leaders—as they had in the 1930s—again voiced vague public support for gun control, insisting that they were in favor of so-called "reasonable" restrictions. Orth, for instance, said that the NRA "has been in support of workable, enforceable gun control legislation since its very inception in 1871" and even went so far as to say that Congress has a "duty" to enact legislation that keeps "undesirables" from obtaining guns.[84] These and similar public declarations have been interpreted by some observers as evidence that the NRA genuinely supported gun control during this period. Its consistent and active opposition when actual regulations were proposed, however, suggests otherwise—namely, that NRA leadership sought to deflect public pressure without actually putting the organization's weight behind new regulations, no matter how reasonable. Taken together, the cases presented in this chapter demonstrate that vague statements in support of hypothetical regulations should not be viewed as evidence that the early NRA was an authentic supporter of gun control, nor should the organization's eventual acceptance of laws that had been substantially weakened as a result of its actions.

These similarities across periods aside, there was also an important change in terms of how the NRA used ideational resources. By the late 1960s, the NRA—which, with nearly a million members, was much larger than it had been in the 1930s—was a controversial organization that many Americans blamed for preventing sensible gun legislation. While this endangered the group's government funding, it was useful for the NRA from a social identity perspective, as it enabled the organization to portray gun owners as a persecuted minority under attack from a number of different out-groups.[85]

The harsh critiques of the NRA that were made during the 1960s paradoxically provided credibility to the NRA's depiction of gun owners as a social group threatened by an anti-gun conspiracy.[86] Unsurprisingly given the importance of perceived threat as a motivator, these developments appear to have actually strengthened the gun owner identity, with NRA membership and *American Rifleman* circulation expanding rapidly around this time.[87] Lee Kennett and

James Anderson's excellent account of these developments—written just after this period—attributes the "vehemence" of the pro-gun crowd to a pattern in which increased demands for gun control led to even more intensity among NRA supporters, who saw gun control as an affront to them personally.[88]

Financial resources played only a supporting role. According to the NRA's annual report, its legislative and public affairs division spent an average of $175,184 per year (around $1.4 million in 2018 dollars) from 1964 through 1966, which amounted to only about 4 percent of its budget. The biggest line item was for salaries; the others were materials (likely consisting of literature describing the NRA's positions), legislative bulletins (sent to members about pending legislation), and "all other" (which comprised around 15–17 percent of the division's spending per year).[89] This spending certainly assisted its mobilization campaigns, allowing it to quickly gather information about a wide range of state and federal legislation, and to then mail communications to members calling them to action. Yet there is no evidence that the group spent money to directly gain some sort of quid pro quo influence. Rather, its spending was used to support the ideational resources it had developed and led to influence only by working in conjunction with identity cultivation efforts. The NRA needed to spend money to communicate with its members, but the *responsiveness* of its members to those communications was a product of their deep commitment to the NRA's cause.

The NRA also benefitted from the institutional design of Congress and the status quo bias associated with it. Because it was fighting to prevent, rather than pass, legislation, the NRA was able to influence policy outcomes by targeting key legislators—such as Commerce Committee Chair Warren Magnuson (who was a key NRA ally and received large volumes of pro-gun mail)[90]—and delaying the legislative process until momentum for gun control had slowed down. Ideational resources were key in exploiting this status quo bias; influential figures like Magnuson, for instance, were NRA allies because of the electoral support of gun owners, and were responsive to the mail they received from constituents on the issue. Similarly, the NRA was able to delay legislative processes in part because it was much harder for legislators to move quickly and quietly on gun control once NRA members found out about it. And the NRA benefitted from these delays in part because its supporters continued to contact their legislators long after the number of letters sent by gun control supporters slowed down.

———

Throughout its quasi-governmental phase, the NRA was consistently able to fend off strong gun control proposals and to substantially weaken the proposals that eventually did pass. Its success was mostly a result of its mass-mobilization campaigns, which used the worldview the organization had built around guns to spur action on its behalf. These campaigns sometimes directly led to gun proposals being defeated or weakened. Other times, their effects were indirect; policymakers, anticipating the NRA's reaction to strong proposals, would preemptively weaken bills—even letting the NRA help craft them—in the hope of avoiding the flood of letters that would come in from gun owners.

Despite this influence, the NRA could not keep gun control proposals off the agenda altogether. It was often on defense, working against the passage of gun control rather than advancing pro-gun policies to weaken existing laws. Lacking influence within a political party, the NRA relied on mass-mobilization campaigns and a relatively small network of bipartisan allies; while this provided it with significant leverage and power, it was not enough to allow the group to control which pieces of legislation would (and would not) be considered by Congress, as well as which would (and would not) be prioritized.

In the 1970s, all of this would change.

6

The Party-Group Alignment of the NRA and the GOP

[Y]ou came through for me, and I am going to come through for you. I was proud to receive the NRA's earliest endorsement in the history of the organization. And today, I am also proud to be the first sitting President to address the NRA Leadership Forum since our wonderful Ronald Reagan in 1983. And I want to thank each and every one of you not only for your help electing true friends of the Second Amendment, but for everything you do to defend our flag and our freedom.
—DONALD TRUMP, NRA ANNUAL MEETING, 2017[1]

By the time Donald Trump took office in January 2017, the NRA had come to occupy an important place in the Republican Party coalition. Yet—as last chapter highlights—the organization has not always been partisan; for many decades, it advanced its pro-gun agenda without taking political sides. What changed? Why did the NRA eventually align with the GOP—and how did it do so?

This chapter seeks to answer these questions and, in doing so, introduces the concept of *party-group alignment*, which describes the set of conditions favorable to partnership that brought the NRA and GOP into a durable, institutionalized relationship.

More specifically—and building directly on chapters 3 and 4— this chapter demonstrates how the NRA's cultivation of a group identity and ideology laid a foundation that would enable its eventual incorporation into the Republican Party coalition. The timing of this alignment was influenced by changing institutional and political conditions—notably a weakening of the NRA's ties to the government and the rise of the insurgent New Right movement. Seizing the opportunity these changes presented, an entrepreneurial group of activist members would dramatically take control of the organization in the late 1970s and rapidly accelerate its alignment with the GOP—forging an alliance that would grow ever deeper, and set the stage for the group to put its full political power into supporting first candidate, and then president, Donald Trump.

Conceptualizing and Measuring Group Inclusion in a Party Coalition

Before diving into the NRA and the GOP specifically, it is helpful to consider what it means for a group to be incorporated into a party coalition, and how membership in a coalition can be measured. How do we know when a group becomes a member of a party coalition? What metrics or empirical indicators can be used to make such a determination?

Some groups—described by political scientist Daniel Schlozman as "anchoring groups"—are so closely intertwined with political parties that they are almost self-evidently members of a party coalition. Anchoring groups—such as, in Schlozman's study, organized labor[2] and the Christian Right—provide the clearest cases of group membership in party coalitions. These groups, in Schlozman's words, "forego autonomous action to ally with major political parties" to whom they provide valuable resources, including votes and money.[3]

However, other groups—not as obviously and deeply intertwined with parties as anchoring groups are—might nonetheless be part of a coalition; measuring the coalitional status of these groups is a more a difficult task. Environmental advocacy organizations, for example, are generally aligned with the Democratic Party, but their ties to it are not as deep, durable, and multidimensional as the ties between the Christian Right and the GOP.[4] Moreover, the extent to which a particular group is aligned with a party can vary over time in important ways. Even if a group's relationship with a party is eventually deep enough to be self-evident—which was probably the case for the NRA by the beginning of the Trump years—it still may not be clear *when* it reached that point (and understanding when something happened is important for understanding why and how it happened). Although challenging, developing empirical measures can be useful for addressing these questions.

Following from the definition of political scientist Katherine Krimmel, I consider political parties to be coalitions of politicians, their subordinates (including staffers and some bureaucrats), and the individuals who comprise the organizations that support their election (such as party committees, like the Democratic National Committee or the Republican National Committee).[5] As discussed in chapter 2, these parties manage coalitions of groups—each of which has an intense desire to advance their preferred policies—with which they have formed durable alliances. In exchange for a party's policy support, these groups provide the party with resources that help them win elections.

Group-party alliances, in other words, involve action on the part of both groups and parties, with groups channeling their resources to one particular party and that party adopting the policy preferences of those allied groups. These alliances are essential features of contemporary parties.

Despite the importance of these alliances, however, it is not entirely clear how to identify whether a particular group is (or is *not*) a member of a party coalition; no single, comprehensive measure exists, and there are a number of distinct ways we might think about this relationship.[6] We need to consider both how committed a group is to a party and how committed the party seems to be to the group. Does the group give most of its support to one party, and, if so, does that party reciprocate by advancing its policy interests? We also want to examine the group-party relationship on different levels. On the organizational level, does the group mostly endorse or donate to candidates from one party? Are politicians from one party more likely to advance the group's policy concerns once in office? On the mass level, how supportive are group members of the party and its candidates? How widespread is support for the group's policy concerns among voters in the party who aren't affiliated with the group?

Given these distinct dimensions, this chapter uses several different indicators to assess the alignment of the NRA and the Republican Party. Each of these indicators measures, either directly or indirectly, some dimension of the NRA-GOP relationship, and, together, they enable us to gain insight into when and in what ways that relationship changed.

Many of these indicators capture the extent of the NRA's commitment to the GOP. One such measure is the list of keynote and political speakers at the NRA's annual meetings. What are the party affiliations of the guests who speak to NRA members and leaders at its convention? Do they change over time? Although we can't assume that the NRA and the politicians who appear at its convention agree on everything, we can learn something about its relationship with each party by looking at patterns in who speaks—if one party is much more frequently represented than the other (and increasingly so), it suggests that the NRA is closer with that party.

Similarly, I again turn to the NRA's *American Rifleman* editorials to see whether they connect gun rights to partisan politics. Do they use explicit partisan (e.g., Democratic or Republican) or ideological (e.g., liberal or conservative) labels while discussing political issues or events? While this doesn't measure the NRA's relationship with the GOP directly, it indicates whether the NRA has seen gun rights as a partisan issue, and how this has changed over time.

The NRA's endorsements of political candidates are also a useful measure. The more a group's endorsements—especially in high-profile elections—go to members of a single party, the more they should be seen as a member of that party's coalition.

A final measure of group-party alignment is the proportion of the NRA's campaign contributions that are spent in support of candidates from each party. A group that is a member of a party coalition would be expected to contribute most or all of its dollars to members of that party.

These indicators mostly measure the commitment of the NRA to the GOP; others capture the commitment of the GOP to the NRA. One such indicator is party platforms. If a group and party are aligned, we would expect the party's official platform to voice support for the group's policy preferences. Similarly, votes in Congress—which demonstrate how often politicians from a particular party vote for a group's favored positions—can also serve as a measure of alignment.

Finally, we can look at the supporters of both the group and the party to measure the NRA-GOP relationship. The partisanship of group members and supporters is one useful indicator; if the NRA and the GOP are aligned, we would expect the NRA's core supporters to identify as Republicans and to support Republican candidates. Another mass-level indicator relates to the gun control preferences of Republican voters. If the NRA is a core group in the GOP coalition, we might expect Republicans on the mass level—even those who don't own guns—to be less supportive of gun control than other Americans.

With these indicators in mind, we can now trace the history of the NRA's relationship with the Republican Party, starting in the 1930s.[7]

1930s to 1950s: Ideology without Party

As we have seen, the NRA was not always a partisan group. During the 1930s, '40s, and '50s, NRA editorials (as well as pro-gun letters to the editor in newspapers) did not associate gun rights with a particular party (or an ideological label associated with a party), and the organization did not favor politicians from one party over the other. Keynote speakers at the NRA's annual meetings (first held as a public event in 1948) were typically military officials, and the elected officials who spoke did not tend to come from one party over the other.

The NRA's nonpartisan approach to politics did not impede its successful efforts at cultivating a gun-centric ideology among its members and supporters, as detailed in chapter 4. Indeed, while the NRA was ideological during this period—in the sense that it connected gun rights to a number of distinct political issues—it lacked a viable entry route into partisan politics. Gun control was not a cleavage issue dividing the parties on the elite or mass levels, meaning that the NRA lacked a clear partisan home.[8]

Perhaps even more importantly, it is not clear that the NRA had anything to gain from entering the realm of partisan politics during these years. It demonstrated notable political clout during the gun policy debates of the 1930s without sacrificing its role (and the associated government support) as the primary administrator of public marksmanship programs. Aligning itself with one political party could have needlessly jeopardized its status as a quasi-governmental institution and the federal support that came along with that status.[9] Further, after the gun policy battles of the 1930s, the 1940s and 1950s saw gun control mostly fall off the national political radar, providing less incentive to enter partisan politics. As a result, the NRA remained nonpartisan throughout these decades.

1960s and 1970s: The New Right Rises

In the 1960s, both gun rights and the ideological perspective the NRA had crafted around them slowly started to attach to mainstream political ideologies and parties. With the return of gun control to the national agenda and the substantial weakening of the NRA's ties to the government, there was an incentive to enter partisan politics. And the rise of the New Right during this period provided a broader ideological movement—one extending beyond the firearms community—to which gun rights could be connected.

THE NEW RIGHT AND THE NRA

The so-called New Right brought together several strands of conservative thought that aligned closely with the ideology that the NRA had propagated for years. Barry Goldwater's successful campaign for the Republican nomination for president in 1964—on a platform that included opposition to gun control[10]—marked the New Right's arrival as an important player in national politics. This ideological movement connected several previously distinct strands of conservatism: it united conservative positions on narrow social issues—like abortion and gun control—with both one another and with hawkish anticommunism, antigovernment populism, and small government libertarianism, which included opposition to civil rights on the stated grounds that it infringed on the rights of states.[11]

New Right leaders did more than just unite intellectually distinct strands of conservatism. They also facilitated connections between (seemingly) single-issue groups, providing space for those groups to identify coherent strategies to advance their respective primary interests. They established think tanks, media outlets, and other formal organizations to provide support to these causes. They also recruited and supported candidates who ran on their platform.[12] They advanced these causes—and were able to act independently of the Republican Party—thanks to highly successful direct mail strategies developed by coalition leader Richard Viguerie.[13]

Support for gun rights was one of the social issue stances the New Right adopted into its platform. The NRA and its gun owning constituency could hardly have been a better ideological fit in this coalition. The organization had already independently advanced many of the New Right's stances, including strong opposition to communism. Moreover, the NRA's ideological emphasis on individual liberty and the centrality of self-sufficiency to the gun owner identity fit well with the New Right's libertarian strand. Finally, the NRA's approach to crime—with its focus on personal self-defense and harsh punishment in lieu of restrictions on access to guns—fit neatly with the "law and order" crime control policies favored by the New Right. Given these affinities, the rise of the New Right in the 1960s presented the NRA with an opportunity to join a broader ideological movement and to attach gun rights to a range of conservative causes and identities.

The NRA's ideological fit with the New Right, combined with the identity-driven political intensity of gun rights supporters, made gun owners attractive to New Right leaders. The NRA's large, politically engaged membership could provide substantial mass-level support to the New Right's candidates, ideas, and fundraising efforts. Indeed, Viguerie—in a 1976 interview about direct mail fundraising—said that "gun enthusiasts are one of the great untapped money markets for the new right."[14] Another New Right leader, who spoke to author Joan Burbick on the condition of anonymity, said that gun rights offered a particularly useful frame for pushing back on liberalism's momentum during and after the civil rights movement. Opposition to gun control offered an opportunity to frame a conservative cause using the language of rights protection at a time when such language was used mostly by liberals.[15]

Another prominent New Right activist—H. L. "Bill" Richardson— also emphasized the crucial importance of gun rights for the conservative cause. During a 1975 lunch with other New Right activists— summarized in a memo written by a staffer of New Right leader Paul Weyrich—Richardson explained that gun rights are "inextricably interrelated with most of the other major issues of the day, such as crime, local control, limited government, deregulation, etc." Describing guns as a "gut issue," the memo recounts Richardson's view that "it is only through the utilization of such concrete matters as gun regulation—i.e., the public's sense of outrage at being deprived of valuable personal property and at being rendered defenseless in one's home—that the evils and real threat of socialism in this country can be made tangible to the people."[16]

However, not all in the NRA were in agreement about the benefits of aligning with a clearly partisan, hardline group, despite the ideological similarities.[17] The NRA's Executive Vice Presidents (the title given to the group's top official)—Franklin Orth until 1970 and Maxwell Rich from then until 1977—strongly opposed gun control and fully supported the organization's efforts to defeat it, but were nonetheless clearly committed to the NRA of an earlier era. Both were former military officers and were part of the so-called old guard faction that was committed to maintaining federal support.

The old guard did not think the that the NRA needed to devote substantially more resources to politics, believed (likely mistakenly) that the organization could continue to succeed without adopting new fundraising methods, and, in general, did not prize the sort of ideological purity associated with the hardline New Right movement.[18] The old guard continued to highlight the importance of government support; *American Rifleman* editorials published throughout the 1960s frequently emphasized the essential role of government funding for NRA programs.[19] The old guard's concern with keeping these programs alive was understandable: although the NRA's federal support was in some cases indirect (for instance, the surplus weapons program, which—by enabling NRA affiliates to purchase firearms at low prices—provided an incentive for individuals and gun clubs to join the NRA), it nonetheless amounted to millions of dollars annually.[20] Moreover, a very large proportion of the NRA's revenue during this era came from membership dues—dues that were almost certainly greater because of membership incentives associated with its federally supported programs.[21]

Nonetheless, the NRA's relationship with the federal government was inarguably in decline. With several hundred thousand members by the beginning of the 1960s,[22] it was a much more prominent organization than it had been during the gun control debates of the 1930s. As a result, its opposition to gun control—even if nonpartisan—drew substantial public attention, and the NRA was widely recognized as the leading opponent of gun regulation in the United States. The group was attacked by authors like Carl Bakal (who wrote an explosive *Harper's* article and later a book documenting the NRA's tactics), received negative coverage on network news programs and in prominent newspapers, and was publicly blamed by some legislators for the failure of gun control proposals.[23]

This bad publicity damaged the NRA's reputation among the general public, which in turn brought greater scrutiny to the government benefits it received (most a result of its involvement with the Civilian Marksmanship Program) from gun control supporters in Congress and from newly formed gun control advocacy groups, like the National Council for a Responsible Firearms Policy.[24] This scrutiny led to the elimination of government support for NRA national matches, substantial reductions in the size of the surplus firearms program, and dramatic cuts to the Civilian Marksmanship Program's budget.[25]

An internal NRA report from the time reveals that the number of NRA-affiliated clubs declined in the years following these cuts. This was likely due to the reductions to the surplus firearms program,[26] which had provided a strong incentive for local gun clubs and their members to affiliate with the NRA because surplus guns could only be distributed through such clubs if they were part of the NRA.[27] The NRA's appeals during this period reflected this trend; as we saw in chapter 4, editorials in the *American Rifleman* that fell into the *Americanism and Guns* topic—which, because it emphasizes the importance of guns for national security, was often used to discuss the NRA's relationship with the government—began to decline deeply and steadily starting in the 1960s.

Despite its weakening relationship with the federal government, the NRA's old guard leaders were hesitant to break with the organization's long-standing approach to politics and fundraising—an approach that was typically nonpartisan and attempted to minimize controversy.[28] Yet a cadre of lower-level—but nonetheless influential—NRA leaders, led by Harlon Carter and Neal Knox, disagreed with this view.

Like the old guard, the "new guard" recognized that the controversy surrounding the NRA compromised its access to federal funds. However, whereas the old guard wanted to soften the NRA's public image to repair this fraying relationship, the new guard, led by Carter, wanted to pursue altogether new fundraising strategies.[29] Further, this group believed that there would be new attempts to pass gun control—given the rise of gun control interest groups and the era's intensifying culture wars—that would require greater political investments on the NRA's part. Lastly, the new guard argued that the NRA's new approach to politics—embodied by the burgeoning themes associated with the *Second Amendment* topics discussed in chapter 4, including the fierce defense of liberty against government intrusion—necessitated an ideologically pure, hardline stance on gun control. The old guard of the NRA's quasi-governmental phase may have strongly opposed gun control, but their willingness to eventually accept bills after they had been weakened was seen by the new guard as unacceptable.[30]

These conflicting views did not immediately come to a head. Initially, the old guard compromised with the new guard by devoting more resources to politics, even creating the Institute for Legislative Action (ILA) in 1975 and appointing Harlon Carter to lead it.[31] Moreover, they allowed Carter and other hardliners to work with the New Right by hiring Richard Viguerie to help with direct mail fundraising for political causes.[32] While the NRA did not formally endorse him, they did invite Barry Goldwater to give a keynote speech at the 1971 Annual Meeting.[33] Beyond Goldwater, other conservative politicians began speaking at the group's meetings during the 1970s, which marked a shift away from the focus on military officials in conventions past.

Moreover, in the *American Rifleman*, the NRA made arguments that aligned with New Right positions and—albeit at low rates—started to explicitly connect the gun control issue to parties and the ideologies associated with them—a move that was also seen among pro-gun letter writers.[34] Prior to this period, as figure 6.1 demonstrates, very few NRA editorials or letters to the editor connected gun rights to partisan politics.[35] Although still infrequent, such connections began during the late 1960s and early 1970s as the NRA's ideological commitments started to intersect with changes in the ideological commitments of the parties.[36]

Just as the NRA came to express more partisan views, starting in the late 1960s the Republican Party took official pro-gun stances for the first time, and its leading officials came to increasingly appreciate the political importance of gun owners. The 1968 Republican platform took an initial step toward support for gun rights by adopting the position—favored by the NRA—that the federal government should stay out of gun regulation and leave it to the states.[37] The 1972 platform went even further, explicitly supporting a right to own and use guns and adopting the "law and order" argument—supported by both the NRA and the New Right—that existing laws should be enforced as strictly as possible but not expanded. The GOP pledged to "[s]afeguard the right of responsible citizens to collect, own and use firearms for legitimate purposes, including hunting, target shooting

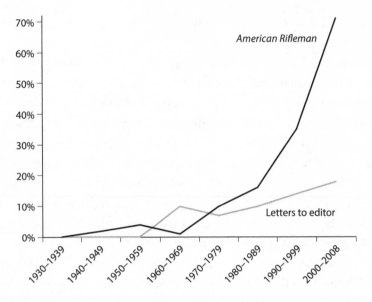

FIGURE 6.1. Proportion of Documents with Partisan Connections

and self-defense. We will strongly support efforts of all law enforcement agencies to apprehend and prosecute to the limit of the law all those who use firearms in the commission of crimes."[38]

President Nixon was a reluctant, tepid, inconsistent, and disingenuous supporter of gun rights; he was (mostly) an opponent of gun control in public and took several stances consistent with the New Right's platform but was nonetheless viewed skeptically by the movement's leaders. Privately, Nixon supported a handgun ban and sometimes even made public anti-gun comments; he never acted on these views, however, due in large part to the advice of deeply pro-gun advisors like G. Gordon Liddy and Patrick Buchanan who saw it as a losing issue due in part to the intensity of the minority of Americans who opposed gun control.[39] Nixon advisers recognized the importance of support from so-called gun-folk and acknowledged that a "culture" existed around guns, which increased the importance of the issue for gun owners.[40] They recognized, in other words, the strength of the gun owner identity—clear evidence that the NRA's work to cultivate this identity was starting to pay political dividends.

When President Ford took office after Nixon's resignation, he too signaled strong support for gun rights despite having favored gun control while in Congress in the 1960s.[41] As a result, the NRA considered endorsing him in 1976.[42] Ford's shift was due in part to pressure put on him by gun rights advocates—including the NRA—in the lead-up to the 1976 election, as well as concerns that a focus on gun rights during the primary would provide an advantage to New Right favorite Ronald Reagan, who competed with Ford for the nomination and was seen as more pro-gun.[43] This marked one of the first instances in which the NRA and its representatives attempted to weaponize the gun owner identity in order to gain influence over Republican officials, explicitly telling Ford's campaign it was "mobilizing a grass roots campaign of thousands of individuals" and that "the President could suffer from this effort" if he chose to support gun control.[44]

For his part, Ford actively solicited NRA support. In a note to Ashley Halsey, editor in chief of the *American Rifleman*, he said he would "oppose any attempt to deprive law-abiding citizens of their traditional freedom to own firearms" and further wrote, "I believe in punishing only those who commit crimes."[45] His letter repeated NRA talking points and language down to the letter. Ford later sent Harlon Carter a note thanking him for a piece in the *American Rifleman* that was critical of Jimmy Carter.[46]

The 1976 Republican platform followed in lockstep, continuing the trend of becoming increasingly friendly to gun rights. Indeed, it not only suggested that individuals have a right to own guns, but went as far as adopting the NRA's Second Amendment language, implying that the Constitution protects gun ownership. It stated, "We support the right of citizens to keep and bear arms. We oppose federal registration of firearms. Mandatory sentences for crimes committed with a lethal weapon are the only effective solution to this problem."[47]

THE REVOLT AT CINCINNATI

Ford lost to Jimmy Carter in 1976, but the election was nonetheless important for the NRA's relationship with the GOP. Reagan, having nearly defeated Ford in the primary, left the 1976 election cycle well-positioned to capture the Republican nomination in 1980. Given both his close relationship with the New Right and his strong embrace of gun rights, Reagan's rise further energized the new guard and made it even more eager to explicitly enter partisan politics.[48]

Around this same time, Gun Owners of America (GOA) was founded by New Right (and gun rights) activist Bill Richardson, who—even after it had made some additional political investments—was dissatisfied with the NRA's approach to politics. Although neither Harlon Carter nor Neal Knox was part of GOA, the new organization gave additional voice to both low-level NRA leaders who were members and to rank-and-file members who favored the New Right's political approach; this, in turn, made the NRA vulnerable to losing its right flank.[49] GOA also served as a venue through which some disaffected NRA members organized.[50]

Moreover, while the creation of the ILA was intended to appease the new guard, ILA staff quickly felt that they were given insufficient resources and objected to the restrictions placed on its activities by old guard leaders.[51] Together, all of this meant that—despite the GOP's gradual movement toward positions favored by gun rights activists as well as the NRA's increased investments in politics—conflict between the old guard and the new guard led by Carter and Knox continued.

This conflict came to a head at the 1977 NRA Annual Meeting in Cincinnati. The year before the Cincinnati meeting, the NRA was engaged in a heated internal battle over whether it should open an outdoors center and new headquarters in the western United States—a move that was supported by the old guard and that many believed would signal a retreat from politics. The old guard—seemingly in response to the intense opposition of Carter and his followers—fired nearly eighty NRA employees, most of whom were aligned with Carter. The firings, occurring on a Saturday, became known as the "Weekend Massacre," and led to the resignation of Carter from his position as leader of the ILA.[52] Outraged, the new guard began to quietly plan an organizational coup, in which rank-and-file supporters of Carter and Knox would take coordinated action to replace existing NRA leadership with new guard leaders.

The plan was executed in May 1977, when the NRA gathered at the Cincinnati Convention Center for its annual meeting.[53] Using radios to communicate with each other and wearing orange vests to identify themselves, new guard leaders and their rank-and-file supporters deftly used procedures defined in NRA bylaws to gain control of the convention's business meeting. The heated battle that ensued lasted eight hours and didn't conclude until 3:30 a.m., at which point the insurgents had voted out nearly all of the NRA's top officials.[54]

Following this Revolt at Cincinnati, new guard leaders took control of the organization, with Harlon Carter elected Executive Vice President and Neal Knox put in charge of the ILA.[55] The NRA quickly moved into closer alignment with the New Right. It deepened its investments in Viguerie's direct mail strategies, and new NRA political operatives—including a young Wayne LaPierre—built ties with other New Right organizations.[56] In the 1978 elections, the mobilization of gun owners on behalf of New Right candidates helped to propel many of them into office.[57] This electoral success enhanced the NRA's standing within the Republican Party, since it increased the proportion of Congress that shared its ideological commitments.

In the language of political science, the new guard leaders who disrupted the NRA's organizational trajectory can be described as *political entrepreneurs*. Political entrepreneurs are individuals who are dissatisfied with the current state of an institution—in this case, the NRA—but lack authority to produce the change they desire. They want to change the status quo, in other words, but don't have enough power within the institution to do so. Instead, these individuals—as political scientist Adam Sheingate argues—take advantage of moments of instability that create openings for change, and use these openings to repurpose existing aspects of the institution in ways that serve their goals. They then find ways to lock in these changes and consolidate their new power moving forward, disempowering the previous authorities.[58]

The NRA's new guard leaders fit these criteria: dissatisfied with the direction the NRA was going in but lacking the authority within existing rules to alter its course, Carter, Knox, and other new guard leaders took entrepreneurial action to set the NRA down a fundamentally different path.

First, they took advantage of the dissatisfaction with current leadership that existed both among other NRA leaders and among rank-and-file members in the 1970s.[59] The new guard seized this opportunity for change, using the instability that existed as a result of internal conflict to create a crisis environment in which an increasingly broad swath of NRA officials and members believed change was necessary. Carter and Knox built a diverse coalition of support, ranging from "obsessive far-right conspiracy buffs to blue-collar union men to constitutional scholars," uniting them behind the belief that "their Second Amendment rights were in jeopardy and that the current NRA leadership could no longer be trusted to protect those rights."[60] Carter and Knox effectively served as "common carriers"—the term political scientist Eric Schickler uses to describe entrepreneurial legislators who unify diverse coalitions in Congress behind institutional reforms.[61]

Second, the new guard leaders repurposed existing elements of the NRA in innovative ways. This included both institutional and ideational innovations. Institutionally, the new guard identified loopholes in existing organizational bylaws, which enabled them to execute an organizational coup d'état in a way that existing leaders did not realize was possible.[62] Upon taking control, the new guard leaders shifted resources within the organization to advance their agendas, devoting more to the NRA's political operations, most notably the ILA.[63] Finally, during both the lead-up to and aftermath of the revolt, the new guard reshaped existing ideas about the purpose of the NRA, elevating its existing role as the defender of the Second Amendment and using that role to sell the need to move in a new direction politically. The NRA, of course, had already opposed gun control and advocated for an individual rights view of the Second Amendment for a long time. The new guard, however, recast these positions in ways that were, as author Michael Waldman puts it, more "dramatic, dogmatic, and overtly ideological"[64] and made the defense of gun rights—and the Second Amendment—paramount to the NRA's purpose.[65]

Finally, the new guard consolidated these changes to ensure the NRA continued in its new, partisan direction. They altered the bylaws that had enabled them to gain control in ways that increased the scope of their organizational power and allowed them to replace leaders throughout the organization.[66] They disseminated and reinforced new ideas to their mass-level supporters about both gun rights and the NRA's ideological and partisan orientation—emphasizing the Second Amendment and its importance to an explicitly conservative movement—and used new fundraising and recruitment tactics to grow the organization—growth that in turn increased the funds available for them to pursue new political efforts.[67] Ultimately, in establishing relationships with conservative and Republican political actors, the new guard set the NRA down a path that was increasingly difficult to reverse; as its relationship with the GOP deepened, in other words, it became costlier and more challenging for the organization to revert back to a nonpartisan approach, thereby making continued alliance more likely.

The impact of the new guard's entrepreneurial efforts on the behavior of NRA members was swift; the organization's partisan shift was quickly followed by an immediate shift in the behavior of its members, with the statistical relationship between gun ownership and voting Republican increasing in the first elections following the revolt.[68] In an internal poll commissioned by the NRA in 1978, 40 percent of NRA members identified as Republicans[69] (compared to just 29 percent as Democrats), and a remarkable 77 percent identified as conservatives[70] (compared to just 22 percent as liberals).[71] Among gun owners generally, only 30 percent and 34 percent of gun owners identified as Republicans in 1976 and 1980, respectively, and 40 percent identified as conservative in 1978.[72] NRA members were thus a particularly conservative, Republican subset of the larger group, and likely an important part of the new alignment between the previously nonpartisan organization and the Republican Party.

RETHINKING THE REVOLT AT CINCINNATI

The Cincinnati meeting is recognized as a watershed moment in NRA history—yet even this understates the impact the event had on the NRA's role within the political system. Without the new guard's actions, the NRA would likely have moved forward with the plan to move its headquarters out west as part of a general organizational emphasis on the outdoors. The ILA, at least in the near term, would likely have remained small, and the organization would have maintained its independence from the New Right. It is even possible that without the revolt, GOA would have eventually become more prominent than the NRA in the political realm. The institutional changes caused by the new guard were a crucial—and necessary[73]—step in the process of partisan alignment.

The revolt is often discussed as though it marked the initial entry of the NRA into politics—as the moment in which the NRA "became the Gun Lobby,"[74] by one account.[75] Yet as this chapter and those before it make clear, the NRA was both highly *political* and highly *ideological* prior to 1977. Moreover, NRA leaders both before and after 1977 shared similar views on politics and connected gun rights to a similar set of political issues. The revolt of 1977 was not the moment that the NRA became politicized, or even a moment of stark ideological change for the organization.

Rather, the revolt marked the NRA's entry into *partisan* politics. The NRA was already political and ideological; what changed in 1977 was the group's decision to embrace rather than avoid partisanship and explicit ideological labels. Crucially, this led the NRA to make investments in the political infrastructure necessary to succeed in an increasingly dense and intense political environment. These institutional changes in the NRA laid a foundation for its future political endeavors.

The 1980s and 1990s: The NRA Joins the Party

Ronald Reagan's successful presidential campaign in 1980 was a momentous event for the NRA. Although the NRA had become increasingly close with the GOP during the 1970s and although the

Republicans, in turn, had included support for gun rights in their party platforms, the NRA had never formally endorsed a presidential candidate prior to 1980—but it had also never seen a presidential candidate quite like Reagan.

Reagan,[76] an NRA member who had won honors from the organization while he was governor of California, showed much deeper and durable support for gun rights than his GOP predecessors.[77] What's more, he accepted the *ideological* connection of gun rights with conservatism—the connection that was embodied by the alliance between the NRA and the New Right. Reagan had it all: he believed in the use of guns for personal self-defense, favored harsh prison sentences in lieu of restrictions on access to guns, saw gun control as a form of big government, and tied all of these to an individual rights view of the Second Amendment holding that the primary purpose of guns is to allow for the protection of individual liberty from the US government.[78] He was also, just like the NRA and the New Right, hawkish on foreign policy and a strong anticommunist.

Beyond his virtually perfect ideological alignment with the NRA, Reagan—both on movie screens during his acting career and in his post-acting life—was a walking personification of the gun owner social identity described in chapter 3. His public image could hardly have been more similar to the NRA's depiction of gun owners as courageous, honest, freedom-loving citizens who patriotically defend an increasingly threatened American tradition. In Osha Gray Davidson's words, "As a Hollywood actor, Reagan often played the part of the slow-to-anger-but-willing-to-fight gun-toting pioneer. . . . Ronald Reagan was the perfect person to ride into Washington and clean out the various varmints who were undermining the American way of life."[79]

When Reagan redefined what it meant to be a Republican in his image, it brought the gun owner identity into closer alignment with Republican partisan identity. This comes through in the words of gun rights supporters, who even years later expressed a personal devotion to Reagan. Frank DeSomma, a producer of AR-15s and gun rights activist, described Reagan as "the only president of my lifetime who really cared about America" and viewed him as "like a grandfather."[80] As another NRA member put it, "To see Reagan come riding in . . . and turn this country around . . . was the most artful thing in the history of mankind to do what he did."[81]

With the new guard at the helm, a close alignment with the New Right, and an "ideological soul mate"[82] running for president, the NRA formally endorsed a presidential candidate for the first time, telling its members in the *American Rifleman* that they should vote for Reagan because he believes "in the people's right to keep and bear arms, and in the right of citizens to be free from the bondage of an oppressive government."[83] The 1980 Republican platform, perhaps unsurprisingly, took its strongest pro-gun stance yet, stating,

> We believe the right of citizens to keep and bear arms must be preserved. Accordingly, we oppose federal registration of firearms. Mandatory sentences for commission of armed felonies are the most effective means to deter abuse of this right. We therefore support Congressional initiatives to remove those provisions of the Gun Control Act of 1968 that do not significantly impact on crime but serve rather to restrain the law-abiding citizen in his legitimate use of firearms.[84]

And gun owners responded to this, with gun ownership being a much stronger statistical predictor of voting for Reagan than it was for previous Republican candidates.[85]

Having won office on a pro-gun platform and with strong support from gun owners, President Reagan's arrival in Washington represented the incorporation of the NRA into a new Republican coalition. This was visible symbolically in Reagan's decision to speak at the 1983 NRA Annual Meeting in Phoenix,[86] which made the new relationship between the NRA and the Republican Party publicly clear.[87] From then on, the Annual Meeting regularly featured Republican politicians, including Vice President George H. W. Bush in 1986.

Beyond the symbolic gestures was legislative action. The Reagan years witnessed not only an absence of successful gun control bills, but the proposal and passage of laws that actually *loosened* gun regulations, along with moves that weakened the BATF, the agency in charge of enforcing gun regulations.[88] Most notable among these was the Firearm Owners Protection Act (also known as McClure-Volkmer)—a longtime NRA priority, which repealed parts of the Gun Control Act of 1968 and passed after the organization mobilized its members behind it.[89] Internal memos sent by Reagan Administration officials illumine their interest in maintaining the NRA's support; one noted that "if NRA members and other gun owners are disillusioned, the political losses will be significant."[90]

George H. W. Bush, the Republican candidate in 1988, likewise recognized that he needed to solve what his campaign termed "the Problem with Sportsman [sic]."[91] Bush carefully took the strong pro-gun stances that would be required to obtain the NRA's endorsement—an endorsement he got, despite some skepticism about him within the firearms community.[92] Whereas Reagan was—or at least genuinely seemed like—an NRA "true believer," Bush's membership in and support of the NRA appears to have been motivated solely by political considerations. Media accounts from the Bush years often misleadingly referred to the president as a "lifelong" NRA member; in fact, he did not join the NRA until May 1985, at which time (in an event publicized by the *American Rifleman*) he purchased a "Life Membership," which simply means that he paid a lump sum for permanent membership in lieu of paying annual dues.[93] (Following his presidency, Bush resigned—in dramatic fashion—after the NRA referred to BATF agents as "jackbooted thugs.")[94]

After Bush won election with the full support of the NRA, his relationship with the group quickly deteriorated. Bush (albeit reluctantly) oversaw and supported a ban on the import of certain assault weapons following the schoolyard massacre that had occurred in Stockton, California, on January 17, 1989—just days before he took office.[95] Despite his action on assault weapons (which deeply angered the NRA and caused some members to attempt to expel him from the group), Bush opposed the "Brady Bill" (a separate effort to enhance gun regulations)[96] throughout his presidency, even though the bill had wide support among both the public and elites—a decision that clearly signaled his desire to keep the NRA's support.[97] But the NRA wasn't mollified, and refused to endorse any candidate in the 1992 election, which Bush ended up losing.[98]

Bush's courting of the NRA (and his loss in 1992 when he could not regain their support) pointed to the further crystallization of the group's relationship with the Republican Party. This was not limited to presidential politics; by the 1990s, opposition to gun control had become a standard position of most Republican candidates, and the partisan gap on the issue among members of Congress increased substantially throughout the 1980s and 1990s, with Republican members supporting gun rights at much higher rates than Democrats (even when statistically accounting for other factors, such as legislators' home regions and public opinion among their constituents). As political scientist David Karol shows, by the end of the Reagan and Bush years—unlike during previous eras—legislators' partisan affiliation was a much stronger statistical predictor of their votes on gun control than public opinion among their constituents.[99] This continued into Clinton's Democratic presidency and beyond; the gap between the parties in Congress kept growing through the end of Karol's dataset in 2000 and has only expanded further in more recent years as partisan polarization has increased.[100]

In line with these voting patterns, the twenty-first century saw a continuation of the trends that started in the 1970s and 1980s. The NRA remained an important member of the Republican coalition, and increasingly endorsed and (discussed in greater depth next chapter) financially supported Republican candidates. The NRA's Annual Meeting became a "who's who" of Republican politicians.

On the mass level, gun owners became even more supportive of GOP candidates. As figure 6.1 demonstrates, the frequency of partisan connections in both the *American Rifleman* and in pro-gun letters to the editor increased rapidly as the relationship between the NRA and the Republican Party grew. Voting patterns bear this trend out; in the 2012 election, for instance, 56 percent of gun owners voted for Mitt Romney, compared to just 26 percent of non-gun owners.[101]

Gun owners' comments in interviews also speak to the increasing alignment between the NRA and the GOP. One NRA member, for instance, commented that "[Gun rights candidates] seem to think the right way in other matters too, you know—individually instead of the state. Anti-big government."[102] Describing his partisan allegiance in clear identity-based terms, another gun owner said, "The Democrat party used to be the party of the workingman ... the gun guy. ... The leadership of the Democrat party [now] criticizes conservatives for our *tastes*."[103]

As gun control measures returned to the legislative agenda under Bill Clinton, and later Barack Obama, support for gun rights among Republican policymakers continued to increase. By the 2010s, Republican opposition to gun control was so strong that any piece of gun legislation was basically dead on arrival. While Clinton was able to pass new gun control laws, Obama's proposals went nowhere— despite horrific incidents of mass gun violence.[104]

Another important development during this period was the broad polarization of mass partisans—that is, Republican and Democratic voters—on gun issues. In the 1970s and '80s, gun control had become an increasingly partisan issue for the NRA, its members and other gun owners, and political elites. In the 1990s, however, the broader public began to split along partisan lines on gun control. Figure 6.2 illustrates this trend. It depicts the difference in support between Democrats and Republicans for a law requiring a police permit to purchase guns and shows that the gap between them on this issue stayed mostly flat, on average, until the early 1990s, at which point it began a steady increase.[105] Change on this issue has mostly been driven by declining Republican support, with support among Democrats remaining constant.[106]

A similar trend is seen on a broader question from the Pew Research Center, which asks respondents whether controlling guns or protecting the rights of Americans to own them is more important. The proportion of Democrats who say protecting the right to own guns is more important has remained stable, but the proportion of Republicans who say this has risen dramatically in recent years.[107] This pattern—in which Republicans drive the partisan opinion gap on gun control—is what we would expect given that there is no gun control advocacy group with influence in the Democratic Party comparable to the NRA's influence in the Republican Party.

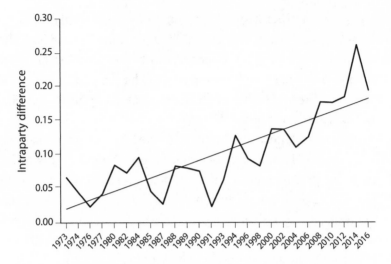

FIGURE 6.2. Party Difference in Support for Requiring a Police Permit to Purchase Guns

More broadly, the higher-level pattern described in this chapter—in which gun owners seemed to switch their party identification based on the parties' gun control stances while the broader public rearranged their preferences on gun control to align with their pre-existing party identification—fits with Thomas Carsey and Geoffrey Layman's study of how the public responds to party position change; in this model, those who care a lot about an issue will, if needed, switch parties based on it, while those who care less about the issue will switch their stance on it to align with their party's position.[108]

The Trump Era: The NRA *Leads* the Party?

The NRA began advocating a conservative brand of populism and nationalism more than a decade before Donald Trump arrived on the political scene—and with Trump, they would find a presidential candidate who in many ways echoed these views. This section digs into the NRA's close relationship with Trump's Republican Party in greater detail. It also further explores gun ownership's (and the gun owner identity's) relationship with other politically relevant group memberships and identities. Recently collected data—which doesn't exist for earlier years—enables a more detailed exploration of these relationships during the contemporary period, and reveals that gun ownership and the gun owner identity (1) are closely related to other group memberships and identities associated with the Republican Party and (2) were statistically significant predictors of approval of President Trump's job performance. Taken together, these additional analyses demonstrate the nature, depth, and breadth of the NRA's alignment with the GOP by highlighting the many ways in which gun ownership and support for gun rights have become wrapped up with the Republican Party.

The NRA was an early and enthusiastic supporter of Trump's candidacy. The organization endorsed Trump in May 2016, before he had officially received the GOP's nomination for president;[109] their endorsements of George W. Bush, John McCain, and Mitt Romney in 2004, 2008, and 2012, respectively, had come much later, in October of those years.[110] The NRA also invested an unusually large amount of money into supporting his campaign—indeed, the NRA bet more on Trump than it ever has on a politician, spending more than $30 million on his behalf.[111] Gun owners shared this enthusiasm; in the 2016 election, 62 percent of gun owners voted for Trump (a rate that was surely much higher among those who are NRA members), compared to just 38 percent of non-gun owners.[112]

On the surface, Trump and the NRA made an unlikely pair. A flashy billionaire, Trump's public image did not align well with the NRA's populist depiction of gun owners; other Republican presidential candidates in 2016—such as Mike Huckabee or Rand Paul—much more closely resemble the NRA's constituency. Moreover, Trump previously voiced support for gun control policies that were staunchly opposed by the NRA, including an assault weapons ban and longer waiting periods prior to firearms purchases.[113]

The NRA's enthusiasm for Trump is much easier to explain, however, when one considers the similarities between Trump's political worldview and the NRA's. As mentioned in chapter 4, Trump espoused a political outlook remarkably similar to the perspective advanced in the *American Rifleman* since the early 2000s. Indeed, it is possible (although difficult to demonstrate) that Trump learned from and adopted some elements of the NRA's approach to politics. Trump's attacks on the media closely echoed decades of NRA appeals in which the organization has derided the so-called mainstream media for being phony, biased, and dishonest. Trump's populist rhetoric attacking elites—even going so far as peddling anti-Semitic conspiracy theories about left-of-center billionaires like George Soros—also echoed NRA appeals that associate gun control with elitism. Further, Trump's racially charged appeals, especially those focused on the threat of violence, also aligned well with the NRA's worldview. This includes the NRA's longtime emphasis on harsh criminal sentencing, its fear-inducing portrayal of urban violence, and its connection of immigration and crime; indeed, the NRA even advocated for building a wall along the United States' southern border as early as October 2010.[114]

After winning the presidency, Trump's rhetoric and policy stances continued to closely align with the NRA's. In one instance, Trump appeared to have outright adopted NRA-generated talking points, discussing school shootings using language that was exceptionally similar to the language used by Wayne LaPierre in a speech delivered just hours before Trump's remarks.[115]

The NRA, for its part, offered Trump its unwavering support on a range of issues that go far beyond gun control. In a series of ominous online videos that garnered millions of views, the NRA defended Trump by attacking his critics, depicting mass-level protestors as violent opponents of American freedom who are taking coordinated action with Hollywood elites and the liberal media. The videos depicted Trump opponents as outsiders—constantly referred to only as "they"—who, it is said, "scream racism and sexism and xenophobia and homophobia to smash windows and burn cars, shut down interstates and airports, bully and terrorize the law-abiding."[116] Other videos attacked the media even more explicitly, calling them "fake news" and depicting them as opponents of America.[117]

In public appearances during the Trump administration, LaPierre advanced themes associated with "deep state" conspiracy theories and made misleading claims about violent crimes committed by undocumented immigrants that were very similar to claims made

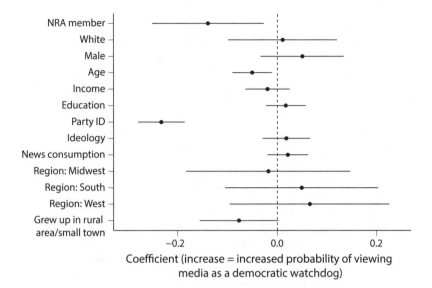

FIGURE 6.3. Relationship between NRA Membership and Views on Media's Role in Democracy. Figure depicts an original OLS regression analysis of data collected by the Pew Research Center in 2017, with standardized independent variables that are weighted to be nationally representative. Because the question about NRA membership was only asked of gun owning respondents, this analysis excludes non-gun owners. A description of the study and all data are available at the following URL: http://www.pewsocialtrends .org/2017/06/22/guns-report-methodology/.

by Trump.[118] Moreover, the NRA's now defunct "NRATV" online news channel—launched shortly after Trump's 2016 victory—was notable for its *lack* of attention to guns.[119] Although short-lived, NRATV espoused ongoing NRA themes in a new medium, focusing on a range of culture war issues—such as NFL players' protests of police violence against African Americans[120]—and often defended Trump against Special Counsel Robert Mueller's investigation into wrongdoing in the 2016 election.[121]

Public opinion polls revealed that mass-level NRA supporters shared these views. As figure 6.3 shows, for instance, NRA membership was a statistically significant predictor of gun owners' views on the role of the media in democracy; even when holding a range of other factors constant, NRA membership was associated with the view that criticism from "news organizations keeps political leaders from doing their job" rather than the view that such

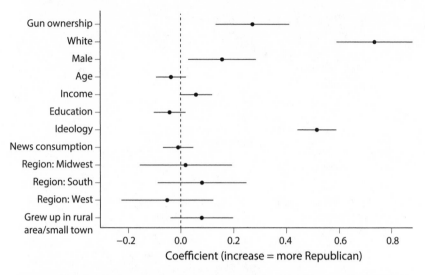

FIGURE 6.4. Relationship between Gun Ownership and Partisan Identification. Figure depicts an original OLS regression analysis of data collected by the Pew Research Center in 2017, with standardized independent variables that are weighted to be nationally representative. A description of the study and all data are available at the following URL: http://www.pewsocialtrends .org/2017/06/22/guns-report-methodology/.

criticism "keeps political leaders from doing things that should not be done."[122]

Trump also demonstrated the extent to which he values the organization's support by frequently speaking to its members. Trump spoke at both the 2015 and 2016 NRA Annual Meetings as part of his presidential run. Then, in 2017, he became the first sitting president since Ronald Reagan to appear at the Annual Meeting, giving a speech in which he thanked the NRA and its members for their support.[123] Trump then appeared at the NRA convention *again* in both 2018 and 2019, marking five straight years of visits.[124]

Trump's attention to the NRA's members and supporters makes sense, as gun owners—especially those who are NRA members— have become increasingly Republican. As of 2017, 61 percent of gun owners were either Republican or leaned Republican. Gun ownership—as figure 6.4 shows—was a strong and statistically significant predictor of identifying as a Republican, even when holding numerous factors—including political ideology (which is itself a strong predictor of party identification)—constant. Notably, gun owners who belonged to the NRA were even more likely to be or lean Republican—77 percent of gun owning NRA members either were or leaned Republican.[125]

The relationship between mass-level NRA supporters and the Trump-era GOP, however, runs even deeper than the statistics presented so far suggest. Gun ownership, NRA membership, and social identification as a gun owner (which, rather than capturing whether an individual owns a gun, instead measures the extent to which gun ownership is part of his or her personal identity) aren't just associated with support for the Republican Party and its candidates, but are instead closely aligned with a wide range of other identities and group memberships tied to Trumpism and the GOP. Using recent surveys, the following pages document many of these relationships, showing the numerous characteristics—such as individuals' views and identities related to race, gender, and religion—associated with support for both Trump and the Republican Party, on the one hand, and gun ownership, support for gun rights, and social identification as a gun owner, on the other. These relationships suggest that the NRA's bond with the GOP has led to a fusion of its identity with other, related identities.

The alignment of all of these identities matters because it serves to reinforce each of them individually—forming what political scientist Liliana Mason, in her pathbreaking work on identity and political polarization, has described as a mega-identity.[126] As chapter 2 notes, some politically relevant group memberships and social identities create cross-pressures for individuals, pulling them in different directions politically. Other group memberships and identities, however, go in the "same direction," which causes them to reinforce one another and increase the strength with which an individual holds each. I find that the gun owner identity and other GOP-linked identities are a clear case of the latter.

The interrelated nature of the various identities associated with the GOP also suggests that political party coalitions—beyond just bringing together groups and their policy views—can also unite the identities associated with each group. The NRA's relationship with the GOP, in other words, has not just involved the party's adoption of pro-gun policy stances, but also an alignment of the gun owner identity with other predominantly Republican identities.

To begin, we can think about race and gender. Regressive views on both racial and gender-related issues are associated with support for Trumpism; indeed, a number of studies have found that racism and sexism were very strong statistical predictors of support for Trump in the 2016 election.[127] Moreover, throughout his 2016 campaign and subsequent presidency, Trump himself made racist and sexist appeals on numerous occasions.[128]

Existing scholarship on gun politics indicates that these same types of views statistically predict individuals' outlooks on gun control.[129] Whites are more likely than others to both own guns and to socially identify with gun ownership.[130] Alexandra Filindra and Noah Kaplan find that racial resentment—which is an established way of measuring, via surveys, the extent to which white individuals are racially prejudiced against Black people—is a statistically significant predictor of whites' gun control preferences, with more racially prejudiced whites less supportive of gun regulations. Numerous other studies have also connected gun ownership and/or gun control preferences to racial prejudice.[131]

Gender is also connected to gun ownership, with men more likely to own guns than women and more likely than women to oppose gun control.[132] Further, numerous scholars have connected guns and masculinity, arguing that gun ownership is a way for some men to assert a masculine identity, especially in the face of perceived threat to their status in society.[133]

The NRA has helped facilitate these connections by linking gun rights to themes associated with white racial and masculine identities and, in so doing, depicting gun owners as patriotic, traditional white men.[134] These themes come through in comments from NRA members interviewed by sociologist Scott Melzer; for instance, one member, connecting a racialized fear of crime to his perceived role as a protector, told Melzer that part of why he needs a gun is that "[i]f three big ol' Black dudes come at you [when you're with your wife and children], you gotta be able to protect your family."[135]

This connection helps explain some otherwise puzzling actions taken by the NRA, most notably its weak defense of Black gun owners. It remained quiet, for instance, in regard to the 2016 killing of Philando Castile by police in Minnesota during a routine traffic stop. Castile, an African American man in his early thirties, was legally carrying a firearm when he was pulled over for a broken tail light and then, shortly after, shot and killed by police. Despite video of Castile informing the officer of his possession of a gun in an attempt to defuse the situation, the officer who killed Castile was not convicted of a crime—a highly controversial outcome about which the NRA said nothing of substance.[136] The NRA's puzzling lack of action on behalf of Black gun owners like Castile is easier to understand when one considers the relationship between gun owner identity, white racial identity, and Republican identity described above. A strong defense of Castile would clash with both white racial identity and (because the protests of Castile's killing were led by liberal Democrats) Republican identity; such a clash could in turn reduce both the strength of individuals' attachment to gun owner identity as well as the alignment of gun owner identity with other conservative identities.

The alignment of the gun owner identity with other predominantly Republican identities is not limited to race and gender—it also extends to religious identity. Like the NRA and gun owners, evangelical Christians are prominently associated with the rise of the New Right and the Reagan coalition, and they also overwhelmingly supported Donald Trump in the 2016 election.[137] The inclusion of evangelicals in the same party coalition as the NRA seems to have impacted their behavior and views in regards to guns. For one thing, they own guns at higher rates than members of other religious groups in the United States; while evangelicalism alone loses statistical significance as a predictor of gun ownership when a robust set of demographic and political controls are included, theological conservatism—which is a measure of the nature of individuals' religious worldview rather than his or her denomination—is significant even when including such controls.[138] Moreover, evangelicals are also unusually supportive of gun rights; surveys show that evangelical

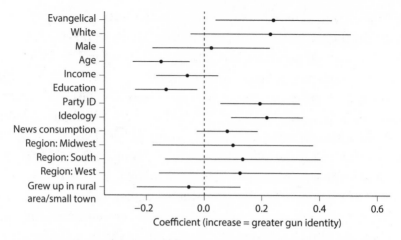

FIGURE 6.5. Relationship between Evangelical Identity and Gun Identity among Gun Owners. Figure depicts an original OLS regression analysis of data collected by the Pew Research Center in 2017, with standardized independent variables that are weighted to be nationally representative. Because the question about gun owner identity was only asked of gun owning respondents, the analysis excludes non-gun owners. A description of the study and all data are available at the following URL: http://www.pewsocialtrends .org/2017/06/22/guns-report-methodology/.

Christians systematically oppose gun control to a greater extent than members of other religious groups, even when holding numerous other factors constant.[139] Finally, among individuals who own guns, evangelical Christianity is a statistically significant predictor of gun owner identity, even when controlling for other politically relevant factors; as figure 6.5 shows, evangelical gun owners are more likely than others to report that their status as gun owners is important to their overall identities.

Closely related, Christian nationalism—a concept that captures the extent to which individuals desire "a close intertwining of Christianity and the public sphere"—is also a very strong predictor of opposition to gun control.[140] Notably, Christian nationalism is also closely associated with having supported Trump in the 2016 election.[141] The connection between guns, Christian nationalism, and support for Trump suggests some individuals hold a worldview that links together particular views about the proper roles of both Christianity and gun ownership in public life, and sees Trump as an advocate for that worldview. This outlook shows up in interviews, in which Christian gun owners often link religion, guns, and politics by arguing that "gun ownership is not a belief" but instead a "God-given right" that the United States, as a Christian nation, is unique in protecting.[142]

Another dimension along which guns are linked to a GOP-aligned identity is community type: gun ownership, support for gun rights, and social identification as a gun owner are all statistically related to rural identity. Individuals who live in rural areas both own guns and socially identify with gun ownership at higher rates than individuals who live in cities or suburbs.[143] They are also less supportive of gun control than others.[144]

Similarly, self-identified conservatives are also more likely than others to own guns, belong to the NRA, and to socially identify with gun ownership. Indeed, identifying as a conservative is strongly associated with identifying as a gun owner, even when statistically accounting for other factors, including one's partisan affiliation.[145] One gun owner, succinctly connecting gun rights to conservative identity, surmised that people like guns "because they piss off the liberals so much."[146]

Lastly, Republican party identification itself is now closely linked with individuals' outlooks on guns. As discussed earlier, over 60 percent of gun owners are now either Republicans or lean Republican, and NRA members are even more likely than other gun owners to be Republicans.[147] Among gun owners, Republicans are much more likely to choose to join the NRA.[148] Further, Republican party identification is a strong and statistically significant predictor of social identification with gun ownership, even when holding other relevant characteristics constant.[149] Finally, Republicans are also much less supportive of gun control than Democrats and Independents.[150]

Perhaps unsurprisingly given the identity-linkages discussed throughout this section, gun ownership, gun owner identity,[151] and NRA membership are all statistically related to individuals' assessment of Trump's job performance. As figure 6.6 shows, all three were associated with increased approval of President Trump's performance in office as of 2017 (when the survey was conducted), even

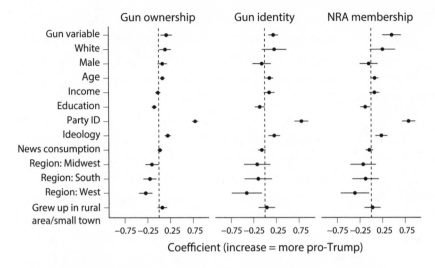

FIGURE 6.6. Relationship between Gun-Related Variables and Trump Approval. Figure depicts original OLS regression analyses of data collected by the Pew Research Center in 2017, with standardized independent variables that are weighted to be nationally representative. Because questions about gun owner identity and NRA membership were only asked of gun owning respondents, those analyses exclude non-gun owners. A description of the study and all data are available at the following URL: http://www.pewsocialtrends.org/2017/06/22/guns-report-methodology/.

when accounting for other crucial factors that would impact support for Trump, such as party identification, ideology, race, and gender.

Together, the patterns described in the preceding paragraphs indicate that the gun owner social identity associated with the NRA fits neatly with other predominantly conservative and Republican identities—especially those closely related to support for President Trump. This close alignment of identities and group memberships— the way in which they are associated with one another and with similar political views—suggests the NRA's relationship with the GOP goes beyond just the ideological inclusion of gun rights in conservatism and the institutional inclusion of the NRA in the Republican coalition. It also involves a unification of the gun owner *identity* with other identities associated with conservatism and the GOP. In this sense, political parties can be thought of as not just coalitions of political actors and groups, but also as coalitions of aligned identities and the themes—the personal values and characteristics—associated with those identities. Put differently, parties are not only capable of fusing together groups and those groups' policy demands, but also the social psychological attachments associated with membership in those groups. Party coalitions, in short, can shape what it means to belong to the groups included in such coalitions.

———

The *party-group alignment* that led to the NRA's incorporation into the Republican coalition was fueled by favorable institutional conditions—the rise of the New Right, the deterioration of the NRA's relationship with the federal government, and the entrepreneurial actions of key NRA leaders—and by mass-level inputs—the gun owner social identity from chapter 3 and the gun-centric political ideology from chapter 4. These ideational, mass-level developments were crucial at every step of the NRA's transition into a Republican coalition.

In short, the NRA demonstrates how groups can (1) cultivate a group-centric social identity along with an ideology that is built around their most important issue, and disseminate both the identity and ideology to their supporters; (2) join a broader ideological coalition as a result of their efforts to cultivate a worldview; and (3) leverage both their affiliation with the broader ideological coalition and the political behavior of their members to get their most important issue adopted by politicians in a party. The NRA's route to party incorporation helps us understand how groups and parties become aligned.

Just how confident can we be that the NRA's efforts to cultivate a group identity and ideology played a causal role in its incorporation into the Republican coalition? As was the case with chapters 3 and 4, this question is difficult to answer with certainty, but the sequence of events described above strongly suggests that the political behavior of NRA members—driven by the NRA—was central to this process. The coherent ideology shared by NRA members, which fit perfectly with the insurgent conservative ideology advanced by the New Right, existed *prior* to both the rise of the New Right and the subsequent changes that occurred within the GOP. Moreover, NRA members—again following the organization's lead—demonstrated high levels of support for conservative Republican candidates before both other gun owners and members of the broader public. And the deep, identity-driven political engagement of NRA members and supporters—described as "an easy voter pool to tap into"[152]—made it an attractive group to Republican candidates, who went to great lengths to receive its support and quickly recognized the political importance of its members.[153]

The NRA has become increasingly prominent within the Republican Party in recent years and played an unusually important role in Donald Trump's successful 2016 presidential campaign. Trump rose to power having adopted a worldview very similar to the NRA's: he advanced a similar brand of nationalistic populism and used racially charged (or outright racist) appeals to mobilize action by making supporters feel threatened. Beyond these similarities—and likely *because* of them—the NRA also made big bets on Trump when other influential actors would not. As a result, Trump demonstrated clear appreciation for the NRA and its supporters.

The alignment of the NRA and the GOP extends to the mass level as well, with gun ownership, membership in the NRA, and social identification as a gun owner increasingly tied to other group memberships, identities, and characteristics that are associated with Trump and/or the Republican Party. This suggests that the social psychological meaning of gun ownership is now clearly aligned with—and perhaps intertwined with—the social psychological meaning of being a Republican. This alignment of identities alters our understanding of the GOP: beyond being an alliance of organized groups whose policy demands have been organized into a broader ideology, it also involves the alignment of the *identities* associated with those groups.[154]

In the Trump era, the NRA may have become an anchoring group.[155] Schlozman does *not* consider the NRA an anchoring group, characterizing it instead as an example of a narrow alliance. In a narrow alliance, as in an anchoring alliance, a group offers a party resources, and the party advances the group's policy demands—but unlike anchoring alliances, the demands only concern single issues and so have little impact on the party's relationships with other groups. Following this logic, Schlozman characterizes the NRA-GOP alliance as narrow because it only impacts the GOP on a single issue: gun control.[156]

For Donald Trump, however, it seems that the NRA's role was much larger. The NRA's relationship with Trump spanned a number of issues and went beyond policy preferences, relating instead to a shared core worldview. Moreover, although the NRA has supported Republican candidates for a long time, its support of Trump's campaign was unusually crucial: Trump's campaign infrastructure was notably weak during the 2016 election cycle, he lagged far behind Hillary Clinton in terms of fundraising, and he was shunned by many of the individuals and groups that Republican candidates had previously relied on.[157] The NRA played a large role in making up for these deficiencies; it spent a record amount in support of Trump's campaign—some of which went to ads that had nothing to do with gun rights—in order to mobilize both its supporters and other conservatives across the country.[158]

It is yet to be seen whether the NRA's current status within the GOP will endure. Moreover, it's possible that its close alignment with the party will eventually have some downsides—a possibility discussed further in the book's concluding chapter. But for now, it is clear that the NRA's position in the GOP is stronger than ever.

The next chapter goes back to the beginning of the NRA's partisan phase in order to explore the effects of this position on the group's ability to influence gun policy outcomes; digging into the gun debate from the 1980s onward, it examines the nature of the NRA's policy influence during a new phase of its history.

7

Gun Policy during the NRA's Partisan Phase

By now, it's well known that 90 percent of the American people support universal background checks that make it harder for a dangerous person to buy a gun. . . . And a few minutes ago, 90 percent of Democrats in the Senate just voted for that idea. But it's not going to happen because 90 percent of Republicans in the Senate just voted against that idea. . . . It came down to politics—the worry that that vocal minority of gun owners would come after them in future elections.

—THEN-PRESIDENT BARACK OBAMA DISCUSSING THE REPUBLICAN-LED DEFEAT OF GUN CONTROL LEGISLATION PROPOSED FOLLOWING THE MASSACRE AT SANDY HOOK ELEMENTARY SCHOOL, 2013[1]

The 1980s marked both the NRA's definitive entry into partisan politics and the return of gun control to the national legislative agenda. The NRA entered the decade in a period of strength: Ronald Reagan, who had a long-standing relationship with the organization and ran on a New Right platform, won the presidency in 1980 after having received the NRA's first political endorsement. This election, as discussed in the last chapter, solidified and deepened the connection between the NRA and the Republican Party that had been slowly developing in earlier years.

The legislative battles over gun policy that would occur in the 1980s were the first during the NRA's partisan phase. How would its efforts to advance its agenda—and the effectiveness of those efforts—shift in light of its new place in the political system? How would the ideational resources it had used in previous gun control battles come into play? This chapter—examining a number of gun policy cases from the 1980s through the 2010s—explores these questions (see table 7.1). As in chapter 5, I again compare the impact of these sources of power to other potential sources of power, such as financial resources.

The NRA, as the cases show, has maintained the ability to mobilize its supporters into political action when needed. But its relationship with the GOP has also opened up new avenues, including influence over both the contents and timing of the legislative agenda—a development that has at times rendered mobilization campaigns unneeded.

The Firearm Owners' Protection Act: 1981–1986

Despite the increasing importance of the gun debate to electoral politics during the 1970s, legislative activity had slowed down following the passage of the Gun Control Act of 1968 (GCA). Most policy disputes pertained to questions about enforcement, including how the GCA would be carried out and whether firearms might be regulated by new agencies, like the National Commission on Product Safety. With Presidents Nixon and Ford eager to court gun owners and wary of crossing the NRA, most of these administrative decisions went the NRA's way,[2] a trend that continued even during the Carter Administration.[3] Moreover, the gun control advocacy groups that were influential in the late 1960s quickly lost steam after the GCA passed and new groups that formed in the mid-1970s were unable to effectively match the NRA's strength.[4]

Simultaneously, the NRA—somewhat paradoxically—used its legislative loss in 1968 to its advantage throughout the following decade. Depicting the GCA as a draconian measure that gun owners

TABLE 7.1. Summary of Cases from the NRA's Partisan Phase

Policy Debate	Years	Summary of NRA Influence
The Firearm Owners' Protection Act	1981–1986	NRA mobilization on behalf of Reagan and other members of the GOP in 1980 encouraged Republican officials to pursue NRA-favored legislation.
		Republican NRA allies in the Senate used unusual parliamentary procedures to bypass Democratic obstructionism in the Judiciary Committee, which enabled the bill to come up for a vote—a decision motivated by a desire to maintain and solidify the electoral support of gun owners.
		Mass-mobilization campaigns pressured GOP leadership to use the procedures described above and further pressured rank-and-file members to vote for the bill.
		The NRA spent substantial sums of money in support of the bill, much of which went toward mobilizing its mass-level supporters.
The Brady Bill and Assault Weapons Ban	1987–1994	Reputational effects were evident throughout, with gun control advocates consistently pursuing incremental measures that were much weaker than they would have preferred as a result of their anticipation of NRA opposition.
		During the 1989–1992 period, mass-mobilization campaigns stalled numerous legislative gun control proposals until they died, led to them being stripped out of broader crime bills prior to votes, or defeated when included in bills that made it to the floor.
		GOP officials—motivated by a desire to maintain the electoral support of gun owners—opposed gun control bills in large numbers and lobbied the White House against including gun control in crime bills; this sometimes led to gun control being stripped out of larger bills or to the defeat of such bills in votes.
		After Democrats gained unified control of government in 1992, the NRA substantially weakened the gun control proposals that eventually passed.
		The NRA made campaign contributions throughout this period—the average size of which was small—and also spent money mobilizing its supporters.

TABLE 7.1. (*continued*)

Policy Debate	Years	Summary of NRA Influence
Columbine	1999–2000	NRA allies in the GOP stalled the post-Columbine gun debate long enough to enable the NRA to launch a mass-mobilization campaign.
		The NRA's mass-mobilization campaign then caused the momentum behind gun control to die, effectively killing the proposed legislation.
		The NRA spent substantial sums to mobilize its supporters and also made campaign contributions, the average size of which was small.
Giffords Assassination Attempt, Sandy Hook, and Beyond	2011–2017	Reputational effects were evident during the Obama years, with many Democrats viewing gun control as a losing issue for them due to the engagement gap between gun rights supporters and gun control supporters, which they believed had harmed them electorally in the past. These effects rendered mass-mobilization campaigns unnecessary during much of this period, as policymakers anticipated the NRA's reaction and decided to not pursue gun control.
		Following Sandy Hook, reputational effects were again present; policymakers crafted weak legislation that included many NRA priorities actually weakening gun laws in the hope of avoiding a mass-mobilization campaign.
		Despite the efforts of policymakers described above, the NRA launched a post-Sandy Hook mobilization campaign, which led to the bill's death.

should work to repeal and using its passage as evidence that they must remain vigilant, the NRA converted a relatively minor legislative loss in 1968 into a tool for expanding its membership and strengthening its group identity moving forward.

The NRA harnessed this energy on behalf of an effort to roll back major provisions of the GCA. During the 1970s, they were thwarted in both the House and Senate Judiciary Committees, which were controlled by gun control advocates Peter Rodino and Ted Kennedy (both Democrats from the Northeast). But with the election of Reagan in 1980, these efforts gained new momentum.

The renewed push for pro-gun reform was led by Idaho Republican James McClure in the Senate and Missouri Democrat Harold Volkmer in the House. Even as the Democratic Party moved toward support for gun control, Volkmer—who represented a rural district—remained a staunch ally of the NRA. His leadership of the bill in the House also made sense given that it was controlled by Democrats, while Republicans were in control of the Senate. The earliest versions of the bill, which was known as McClure-Volkmer, had some initial success during the committee stage, but were slowed by the creative obstructionism of gun control supporters, particularly Kennedy.[5] And the bill had little success in the House, where Rodino still controlled the Judiciary Committee.

After a near success in the Senate in 1984, the NRA ramped up efforts to advance the legislation in 1985. It began describing McClure-Volkmer as the "bill of rights for America's gun owners" and increased its mobilization efforts on behalf of the proposed legislation.[6] These efforts led Senate Majority Leader Bob Dole—encouraged by McClure and Utah Republican Orrin Hatch—to use parliamentary procedures to place the bill directly on the Senate's 1985 legislative calendar, bypassing the Judiciary Committee and a public hearing.[7] A July 9 vote was announced in late June, at which point the NRA led an intense, two-week-long, identity-driven mobilization campaign, warning gun owners that "this could be your last chance." Following the campaign—which gun rights supporters responded to in large numbers—the bill passed through the Senate by a wide margin, an outcome for which the NRA was credited.[8]

The bill's passage—and the use of an unusual procedure to bypass committee proceedings pertaining to it—showed that the NRA now had another powerful force working in its favor. In addition to the identity-driven mass mobilization it had used successfully in past legislative fights, it now also benefitted from its position in the Republican Party. Republican senators voted for the bill at a much higher rate than Democrats, especially in regions, like the

East, in which fewer gun owners lived.[9] An internal memo prepared by Dole's staff prior to his meeting with NRA leaders emphasizes that advancing the bill will deepen the GOP's relationship with the NRA—and thus encourage the organization to continue mobilizing its members in support of Republican candidates. The memo contains prepared talking points instructing Dole to stress the important role that many Republican senators played in passing the bill, and notes the 1986 midterms will give the NRA an opportunity "to demonstrate that support for the positions of the NRA's membership can translate into support at the polls." Finally, it notes, "if the NRA mobilizes and its members vote on the basis of the issues, Republicans will benefit."[10]

The bill faced a much tougher road in the Democratically controlled House. To get around the opposition of Judiciary Committee Chair Rodino, Volkmer pursued a discharge petition, which could force a vote on the bill without it receiving committee approval if a majority of House members—218 total—signed. The NRA again launched a mobilization campaign, this one even bigger than the campaign it had directed at the Senate. It told gun owners to "contact their representatives and ask them to sign the discharge petition so that the right to keep and bear arms for all law-abiding citizens can be protected"[11] and sent out personalized appeals to NRA members whose representatives had not yet signed the petition, describing support for the bill as a "litmus test" on which one's member of Congress "either . . . is for us or . . . against us."[12]

Although White House mail statistics are not publicly available for this period, accounts of the process all indicate that NRA supporters put tremendous pressure on policymakers. As this pressure grew, the number of signatures on the petition began to approach the magic number of 218. Some members privately indicated that they only supported the bill because they could not afford to vote against the NRA. One told a reporter that, because of the NRA, gun control is "the kind of issue that could defeat me when nothing else could."[13]

Volkmer's discharge petition was successful, and the House passed the bill in early April by a vote of 292–130. As was the case in the Senate, support for the bill was much greater among Republicans than Democrats; only 15 House Republicans voted against it, with stronger Republican than Democratic support across all regions of the country.[14] The Senate then quickly passed the House version of the bill—officially named the Firearm Owners' Protection Act (FOPA)—and President Reagan signed it into law on May 19, 1986.[15]

Passage of FOPA—which repealed or weakened numerous provisions of the GCA—was a major victory for the NRA. The law allowed for interstate gun sales under certain conditions, made it easier for gun owners to transport firearms across state lines, loosened record-keeping requirements for dealers, reduced licensing requirements, and relaxed restrictions on sales at gun shows. It also constrained the enforcement capabilities of the BATF by limiting the number of unannounced inspections it could conduct and prohibiting the creation of any sort of centralized gun registration system.[16]

FOPA represented the first prominent instance in which the NRA relied not just on identity-driven mass mobilization but also on its position within the Republican coalition to advance its political goals. Although the pressure gun owners put on House members to sign Volkmer's discharge petition was crucial, it is unlikely FOPA would have passed if Majority Leader Dole, the Republicans' leader in the Senate, hadn't used the prerogatives of his office to advance the NRA's cause. That Dole was willing to do this indicates the rising importance of gun owners to the party.

Indeed, unlike during earlier periods, Republican leadership saw the collective interests of the party as connected to the support of the NRA. As an internal Reagan Administration memo argued while discussing the importance of the NRA's endorsement in 1980, if "Reagan is perceived as backing off his earlier commitment [on McClure-Volkmer], the impact will be both a political loss to his Administration and to the overwhelmingly Republican Senators and Congressmen who have benefitted, and will otherwise benefit, from the NRA's political operations."[17]

The influence the NRA had within the GOP was undergirded by its ideational resources; beyond just being useful for rallying gun owners into action, they provided the NRA with leverage over Republican policymakers, who viewed the organization's mobilizational capabilities as both a source of promise and peril. The Reagan Administration, for example, was very concerned with maintaining the benefits of the NRA's operational capabilities during elections, noting the importance of its massive "get out of the vote" campaigns and the power of magazine editorials for swaying voters. The internal memo mentioned above explicitly states that "if NRA members and other gun owners are disillusioned, the political losses will be significant."[18] This suggests that the NRA's influence within the Republican coalition was related to the political dedication of its members; Republican leaders recognized that they could not simply include support for gun rights in their platform, but had to actually follow through on policy commitments made to the NRA in order to maintain the support of its members.

Support for gun control was still not entirely partisan on either the mass or elite level; some Republican policymakers from particularly anti-gun areas, for instance, still supported gun regulations, and many Democrats from pro-gun areas opposed them. Nonetheless, the NRA's membership in the Republican coalition was clearly starting to impact gun policy, most notably by influencing the legislative agenda. With the passage of FOPA, the relationship between the NRA and the GOP deepened. Shortly after President Reagan signed the bill, for example, Vice President Bush opened the NRA Annual Meeting, and Senate Majority Leader Dole was the meeting's keynote speaker.[19]

The NRA did not just rely on mobilization efforts and its budding influence within the Republican Party—it also deployed significant financial resources. NRA spending on politics increased substantially following the creation of the ILA and Political Victory Fund (PVF) PAC in the mid-1970s. The PVF spent $1.7 million on 1986 Congressional races—mostly on Republicans[20]—and $1.6 million in support of FOPA via advertising and lobbying, and there is evidence that the NRA's financial contributions impacted legislators' votes on FOPA.[21]

Nonetheless, the NRA's influence during the debate over FOPA cannot be explained solely by its political spending. Much of its spending was geared at mobilizing and persuading its own supporters—spending that was likely more effective as a result of the gun owner identity, which led NRA members to take the organization's directives seriously. It spent great sums of money, for example, on internal communications to its members, and about half its campaign spending was actually independent spending rather than the sorts of direct contributions that would be expected from an organization attempting to "buy" votes.[22] NRA financial contributions during this period, in sum, were a complement to its deployment of ideational resources, not the driver of its influence.

The debate surrounding FOPA demonstrated that the NRA's influence was not limited to preservation of the status quo. Whereas the cases in chapter 5—focused on the NRA's quasi-governmental phase—explored instances in which the NRA attempted to *prevent* the passage of new laws, this case is one in which the NRA helped *pass* a new law that loosened regulations on guns. Given the relative difficulty of passing—as opposed to preventing—legislation in the United States, this highlights why the NRA's entry into the Republican coalition was crucial. FOPA was also the first instance in which the NRA's efforts at ideological cultivation and its related transition into the GOP coalition directly enhanced its policy influence, while also working in conjunction with its cultivation of a group identity. In this sense, the *source* of the NRA's power in this period was still ideational—it can be traced back to its long-running efforts at ideological cultivation—but it took a new *form*: influence within a political party.

The Brady Bill and Assault Weapons Ban: 1987–1994

Ohio Democrats Howard Metzenbaum (Senate) and Edward Feighan (House) first introduced the Brady Bill in 1987. The bill was named after former Reagan Press Secretary James Brady, who became permanently disabled when he was wounded during the 1981 assassination attempt on Reagan. Brady's wife, Sarah, became a gun control activist and, working with Handgun Control Inc., played a prominent role in advocating for passage of the proposed legislation.

The very genesis of the proposal demonstrates the NRA's growing clout. The bill—which focused on instituting waiting periods prior to gun purchases and enhancing background checks—was itself a watered-down version of legislation that Kennedy and Rodino cosponsored throughout the 1980s but were unable to advance, largely thanks to the NRA's opposition. Anticipating the group's resistance, policymakers adjusted their approach and constructed, with the Brady Bill, much weaker legislation than they had previously sought.[23] This is a distinct form of influence—related to the second dimension of power—in which the NRA's reputation helped shape the nature of the subsequent policy debate in its favor.

Despite its relative weakness, the bill still failed to advance initially, with the NRA once again rallying gun owners in opposition. As in the past, numerous legislators privately admitted that they personally supported the legislation but could not vote for it due to the mass opposition generated by the NRA.[24]

Major efforts at gun control might have stalled indefinitely if not for what happened in Stockton, California, on January 17, 1989. That day—just three days before Bush's inauguration—a mass shooter used a semiautomatic, Chinese version of an AK-47 to kill five students, all under the age of ten, and wound thirty-three others plus a teacher on the playground of Cleveland Elementary School.[25] The shooting received extensive media attention and thrust gun control back onto the agenda, reinvigorating support for the Brady Bill and generating calls for other measures, most notably a ban on so-called "assault weapons" like the gun used in Stockton. This put Bush—who had not yet even taken office—into a tight spot between those demanding stricter regulations and the NRA, whose support he had courted and gained despite gun advocates' initial skepticism of him. The pressure on Bush increased further when First Lady Barbara Bush publicly stated her support for an assault weapons ban.[26]

Bush's initial response was to reaffirm his support for gun rights, sticking with the NRA's favored approach of advocating harsh punishment for offenders in lieu of restrictions on gun ownership. As public pressure continued to build, however, Bush reversed course, banning the importation of the weapon used in Stockton and others like it via executive order in mid-March. Initially temporary, the ban was made permanent in July.[27] It only applied, however, to foreign-made weapons and therefore did not actually prevent the sale of assault-style weapons to Americans; indeed, its actual effect may have primarily been to increase demand for American-made guns. Nonetheless, it provided momentum to legislative efforts to pass more meaningful restrictions on assault weapons.

The NRA reacted to these efforts swiftly, organizing a massive campaign against proposals calling for broader, much more effective assault weapons bans. The April issue of the *American Rifleman* contained a special cover insert imploring members to contact their representatives. The insert used threatening black and red lettering, referred to proposed assault weapons legislation as a "semi-auto gun ban," included a list of specific firearms that were marked "banned" in red capital letters, and stated that the real goal of the "anti-gunners" was to ban all guns—"Your guns."[28] The issue also contained a "Firearms Fact Card"—a list of pro-gun talking points members could use in conversations with others. The May *American Rifleman* contained several more inserts, again printed in threatening red and black letters and this time with perforated edges to encourage members to remove, copy, and distribute the materials to others. The NRA wrote, "[I]f you're one of the 30 million law-abiding Americans who owns a semi-automatic firearm, *you must act now—before you become a criminal.*"[29] Similar inserts also appeared in the August and September 1989 issues.

The NRA's appeals reflected its increasing emphasis on the Second Amendment, continuing a trend (as described in previous chapters) that began in the 1960s. Its appeals against an assault weapons ban, for example, used the tagline, "Don't sacrifice the bill of rights for a bill that's wrong." The "Firearms Fact Card" included an entire section on the Second Amendment.[30]

The NRA's pro-gun arguments aligned with broader conservative issue positions, such as harsh criminal sentencing. The September 1989 special cover insert, for instance, said, "Tell your Senators to vote for more prisons, tougher judges, less plea bargaining, tough sentences and more police officers. Not gun bans."[31] This emphasis on crime and liberty was increasingly related to the Second Amendment, suggesting that the Second Amendment was necessary not just to protect gun rights specifically, but also individual liberty more broadly.

As in earlier periods, these appeals tended to greatly exaggerate the severity of proposed regulations and frame them in identity rather than policy terms, depicting gun owners' identities, values, and traditions as under dire threat.

During this same period, the NRA led similar mobilization efforts aimed at defeating the Brady Bill, which gained new momentum in 1991. The NRA began its mobilization efforts via the *American Rifleman* in May 1991, while the House was considering the Brady Bill as part of a broader crime bill; it ramped them up substantially in the July 1991 issue after the bill had passed in the House and moved into the Senate. In another two-page, bold red and black lettered call to action printed in the July issue, the NRA again exaggerated the threat posed to gun ownership while invoking the Second Amendment and making strong identity appeals. It wrote, "At stake is nothing less than your ownership and use of firearms," and noted, "Passage of any or all of this anti-gun laundry list would strangle the rights of 70 million law-abiding Americans. That means you, your friends, and your neighbors. No guns. No ammunition. No Second Amendment." It connected these appeals to explicit calls to action while again advocating for conservative crime control approaches.[32] The NRA ran multipage appeals in September and October that included similar themes, telling members that "Second Amendment freedoms will not exist for you or your children unless gun owners stand united."[33]

As they had before, gun owners responded strongly to these appeals, flooding policymakers with mail opposing both proposed assault weapons bans and the Brady Bill. In the two months after the NRA campaign against the assault weapons ban began, the White House received over 9,000 phone calls in opposition to it (versus less than 1,000 in favor of it).[34] The White House received over 54,000 NRA-inspired letters in April 1989 alone.[35] A similar pattern played out for the Brady Bill. The NRA's initial call to action came in the May 1991 *American Rifleman*, which members would have likely received in April; in the last two weeks of April, 5,242 phone calls were made to the White House in opposition to the Brady Bill, as opposed to only 92 in favor of it. The White House did not appear to record calls or letters on the issue prior to this period, which suggests that they spiked in response to the NRA's efforts. Similarly large imbalances were seen in the number of letters sent to President Bush. From January to October, the White House received almost 23,000 letters in opposition, versus about 4,600 in favor.[36]

The magnitude of the response to the NRA's calls to action demonstrates how successfully such appeals activated the gun owner identity. Beyond the size of the response, the content of the letters sent to President Bush also provides evidence that writers were motivated by perceived identity threat and, further, saw gun rights as connected to conservative issue positions. Just as the NRA did, letter writers framed the proposed regulations in identity terms and clearly felt personally attacked by the regulations; their appeals emphasized emotion more than policy, and many letter writers appeared misinformed about the legislation. They also tended to pair gun rights advocacy with support for other conservative issue positions and articulated the Second Amendment as core to their political worldview.

One letter writer, for example, introduces himself as a "law-abiding American citizen"—a classic NRA in-group phrase. He then immediately connects firearms to his personal identity, describing the role they played in his upbringing and the role he would like them to play in his children's upbringing. The writer then—as would be expected by someone motivated by identity threat—moves away from specific complaints about Bush's ban on a relatively small number of weapons and toward a broad defense of the Second Amendment, writing, "This letter is not written to defend the ownership of a specific firearm, but to defend the Second Amendment rights of law abiding American citizens to legally operate a firearm." Finally, the letter, echoing NRA appeals, blames the "media's anti-gun hysteria" and notes that the "real issue" is the "lackadaisical attitude the government has towards criminals."[37]

Writers of newspaper letters to the editor used similar themes. A letter printed in the *Atlanta Journal-Constitution* in early April 1989, for example, also mentions media "hysteria" and advocates for conservative criminal justice reforms. Again, as would be expected by someone motivated by perceived identity threat, the writer overstates the potential impact of proposed legislation and portrays it as an attack on gun owners. He writes, "Is it any wonder we have the crime problems that we do when our criminal justice is so ready to slap the maximum to law-abiding citizens, confiscate their private property and their means to self-defense and then placate the criminal by saying, 'Oh! It's not your fault. It's our rotten society's fault. We'll punish society.'"[38]

As was the case during the debate over FOPA, the NRA's mass-mobilization campaigns against assault weapons legislation and the Brady Bill worked in conjunction with its increasing prominence in the GOP coalition. Republican policymakers were very concerned about losing the NRA's support. Early in the debate, Republican lawmakers—such as NRA board member and then-House Representative Larry Craig—informed President Bush they would be forced to oppose any crime bills that also included gun control provisions.[39] Craig also sent a very similar letter to the White House that was cosigned by nearly seventy-five members of Congress.[40] As meeting transcripts from the George H. W. Bush archive indicate, some Republican lawmakers expressed the sentiment that they needed to "dance with them what brung ya"—which, in this instance, meant sticking with the NRA as a result of its electoral support.[41]

Some Republican members of Congress specifically cited mail from gun owners while asking the president to not include gun control provisions in any crime legislation he pursued. Bob Stump, a Republican member of the House from Arizona (who, as a longtime conservative, switched his party affiliation from Democratic to Republican in the early 1980s), wrote to President Bush in opposition to the Brady Bill, telling him, "In the past few weeks alone, I have received more than 1,500 letters from my fellow Arizonans opposing passage of the Brady bill."[42]

This concern among Republican policymakers was likely well-founded given last chapter's discussion of the increasing rates of opposition to gun control among Republican voters as well as the increasing proportion of gun owners who—so long as the party opposed gun regulations—supported GOP candidates. Some of the gun owners who contacted the White House in opposition to gun control made clear that they were loyal Republicans—but also that both their loyalty to the party and their decision to vote for President Bush were related to their opposition to gun control. One writer, for example, told Bush that if he signed gun control provisions into law, he would "lose my vote as well as everyone I can influence. I will also leave the Republican party after more than forty years."[43] Another letter writer, who noted his affiliation with the party, asked the president to oppose the Brady Bill in part because of his belief that it would cause electoral harm to Republicans.[44] In making these arguments, gun owners were linking the collective interest of the Republican Party—not just individual politicians—to opposition to gun control.

Ultimately, the combination of the NRA's standing in the GOP and the actions of its mass-level supporters led to the failure of both the Brady Bill and assault weapons legislation throughout the entirety of the Bush years. When these proposals were voted on, large proportions of Republicans were unified in opposition to them—a pattern that was crucial to their defeat on numerous occasions. One such instance occurred when Republicans threatened to filibuster the 1991 crime bill (mentioned above) that contained Brady Bill provisions and defeated an attempt to invoke cloture on it—thereby killing the legislation and effectively marking the end of the road for the Brady Bill during the Bush presidency.[45] In this case and others, the NRA could not exclusively rely on having a small number of very loyal allies in Congress; it took widespread Republican opposition to prevail. Beyond votes, NRA-influenced Republicans—following the near passage of Brady Bill provisions in 1991—were able to prevent gun control from getting to the floor in 1992.[46] Reflecting on the demise of the Brady Bill, several participants in the legislative process ultimately credited the NRA's efforts with having defeated the proposal; Democrat Chuck Schumer, then a member of the House, said that President Bush (who had threatened to veto the legislation) now "can whisper to the National Rifle Association, 'I did your bidding,'" and then-Senator Joe Biden—also a Democrat—said that Bush was "toeing the line" of the NRA.[47]

In the case of assault weapons proposals, the previously mentioned legislation introduced in 1989 was—following the NRA's mobilization campaign against it—stalled until 1990; this was another instance in which the NRA, as it had at times in the 1960s, deployed ideational resources to sustain a mobilization effort long enough to delay pending legislation until the momentum behind it died down. A similar pattern occurred when assault weapons provisions were later stripped out of crime bills in 1990 and 1991 following additional NRA mobilization efforts.[48] In the aftermath of these episodes, members of Congress pointed to NRA mailings and the actions of its members as factors that prevented the advance of a legislatively enacted assault weapons ban.[49]

Gun control advocates concurred with this assessment. Sarah Brady, for instance, said that several members of Congress told her that they privately supported the legislation but felt that they could not vote for it because of their constituents. Brady commented, "You talk to any number of them and you would think that all the gun owners are in their district."[50] Brady's comments are notable since—as discussed in chapter 2—legislators' overestimation of opposition to gun control among their constituents is one way that the NRA's mobilization efforts can impact policy outcomes; when legislators are contacted by opponents of gun control much more frequently than advocates, they may end up with a skewed opinion of actual support for gun control in their districts. Some legislators also said that they believed the NRA caused members of the public to overestimate the strength of the proposed legislation, which represents another distinct form of NRA influence, in this case on the third dimension of power.[51]

Although the NRA had succeeded at holding off efforts to pass gun control during the Bush years, the 1992 election of Bill Clinton quickly turned the page on the gun debate. Clinton supported stricter regulations on guns during the 1992 campaign; unsurprisingly, the

NRA strongly opposed his candidacy, but also refused to endorse Bush for reelection as a result of his actions on assault weapons.[52] Once in office, President Clinton quickly revived—and eventually passed—both the Brady Bill and, as part of a broader crime bill, a ban on assault weapons. Among other things, the provisions of the Brady Handgun Violence Prevention Act of 1993 and the assault weapons ban (which was contained in the much larger Violent Crime Control and Law Enforcement Act of 1994) together prohibited the manufacture, sale, and possession of certain firearms deemed "assault weapons" for a period of ten years, mandated a five-day waiting period prior to purchasing guns for a five-year period, increased licensing fees for dealers, and encouraged expanded background checks.[53] This amounted to the first successful passage of substantial gun control legislation since 1968.

The passage of both gun control laws raises two questions. First, what changed that enabled gun control legislation to pass in 1993 and 1994 after having failed since 1987? Second, despite losing, to what extent (if any) was the NRA able to weaken the legislation that passed?

One important factor was that the Democrats had unified control of the government in 1992 for first time since the Carter Administration. During the intervening period, gun control became much more polarized along partisan lines. Although the NRA had gained substantial benefits throughout the 1980s as a result of its influence within the Republican Party—most notably the 1986 passage of FOPA—the cost was that Democrats, in response, became increasingly *supportive* of gun control. As a result, unified Democratic government substantially increased the likelihood of gun control passing. Indeed, strong support among Democratic members of Congress was key to the passage of the Brady Bill in 1993. And, although the crime legislation that contained the assault weapons provisions received some crucial Republican support, it nonetheless required the Democrats to invoke cloture in order to overcome a filibuster led by the Senate GOP.[54]

Increased support for gun control among Democrats, however, would likely not have been sufficient if not for (1) a combination of high-profile instances of gun violence and a large increase in over-all rates of gun violence, which together garnered substantial and sustained media coverage; and (2) an increasingly active and stra-tegically savvy set of organized groups dedicated to the passage of gun control.

The Stockton schoolyard shooting served as a "focusing event" that thrust gun control onto the political agenda, and it was followed by other, similar events that reinforced its impact.[55] Simultaneously, overall rates of gun violence soared, with a 40 percent increase in gun homicides and a nearly 30 percent increase in armed robberies. As a result, crime—particularly gun crime—and proposed gun con-trol legislation garnered a great deal of media coverage, and became a bigger priority for both voters and politicians during this period.[56]

Not only was gun-related crime more salient, but gun control advocates also took a savvier approach than in the past. Kristin Goss—in her authoritative analysis of gun control advocacy efforts—demonstrates that organized gun control groups (led by Handgun Control, Inc.) pursued a more effective strategy, focusing on incre-mental (rather than sweeping) policy changes and devoting much more attention to the development of grassroots support as well as alliances with other groups, such as law enforcement. Goss's analysis also shows that efforts to reframe gun control as a matter of "child protection" were successful, which in turn were associated with more widespread political participation on behalf on gun control.[57]

These two factors were necessary for gun control to be a legisla-tive priority for Clinton and Congressional Democrats, who could have chosen to not pursue gun control early in the Clinton Admin-istration. And had they delayed the pursuit of gun control, it likely would not have passed at all, as the first two years of the Clinton Administration ended up being the only two years of Clinton's presi-dency in which Democrats controlled Congress.

Beyond the impact of unified Democratic government, gun vio-lence, and gun control advocacy efforts, gun control laws passed in part because they were weakened over time in order to overcome NRA opposition. The Brady Bill's five-day waiting period prior to handgun purchases (which originally had been proposed as a seven-day period), for instance, expired after five years, at which point it was to be replaced by an instant, computerized background check that was under development at the time.[58] Similarly, the assault weapons ban contained in the 1994 crime bill expired ten years after enactment and contained numerous loopholes. As part of the compromise needed to pass that 1994 legislation, the recently passed Brady legislation was further weakened.[59] In the end, the legislation passed in early 1993 and 1994 was substantially weaker than many other gun control proposals from the 1980s. Clearly, despite losing, the NRA nonetheless exerted important influence.[60]

As it had during the McClure-Volkmer debate, the NRA again used financial resources in conjunction with its mobilization efforts and its influence within the Republican Party. In the 1990 election cycle, for instance, the NRA spent nearly $875,000 (compared to $178,000 spent by Handgun Control).[61] In 1992, that gap grew, with the NRA spending over $1.7 million compared to Handgun Control's $163,000.[62] This spending likely reinforced its relationship with legislators to whom it contributed. Nonetheless, although these sums may seem large, the NRA spread its contributions across a large number of candidates, meaning that its contributions to particular candidates were unlikely to have comprised a substantial proportion of those candidates' war chests. In 1990, for example, winning House candidates spent an average of $423,000, and winning Senate candidates spent an average of $3.3 million.[63] That year, the NRA contributed a total of $480,174 to 162 House campaigns and a total of $135,450 to 25 Senate candidates, which amounts to an average contribution of just under $3,000 in the House and around $5,400 in the Senate. In 1992, when it cost nearly $557,000 to win a House seat and $3.5 million to win in the Senate, the NRA spread $913,342 across 193 House candidates and $147,150 across 26 Senate candidates—an average of $4,732 (House) and $5,659 (Senate).[64] When put in this perspective, the NRA's sizable aggregate contributions to candidates seem less impressive—and less likely to explain its influence.

The NRA, as it had in the past, spent similar sums on messaging campaigns designed to mobilize gun owners.[65] As discussed earlier, the effectiveness of this type of spending—the goal of which is to spur mass-level political action among gun rights supports—is related to the NRA's development of a gun owner identity, as this identity increases the responsiveness of gun owners to the NRA's appeals. This view is supported by insiders from this period, who believed that members of Congress cared more about the political action the NRA could generate than its contributions to their campaigns. As one congressional aide put it, "I don't think [politicians] care about the contributions they get from the NRA. They care about the piles of mail, these nasty calls, people picketing at their state offices."[66]

Taken together, the multiyear battles over both the Brady Bill and assault weapons bills were another instance in which the NRA effectively deployed ideational resources on behalf of its agenda. When combined with its increasing influence within the Republican Party, these mobilization efforts enabled the NRA to defeat proposed regulations on several occasions during this period. Simultaneously, however, the eventual passage of both the Brady Bill and the assault weapons ban demonstrate limits on the NRA's influence; although it was successful at weakening both sets of regulations prior to their passage, these laws nonetheless passed in the face of real opposition from the NRA. A combination of unified Democratic government, high-profile instances of gun violence that garnered substantial and sustained media coverage, and improved strategy on the part of gun control activists was sufficient to overcome the NRA's efforts.

Columbine: 1999–2000

The NRA didn't stay down for long: following passage of the assault weapons ban in 1994, Republicans won a dramatic victory in the 1994 midterm election, taking over both chambers of Congress for the first time since the 1950s. Republicans would continue to maintain control of Congress during the remainder of Clinton's term. In response to its losses in each of the previous two years, the NRA made a strong electoral push on behalf of pro-gun Republicans. President Clinton later said that he believes the NRA played a major role in the "Republican Revolution" of 1994, telling the Cleveland *Plain*

Dealer that year, "The NRA is the reason the Republicans control the House" and later writing in his memoir that the NRA "could rightly claim to have made Gingrich the House Speaker."[67] Statistical analyses support Clinton's intuition, indicating that the NRA's endorsements had significant impacts on the success of Republican candidates that year.[68]

To achieve this level of electoral influence, the NRA used its legislative losses in 1993 and 1994 to its advantage. The passage of new gun control laws—as it had in the late 1960s—provided credibility to the NRA's claims that gun owners were under attack and may have enhanced the strength of the gun owner identity among those who held it. Former NRA lobbyist Richard Feldman described the Assault Weapons Ban as a rallying issue for the gun owner community, and recalls seeing two lines at gun shops following the ban: one to buy the remaining stock of banned weapons and the other to sign up as volunteers for Republican candidates.[69] Other accounts depict the same dynamic and note the irony of it, given that the law was largely "toothless" and its provisions easily avoided.[70]

The NRA's relationship with the GOP continued to strengthen during the mid-to-late 1990s. The legislative momentum behind gun control stalled, and there were even (ultimately unsuccessful) attempts in the House to repeal the Assault Weapons Ban of 1994.[71] The NRA then won a victory in 1997, when Congress stripped funding for a Center for Disease Control program—deemed anti-gun by the NRA—that studied gun violence as a public health issue; although this move did not technically ban future publicly funded research on gun violence, it produced a chilling effect that successfully discouraged such research for decades afterward.[72]

The gun debate reignited, however, following the early 1999 shooting at Columbine High School in Colorado. In what was the deadliest school shooting in US history at the time, two students killed twelve of their classmates, one teacher, and themselves, while wounding many others. The Columbine massacre deeply shocked the country and immediately put tremendous pressure on legislators to take action. In response to this pressure, juvenile crime bills were quickly introduced in both the House and Senate. The Senate version of the bill—which was passed very quickly—contained several gun control provisions, including, among other things, the mandatory inclusion of child trigger locks with newly sold handguns as well as required background checks at gun shows.[73]

The speed with which the Senate moved following Columbine—drafting, debating, and passing a bill within a month of the shooting—made it difficult for the NRA to mount a strong mobilization campaign against the legislation.[74] The bill was further assisted by what some described as mismanagement on the part of Senate Majority Leader Trent Lott—a Republican—who seemed to have lost control of the process in the Senate.[75]

The process played out very differently in the House, which was also controlled by Republicans at the time. Although House Speaker Dennis Hastert signaled a willingness to consider "common sense" gun control provisions, other influential Republicans in the House—like Majority Whip Tom DeLay—opposed any bill that contained gun control. This internal debate among Republican leadership slowed the process considerably, which some Democrats said was done intentionally as a way to give the NRA more time to mobilize its supporters.[76]

The NRA did indeed use the delay—along with a post-Memorial Day recess—to rally its members in opposition to the bill.[77] In his column in the July 1999 *American Rifleman*, Wayne LaPierre used heavy identity appeals as part of a call to action in opposition to the proposed legislation, referring to gun control advocacy as "[a] hateful and bigoted war" against owners that amounts to a "'cultural cleansing'—specifically targeting the bedrock Second Amendment beliefs of firearms owners for extinction."[78] Outside of the *American Rifleman*, the NRA launched a large mail, phone, and advertising campaign to mobilize its supporters.[79] LaPierre also appeared on numerous cable news programs to advance the NRA's PR campaign, telling CNN, for instance, "I think that what they're really after is trying to dismantle this great American freedom, the Second Amendment, piece by piece."[80] As in the past, Congress received large quantities of letters and calls in opposition to the legislation, and some members said that they were swayed by the intensity of the opposition.[81]

Although no examples of public mail are available in the Clinton presidential archive, newspaper letters to the editor written in opposition to post-Columbine gun control proposals contain NRA-driven identity themes, suggesting that the NRA's appeals successfully primed gun owner identity. One *Atlanta Journal-Constitution* letter writer, for example, used identity-based language and logic associated with the NRA to argue that proposed controls would mostly impact lawful gun owners:

> Gun control whiners are calling for more gun control laws. It has been reported that the teenagers responsible for the Columbine shootings violated no fewer than 19 current gun control laws, so why do people think that more gun control laws would have done anything to prevent this tragedy? The unbalanced kooks and nuts in our society will always get guns if they want them. . . . The only people who are truly affected by gun control are law-abiding citizens. We don't need more gun control. We need more kid control.[82]

Another letter writer referred to the Second Amendment to argue against new controls, while again using both in-group and out-group identity language, including an identity frame, and repeating NRA-favored logic about harsh sentencing:

> A recent editorial advocating a ban on semiautomatic assault weapons shows how little you really know about our U.S. Constitution and Bill of Rights. . . . It boils down to the fact that you anti-gun people are using every means possible to take guns from honest law-abiding citizens. Instead of trying to make felons out of people who would never use a gun criminally, why don't you put your effort into keeping the 6 percent of violent repeat offenders in prison and quit trying to make the gun the criminal?[83]

The NRA's relationship with the GOP also helped its cause; although some Republicans did defect, the NRA nonetheless relied on much stronger support among Republican members of Congress than Democrats, and key Republicans in the House—both leaders and rank-and-file members—provided important assistance.

Majority Whip DeLay's initial anti-control efforts stalled the debate and reduced legislative momentum in the House. Although Speaker Hastert did introduce a legislative package containing some gun control provisions (along with some harsh crime control provisions that Democrats were unlikely to support) just prior to the Memorial Day recess, he did not pressure Republican House members to support it following the recess; his decision to not push the legislation came after both DeLay and House Majority Leader Dick Armey announced that they would oppose it. Beyond the defection of key Republican leaders, David Karol's aforementioned study more broadly indicates that Republicans in Congress were increasingly unified in their opposition to gun control by this time.[84]

The NRA's mass-mobilization efforts and its influence within the Republican Party also worked in conjunction with the status quo bias inherent in the design of Congress. Pressure for gun control was extremely high in the months following the Columbine massacre, and many members of Congress—clearly a majority in the Senate and perhaps, with the right set of a provisions, a majority in the House—were open to passing new regulations. A small number of gun rights advocates in a single chamber of Congress, however, were nonetheless able to slow down the legislative process long enough to provide the NRA an opening, which it then used to prevent the inclusion of gun control provisions in the House bill.[85]

The House did ultimately pass a juvenile crime bill, but it contained no gun control provisions. And once the juvenile crime bills from each chamber went to conference, a relatively small number of members with particularly strong dedication to gun rights were again able to stall the process long enough to kill the legislation. The conference committee was unable to produce a compromise bill and never revisited the issue during the 2000 election year.[86]

Throughout this process, the complex nature of the legislative process enabled Republicans to simultaneously voice support for the Second Amendment and to appear to take gun control seriously (without actually holding tough votes that might cause them problems with the NRA). During the conference process, for example, the

House overwhelmingly supported two separate motions instructing the conference committee to include gun control provisions in the final bill; these motions, however, were nonbinding for the committee, and members who supported them could still obviously vote against the eventual conference bill (and some of them were actually more likely to do so if it contained gun control provisions). Further, the House—talking out of both sides of its mouth—also overwhelmingly supported a motion instructing the conference committee to exclude any provisions that "impose unconstitutional restrictions on the Second Amendment rights of individuals."[87]

The NRA also used financial resources to advance its cause. As in prior periods, it spent money in attempts to mobilize its members into action, devoting over a million dollars during the summer of 1999 to mailings, phone calls, and advertisements asking its supporters to contact their members of Congress.[88] This spending may have enhanced the effectiveness of its mobilization campaign by increasing the number of and frequency with which its supporters were exposed to its calls to action. In this sense, its spending, as in prior periods, may have worked in conjunction with its identity-based mobilization efforts. The NRA also continued to make campaign contributions during the second half of the 1990s, the modest average size of which had not changed since the beginning of the decade. Its contributions did, however, continue to become increasingly partisan; for instance, 86 percent of its 1998 contributions went to Republicans compared to 80 percent in 1994 and just 63 percent in 1992.[89]

In the end—despite the public attention that the tragedy drew and the support it spurred on behalf of gun control—the post-Columbine debate in Congress was effectively over within a few months of the massacre.[90] A combination of the NRA's partisan influence and its ideational resources proved crucial; its place in the GOP provided it with influence over the legislative agenda—not just in terms of the substance of what was considered but also the timing of it—which gave the organization a chance to launch a mobilization campaign using ideational resources that ultimately led to the legislation's demise.

Giffords Assassination Attempt, Sandy Hook, and Beyond

Despite no new federal level gun laws having been passed following Columbine, the NRA—as it had before—used the specter of gun control to boost the size and political dedication of its base, reporting both substantial growth in membership and fundraising in the year after the massacre—trends it attributed to fear of new gun regulations.[91] The NRA used this strength on behalf of George W. Bush's successful presidential campaign in 2000.

With Bush in office, the NRA once again had a reliable partner in the White House, and its relationship with the Republican Party continued to deepen. Particularly after the GOP gained unified control of government following the 2002 midterm, the NRA—as was the case during the Reagan years—was back to playing offense rather than defense. It not only successfully kept *stricter* gun control laws off the agenda, but also won two major victories that actually *weakened* them: (1) the expiration without renewal of the assault weapons ban in 2004, and (2) the 2005 passage of a law that limited the legal liability of gun dealers and manufacturers in lawsuits related to gun violence.[92]

Although a source of strength during the Bush years, the NRA's increasing alignment with the GOP was a potential liability following the 2008 election, in which Democrats won unified control of government. With gun control supporter Barack Obama in the White House and Democratic majorities in both chambers of Congress, the early Obama years were seen as cause for hope among gun regulation advocates and cause for alarm among gun rights advocates.

The Democrats' initial priorities following the 2008 election, however, were focused on other issues, most notably healthcare reform. And the window of opportunity provided by unified Democratic government proved short-lived, as the Republicans won the House of Representatives in 2010, which they would then control for the remainder of Obama's time in office (along with the Senate during the last two years of his presidency). This frustrated some gun control advocates who thought that Obama should have pushed harder to pass new regulations on firearms when he had the chance.[93] Although Obama did voice support for gun control after the early 2011 shooting in Arizona that critically wounded US House Representative Gabrielle Giffords and left six people dead, the president and his team realized that it was unlikely to pass in Congress and that it would be best for the president and the party to wait at least until after the 2012 election cycle.[94]

The reaction of President Obama and the Democrats following the Giffords shooting reflected a political reality that had also been present following the 2007 massacre of thirty-two people at Virginia Tech. Although Virginia Tech was, at the time, the deadliest mass shooting in US history and although the Democrats controlled both chambers of Congress, the GOP's control of one branch of government—in this case the White House—was seen as sufficient to prevent the advancement of gun control.[95] Moreover, the Democrats—despite their control of Congress—saw little political incentive to pursue new regulations; they believed that support for gun control had contributed to their major losses in the 1994 midterms as well as Al Gore's loss in the 2000 presidential election.[96] That the NRA's electoral influence in prior elections continued to discourage policymakers from pursuing gun control more than a decade later represents a clear but somewhat hidden form of influence on the second dimension of power, in which its earlier efforts continued to keep gun control off the agenda in the future.

Further, the Democrats' belief that gun control was a losing issue—despite public opinion polls showing majority public support for it—is understandable given the gun owner identity's effects on the gun control debate; the Democrats felt that relatively few votes could be gained from single-issue anti-gun voters, but that many more could be lost from single-issue pro-gun voters. And, even if their support for gun control did not *lose* them many votes (which is possible given that most gun owners by this point were Republicans), they may have feared that making gun control salient would enable Republicans to more easily rally their base. They had also lost potential partners, since the gun control advocacy groups that played important roles during the debates of the early 1990s had by this point faded from prominence.

Notably, the NRA did not even need to launch large mobilization campaigns following the Virginia Tech and Tucson shootings because politicians at this point anticipated—and feared—the reaction they would receive from NRA supporters for pushing new gun control proposals.[97] In this sense, the NRA's influence over firearms owners on the third dimension of power—its ability to shape their political behavior—had again enabled it to protect its policy interests in Congress on the second dimension of power: gun control was off the political agenda because politicians anticipated the reaction they would get from gun owners for pursuing it.

Despite all of this, President Obama changed his mind and decided to push hard for gun control following the December 2012 massacre at Sandy Hook Elementary School in Newtown, Connecticut.[98] The shooter, who unleashed 154 rounds in under five minutes, killed twenty children—many of them very young—along with six teachers. In response, Obama called for a broad range of new controls on guns—including expanded background checks that would apply to private sales and a renewed assault weapons ban—and tasked then-Vice President Joe Biden with leading the effort.[99]

Even before President Obama announced his proposal in mid-January, the NRA had launched a campaign against it in the *American Rifleman*. The February 2013 issue—which would have come out prior to Obama's proposals and was the first to press after the shooting—contained a transcript of Wayne LaPierre's speech shortly after the shooting, in which he infamously called for armed guards in schools across the country, saying that "the only thing that stops a bad guy with a gun is a good guy with a gun." It also included a feature article entitled "Siege: Gun Owners Face an Unprecedented Assault on their Rights" and a special essay from LaPierre entitled "Stand and Fight." Both articles used intense identity frames while depicting gun control proponents as out-of-touch elitists willing to do anything to advance their "anti-gun agenda." The "Siege" article ends by saying, "If the Second Amendment does survive, it will only be because NRA Members and friends of liberty politically and socially mobilized like never before."[100]

LaPierre's essay emphasized in-group pride and, in addition to asking members to take direct political action, also asked them to help expand the NRA's reach and political power:

> it is *you*, proud NRA members, who are the key to enlisting new members in the ranks of our army of freedom. NRA grassroots has always been our Association's greatest strength.... As we Stand and Fight, let's continue to make the shooting sports one of the fastest-growing recreational activities in America. . . . We can't win the political war if we lose the cultural war. One of the great protectors of the Second Amendment is the popular, active, responsible use of firearms for shooting and hunting. . . . We have so much to be proud of as gun owners, shooters and freedom lovers. That pride, especially when it's not hidden in the closest, is itself a form of protection for the Second Amendment.... We will grow the NRA more than ever. And we will be prouder than ever to be freedom-loving NRA patriots.[101]

Later in the legislative process, the NRA made more specific calls to action that contained similar identity appeals, including specific instructions for contacting one's representative in Congress, as well as another special essay in which LaPierre referred to President Obama as "King Pinocchio."[102]

Despite this campaign against new gun regulations, the NRA was hedging its position during the debate's early stages; while taking its usual "no compromise" public position, it also quietly worked to influence the bills being produced in Congress. (The March *American Rifleman* reflects this; it still attacked the media and anti-gun politicians while discussing the post-Sandy Hook reaction, but the intensity, prominence, and specificity of such discussions were reduced relative to the February and April issues.)[103] The Democrats knew that the NRA would not *support* any proposals they put forward, but went out of their way to produce a bill that they hoped it would choose to not strongly *oppose*. To do so, they convinced Senator Joe Manchin—a conservative Democrat who had previously received NRA support—to sponsor the legislation. He, in turn, convinced Senator Pat Toomey—a Republican who also had previously received NRA support—to cosponsor the bill with him.

The contents of the Manchin-Toomey bill were specifically designed to try to win private NRA approval and thus avoid strong public opposition. The main gun control provision was expanding background checks to gun shows and private sales—an incredibly popular position among the public. The bill also included a number of longtime NRA priorities that would actually *loosen* regulations on guns; these included—but were not limited to—reducing the waiting period for background checks from seventy-two hours to forty-eight hours (with sales going through if the report could not be completed within that time frame), making it easier to transport and sell guns across state lines, and legally prohibiting the government from using gun sales records to create a gun registry. Moreover, the Democrats seemed willing to weaken the new language on background checks if doing so would help passage.[104]

This illustrates the power the NRA now held. Without it even making a firm commitment to stay quiet on the bill, Senate Democrats went out of their way to court the NRA, appointing its allies to cosponsor the legislation, giving it tremendous influence over the bill's actual contents, and ultimately producing a bill that—in net—may have actually *weakened* existing gun control laws. Importantly, the NRA's behind-the-scenes access during this process was a product of its long-term use of ideational resources—its ability to influence mass political behavior—and its role in the GOP. The Democrats knew that if the NRA came out strongly in opposition to the proposed legislation, its members would flood Congress with calls and letters, and that rank-and-file Republicans would be too scared of potential electoral consequences to support it. This should be seen as another prominent instance in which the NRA used its proven ability to exert influence on the third dimension of power to exert influence on the second dimension of power: the reaction that policymakers anticipated from the NRA and its supporters dictated both the process used to craft the bill and the ultimate contents of it—that is, the gun control agenda. In this sense, even if the bill had ultimately passed, the process used to produce it and the contents of it would be testaments to the NRA's power.

But the bill did not pass. Despite its influence over the creation of the proposed legislation as well as its private approval of it, the NRA eventually came out strongly against it. It is unclear whether the NRA was pressured from its own right flank—which reacted negatively when they heard that the NRA had been negotiating with "anti-gunners"—or whether its negotiations with Congress were done in bad faith.

In any case, once the NRA made clear to its supporters that it specifically opposed the Manchin-Toomey bill and that they should contact their representatives in opposition to it, the legislative process changed dramatically. Accounts from the time indicate that, as in the past, the NRA's campaign succeeded in mobilizing its members. Especially after the NRA made its opposition to the legislation clear and specific, large volumes of calls opposing it came into the offices of members of Congress. Calls to Toomey's office were nine to one against the bill. In Manchin's office, they were two hundred to one against it. The NRA also sent an email to the Senate informing members that their stances on the bill would be used to calculate their letter grade in the following election, which caused additional concerns about the electoral consequences of supporting the bill.[105] The bill—which, even if it had passed in the Senate, would have faced a tough road in the House—died shortly after.[106]

The general pattern that dictated the legislative outcomes of the debates after Virginia Tech, Tucson, and Sandy Hook was then repeated following subsequent mass shootings, including the 2016 Pulse Nightclub massacre in Orlando (which was, at the time, the deadliest mass shooting in US history), the Las Vegas concert shooting in 2017 (which eclipsed Orlando, with 58 killed and an incredible 851 wounded), and numerous others. In all of these instances, GOP control of either the White House or one chamber of Congress was sufficient to prevent the advancement of gun control. This influence appears to be a product of the electoral importance of gun rights supporters for Republicans, the NRA's ability to affect mass-level political behavior, and the general importance of both the NRA and the gun rights issue to contemporary conservatism. With the exception of Sandy Hook, NRA influence over Republicans has often caused Democrats to prioritize other issues and avoid costly gun regulation debates; Democrats (at least prior to 2018, as discussed below) seemingly have not felt they would receive either the benefits (or punishment) from gun control advocates as a result of their actions on the issue that Republicans receive from the NRA.

The NRA has continued to devote large sums of money to supporting Republican candidates (and opposing Democrats) but—as in the past—most of this spending goes toward mobilizing its members into action. As former NRA president David Keene points out, it is "difficult to disentangle the influence of popular support from the influence of money . . . because about half of its [the NRA's] revenue comes from its five million dues-paying members and fee-generating services." Indeed, says Keene, "80 percent of the NRA's contributions come from its members. So in a sense, for the NRA popular support and money are inextricably interrelated: the NRA has more money because it has more popular support."[107]

The NRA's power has also been enhanced by the design of both electoral and legislative institutional rules in the United States. Electoral rules favor the NRA because they cause its mass-level supporters and elite Republican allies to be overrepresented in both chambers of Congress. In the House, this is a result of geographic sorting—with Democratic voters more concentrated in particular areas (and therefore Congressional districts) than Republicans—and gerrymandering. In the Senate, it is caused by the equal apportionment of seats to each state regardless of population, which has advantaged the GOP in the contemporary period.[108] Legislative rules favor the NRA because it generally supports maintenance of the status quo, which enables the advancement of its agenda even when Republicans only control one branch (or even just one half of one branch) of government.

———

Although no new gun laws passed following the Sandy Hook shooting, it did have an important legacy: a reinvigoration of the gun control movement. Following Sandy Hook, gun control advocates—along with wealthy patrons like Michael Bloomberg—founded several new groups, most notably Everytown for Gun Safety as well its subsidiary group, Moms Demand Action. These groups could not grow quickly enough to make an immediate post-Sandy Hook impact, but they gradually built a strong foundation. After several more shootings—those in Orlando and Las Vegas, as well as the 2018 shooting at Stoneman Douglas High School in Florida—these groups gained momentum.[109] This momentum did not immediately produce new laws—the GOP controlled one or more branches of government when all of them occurred—but, at the time of writing, the gun control movement appears to be reinvigorated, with Democrats much more willing to push the issue than they had been previously.

The next chapter—the book's conclusion—further ponders what the future holds for the NRA and its opponents, while also reflecting on the broader lessons it has for politics and American democracy.

8

Conclusion

When Donald Trump spoke at the NRA's 2017 annual meeting in Atlanta—the first meeting convened after his victory the prior fall—the organization was in many ways at the pinnacle of its political journey. Having played an integral role in Trump's election, the NRA found itself at the center of a political party that now had unified control of government and was led by a man whose political worldview aligned closely with its own. Trump's appearance was a celebration—and, in many ways, a culmination—of an ongoing relationship between the NRA and the GOP that had started several decades earlier. Aligning with the conservative movement and Ronald Reagan's Republican Party had enabled the group to play an important role in a long-term political effort that reshaped American politics—the NRA, as a result, had not only advanced gun rights, but also gained wider prominence.

Yet, in the years following the celebration in Atlanta, the NRA faced several major challenges, many of which were still ongoing as I concluded work on this book. In 2019, an internal battle pitted NRA chief Wayne LaPierre against its then-President Oliver North. LaPierre triumphed, but the conflict—and the bad press it generated, including accusations that LaPierre had used NRA funds inappropriately—damaged the organization. Fundraising and succession planning were thrown into chaos with the resignations of both North and NRA-ILA chief Chris Cox (who had been considered LaPierre's heir apparent), and the NRA publicly split with—and ended up in a legal battle against—its longtime advertising, PR, and media production partner, Ackerman-McQueen.[1] Adding to the group's woes was an investigation and lawsuit launched by the state of New York for alleged financial wrongdoing—threatening the group's status as a nonprofit organization and even its very existence.[2]

These conflicts—and the costly litigation associated with them—put the organization in a dire financial situation. In a leaked recording of an NRA board meeting, LaPierre reported in early 2020 that the lawsuits the organization faced had already cost it $100 million—a very sizable amount for a group that had a total revenue of just over $400 million in 2018.[3] These troubles were compounded by the Covid-19 pandemic, which forced the cancellation of the 2020 annual meeting and numerous fundraising events. The NRA, already in financial straits, was forced to lay off or furlough employees and reduce the salaries of those who remained.[4]

While the NRA was plagued by internal troubles, its political opponents were multiplying and growing stronger. In her 2006 book on the "missing movement" for gun control, Kristin Goss identified several issues that have historically plagued gun regulation advocates, including insufficient funding and the lack of a compelling narrative. But she has argued that recent efforts, started after Sandy Hook and energized following subsequent mass shootings, seem to have what it takes to overcome these challenges and build a genuine political movement.[5] Together, relatively new groups formed in the aftermath of mass shootings (e.g., post-Giffords, Everytown for Gun Safety and its subsidiary Moms Demand Action, and the student-led Never Again MSD) along with longer-standing groups (like Brady and the Coalition to Stop Gun Violence) outspent the NRA in the 2018 midterms, and the candidates they supported generally fared well.[6]

What should we make of all of this? Is the end nigh for the NRA?

The challenges the organization faces are considerable, as is the threat posed by New York's lawsuit against it—but by and large, the findings of this book suggest that, barring new developments, it would be premature to write the NRA off. Throughout the preceding chapters, I have argued that the NRA's influence is fueled by the actions of its members and supporters who—sharing a group identity and ideology—are unusually politically dedicated and active. The NRA's financial struggles do not strike at the heart of its main source of power, which is its people, not its money. As the case studies in chapters 5 and (especially) 7 showed, financial resources are a useful complement to mobilization, making it easier for the NRA to frequently and repeatedly reach its supporters and encourage them to act; having less money to spend is certainly not helpful to its cause. Nonetheless, its ability to mobilize large numbers of gun owners on behalf of gun rights predates and does not rely on its development of a large political war chest.

Moreover, the NRA has not just recovered from setbacks in the past, but has at times actually used them to its strategic advantage. The NRA used the passage of the Gun Control Act of 1968 as well as the Brady Act and assault weapons ban in the early 1990s to reinforce a sense of identity among gun owners and grow its membership ranks. This pattern makes sense in light of chapter 3, which showed that the NRA has built and used a group identity by portraying gun owners as a distinct social group that has its own values and interests—its own identity—and by arguing that the identity is under dire threat from gun control supporters. Counterintuitively, political setbacks can actually legitimate the NRA's consistent refrain that gun owners are under attack. This has historically occurred in the aftermath of policy losses, but may occur again in response to the growing strength of gun control advocacy groups and investigations into the NRA's finances. (I have a bit more to say about the book's lessons for the contemporary gun debate later in the chapter.)

Even grift of the sort that Wayne LaPierre has been accused of isn't new to the NRA. Putting aside the Revolt at Cincinnati—certainly the most dramatic internal conflict in its history—the NRA has faced (and overcome) organizational turmoil before. G. Ray Arnett, who became the NRA's Executive Vice President in 1985, was forced to resign only a year later amidst accusations that he was often absent from the office, had used NRA funds for personal hunting trips, and had promoted someone with whom he may have been having an affair.[7] Arnett's successor, J. Warren Cassidy, was *also* forced out of the organization after a relatively brief tenure, having been accused of sexual harassment, improper romantic relationships with NRA employees, and financial mismanagement. He resigned in 1991 and was replaced by Wayne LaPierre, whose own (much longer) tenure has now been similarly marked by internal conflict and accusations of wrongdoing.[8]

While it's possible that the NRA's struggles may stymie the organization's political effectiveness moving forward, such issues are not unprecedented, and putting them into historical perspective is helpful for understanding their potential longer-term effects. Why is it that the NRA has been able to weather these storms throughout its history?

One likely reason for the NRA's staying power is its place in the world of firearms, politics aside. The NRA, as noted throughout the book, does not just advocate for gun rights, but also offers firearms training and education programs, administers shooting competitions, and provides gun owners with a wide range of services. Because the NRA has reasons and means to exist beyond politics, it's able to maintain itself even when its political fortunes take a turn for the worse. Moreover, because many of its supporters share a gun-centric worldview that informs their political behavior, their commitment to the gun rights cause—and their willingness to act on behalf of that cause—remains even during the NRA's downturns.

Trumpism and the Future of the NRA

While the NRA has been confronted with organizational turmoil and political setbacks in the past, it now also faces a new threat that stems from one of its greatest recent strengths: its exclusive, institutionalized relationship with the Republican Party. The NRA's gradual alignment with the GOP has to date been very beneficial; its place in the Republican coalition has, directly and indirectly, made the passage of new gun control laws less likely, led to legislation that actually weakens existing regulations, and, more broadly, increased the importance of both the NRA and gun rights in national politics. Yet the NRA's relationship with the GOP—an important *source* of its power—may well become more of a burden than a boon.

One reason is the increased potential for the NRA to become "captured" by the GOP. Capture—as discussed in chapter 2—refers to a situation in which a group is so closely associated with one party that the competing party would rather oppose it than seek its support. This reduces the group's leverage over the leaders of the party it is aligned with since it cannot credibly threaten to switch allegiance to another party. Lacking such leverage, the party can deprioritize the group's policy interests without suffering major negative consequences.[9]

The NRA has avoided capture so far—but this may not last. In the Reagan years, early in its partisan phase, the NRA still supported a number of pro-gun Democrats, and continued to do so throughout the following decades. Starting in the 2010s, however, it shifted from giving *most* of its support to Republicans to giving virtually *all* of it to them.[10] In other words, the NRA has gone from having a close relationship with the GOP to having an exclusive relationship with it. This may reduce its leverage over Republican politicians, who are potentially less likely to believe that the NRA is willing to support Democrats if and when it is dissatisfied with Republicans.

Together with the NRA's exclusive support for the GOP, increasing partisan polarization on gun control has constrained the group's ability to build and maintain working relationships with members of the Democratic Party. The NRA, of course, has contributed to this polarization: its actions have helped fuel the growing gap between Republican and Democratic politicians on gun control. The upside of this polarization is that Republican officeholders are increasingly unified in their support of gun rights—a trend that, as last chapter showed, has had substantial benefits for the NRA. But there are also downsides. With so few pro-gun Democrats left in national politics, the NRA has few Democratic allies to which it can threaten to defect. Further, as the NRA's favorability rating among Democratic voters has decreased, fewer Democratic politicians have an incentive to even *want* its support;[11] many Democrats now see an advantage in explicitly running against the NRA, with some going so far as to wear their "F" ratings from the NRA as badges of honor. Indeed, the candidates who sought the party's 2020 presidential nomination were unusually strong and unified in their support of gun control.[12]

Beyond increasing the potential for the NRA to be captured, these developments also increase the likelihood that Democrats will prioritize gun control if and when they gain unified control of government. More than ever, the NRA's political fortunes are wrapped up with the political success of the Republican Party—its political fate is in no small part linked with that of the GOP.

As a result, another threat to the NRA's power is the potential decline of the GOP itself. The NRA's close association with Trump and his Republican Party—a source of power during the Trump presidency—could become a liability given the controversy associated with Trump's time in office. Indeed, the NRA's outspoken support for increasingly hardline positions wholly unrelated to guns has already alienated not just its opponents but some of its own members and lower-level officials.[13] As chapter 4 showed, the NRA has long taken political stances that go beyond gun rights, but these stances— especially as articulated on NRATV prior to its demise—became more pronounced and controversial after Trump's election. If the Democrats eventually gain power by repudiating Trumpism, and the GOP, sensing a need for change, shifts away from Trump's vision in response, the NRA may find itself in a less than desirable position.

More broadly, the NRA's relationship with the Republican Party began at a propitious moment—during a Reagan presidency that in many ways marked a transformative shift in American politics. The political order associated with the New Deal Democratic Party, which had maintained a robust electoral coalition and defined the political agenda for decades, was faltering in the face of deteriorating economic conditions and substantial internal divisions. This decline provided an opening for Reagan, who fundamentally and durably altered the political landscape by rejecting much of what came before him. Casting skepticism on "big government," undermining some of the institutional pillars of the New Deal, and building a new electoral coalition (which, of course, included gun rights supporters), Reagan laid a foundation that would benefit Republicans for years to come. This new conservative coalition and vision—a vision that aligned with the NRA's worldview—outlasted Reagan's presidency, marking a new, conservative era of American politics and establishing a trend in which subsequent Republican presidents, including Trump, would seek to assume the mantle of Reaganism.[14]

Some scholars, however, believe that Trump's presidency may usher in the end of the Reagan era.[15] The electoral coalition that Reagan built in the 1980s—which was, by and large, the same coalition Trump relied on in 2016—represents an increasingly small proportion of the US electorate.[16] Although Trump won the presidency in 2016, he failed to win the popular vote, taking a narrow path to an Electoral College victory that subsequent Republicans may struggle to replicate. And after taking office, Trump doubled down on a base-mobilization strategy in lieu of attempting to broaden the GOP's coalition by appealing to new groups.[17]

Moreover, while Trump and Republican leaders in Congress found ways to work together on some issues, his right-wing populist appeals—geared toward the white working-class part of the Republican base—clash with some of the party's long-standing priorities geared toward the part of its coalition (and donor base) comprised of wealthy fiscal conservatives and business interests. The Reagan coalition's internal contradictions, in other words, have produced some visible cracks, which—in combination with the narrowing of its electoral base—call into question its sustainability.[18]

Despite these challenges, it is certainly possible that Trump's worldview—the ways in which he has built onto, rejiggered, and adapted the vision set out by Reagan—will not only come to define the GOP moving forward, but also that its proponents will find ways to build durable governing majorities. If so, the NRA—given its place in Trump's GOP—will likely maintain and strengthen its position in the American political landscape. But if Trumpism does mark the last gasp of Reagan's conservative order, then this book's publication may coincide with what will turn out to be the apex of the NRA's power.[19]

Is the NRA Unique?

While the durability of the NRA's power isn't certain, there is no doubt that it stands apart from many other interest groups in American politics in its cultivation and mobilization of a group identity and ideology. Is the NRA unique in its success at cultivating ideational resources—and what lessons might the NRA have for groups that seek to do the same?

As chapter 2 noted, we all hold numerous, potentially overlapping social identities. These identities can be based on race, gender, or sexual orientation, but can also be related to our occupations, hobbies, sports allegiances, or places of residence—any group membership that we use to derive a sense of who we are. That gun ownership is associated with an identity, then, does not make the NRA unique in itself.

However, just because all group memberships can lend themselves to identities does not mean that what the NRA has accomplished—the ways it has developed and used ideational resources—is typical.

For one thing, not all identities are relevant to politics; many identities may be important to people in particular contexts without impacting their political decisions. Being part of a running club may give you the opportunity to improve your fitness with other runners and provide a sense of meaning, purpose, and belonging—an identity—but that does not mean that this group membership is relevant to your politics.

And those identities that are relevant to politics may not be defined by or intimately tied to organizations that represent group members. Some identities, in other words, may inform individuals' political actions, but—unlike in the case of the NRA and gun owners—have not been shaped over time by an organized interest group. Your Latinx identity may inform your political beliefs, and you may even be part of an organization that advocates politically on behalf of Latinx interests. Yet there is no unified interest group that systematically shapes what it *means* to be Latinx in the way that the NRA has shaped the social and political meaning of gun ownership. This is likely the case for many ascriptive identities—organizations can appeal to them in order to mobilize action, but may find it difficult to mold what they mean to group members.

In other cases, particular identities become politically relevant and lead to widespread mobilization, but only for relatively brief periods, failing to maintain salience over time in the way that the gun owner identity has. In 2017, for example, conservationist and environmentalist organizations were able to mobilize outdoor enthusiasts and hobbyists—hikers, fishers, hunters, canoers, and rock climbers, among many others—to take action against a bill that would have led to the sale of some federal lands to states, thereby making them easier to develop. The bill was pulled in response to the backlash, but the episode does not seem to have durably increased the political salience of the "outdoor enthusiast" identity; once the moment passed, in other words, the political relevance of the identity dissipated.[20]

Finally, even among identities that are consistently politically salient and linked with organizations, not all are reinforced by ideologies that position them as part of a broader political worldview. Older Americans, for example, comprise an important political constituency and are represented by AARP, which has lobbied on behalf of their collective interests for many years. AARP is effective at mobilizing older Americans into action by appealing to a group identity built around their shared interests. As political scientist Andrea Louise Campbell has demonstrated, the creation of Social Security in 1935 was responsible for spurring the establishment of both AARP itself and a shared political identity among older Americans, and the organization has played a role in shaping this identity over time—and in harnessing it for political ends.[21]

In 2005, for example, it led the charge against an ultimately failed attempt by the Bush Administration to partially privatize Social Security; its supporters, encouraged by a large mobilization campaign, flooded Congress with calls and letters in opposition to the plan, contributing to its demise.[22] Like the NRA, this mobilization was possible thanks to a strong communications infrastructure—including one of the most widely circulated magazines in the country—which it uses to frame the protection of government benefits not just in terms of seniors' material interests, but also in terms of identity. Medicare and Social Security are benefits seniors have, in AARP's words, "earned and paid for through long years of work" and should therefore fight to protect.[23]

Yet the political identity shared by older Americans doesn't seem to be accompanied by a political ideology in the way that the gun owner identity is, and AARP generally has not framed the interests of seniors as part of a broader political worldview. Moreover, as a group, older Americans do not lean strongly toward one party or the other, and AARP has avoided partisan politics.[24] This truly single-issue focus has certainly aided AARP in some ways—helping the group avoid capture as both parties compete for the support of its members—but has also likely narrowed the scope of its influence. It has a lot of power over one policy area, but the age-based identity shared by its supporters is not necessarily the central lens through which they make most political decisions, and their views on other policy issues are not highly unified. As a result, if an organization like AARP wanted to align with a political party—as the NRA has—it would struggle to do so without alienating many of its supporters.

Considering all of this together, what is most notable about the NRA is not the mere existence of a gun owner identity. Rather, it is the consistent political salience of the identity for the NRA's supporters and its savvy use of that identity to mobilize them into action. It's the active role that the NRA has played in shaping a more comprehensive worldview around guns. And it's the fact that the worldview is composed of both an identity and a reinforcing ideology, and is therefore amenable to alignment with a political party.

Nonetheless, it's certainly possible that other groups are similar to the NRA across all of these dimensions. In particular, the anchoring groups studied by Daniel Schlozman—the Christian Right and organized labor—are likely candidates. Both cases include a strong, organizationally led movement of individuals who share a common political identity. Moreover, in both cases, that identity is central for many group members, informing their political attitudes and actions not just in specific contexts and during fleeting moments, but broadly and durably. Further, in both cases the identity is linked with a more comprehensive ideology, which suggests that each group's core issues are wrapped up with a wider array of political stances. And finally, both cases have witnessed the group's alignment with a political party. Further study of these groups could help determine the extent to which they mirror NRA strategies in terms of the intentional cultivation of a political worldview.

Lessons for Other Groups

Leaving aside the question of whether the NRA is unique in its production of ideational resources, it's undeniable that the group has been successful in deploying them to advance its agenda. What lessons might other groups learn from the NRA in terms of cultivating and using ideational power?

The NRA has certain qualities that aren't easily replicated. It is not just an interest group, but also a provider of educational and recreational programs, and has an industry that is eager to cater to its members. Many of its programs bring people together in person, which certainly helps to build a sense of identity among group members. Finally, the NRA has a much more prominent position in the gun rights realm than any single organization does in many other political realms; no one group speaks for the environmental movement, for instance, in the same way that the NRA does for the gun rights movement.[25]

However, even if other groups lack the NRA's advantages and, as a result, cannot adopt its model outright, they can learn lessons from it. To build identity, groups can encourage members to meet each other by developing programs that offer opportunities to interact in person (rather than, for example, interacting with the group exclusively through fundraising appeals). Indeed, as Hahrie Han demonstrates in her study of the development of civic activists, successful organizations stand out in part due to their focus on bringing members together and developing their ability to recruit and lead others, something that the NRA does through its programs and affiliated clubs.[26] Further, groups can also tap into existing social

networks and tie the issues they are interested in to identities related
to those networks—something anti-abortion groups have done with
great success.[27] Finally, groups can frame their appeals to members
in ways that prime existing identities, even if those identities are not
explicitly related to the group's mission.

The NRA also has lessons for how groups can overcome collective action problems. All organized groups must offer incentives
that help them avoid free rider problems related to both recruiting
and mobilizing members. Although the NRA offers some financial
incentives—such as discounts with retailers—its real draw, as noted
in chapter 2, is the gun owner identity and gun-centric ideology it
provides members. As former NRA lobbyist Richard Feldman put
it, "Nobody's joining NRA to get a discount at Hertz. . . . Joining
NRA is like making a religious commitment; it's a statement about
where you stand not just on guns, but on one view of what it means
to be an American. It's a powerful symbolic move."[28] Other organizations can try to follow the NRA's lead here, framing themselves in
terms of the social psychological benefits they offer, such as group
camaraderie and a sense that members are contributing to a cause
in which they deeply believe.

Some groups—even those that often oppose the NRA—are
already trying to adopt its tactics.[29] In an interview with the *New
York Times' Daily* podcast, for instance, Anthony Romero—executive
director of the American Civil Liberties Union (ACLU)—explained
how his organization has started to model its approach after the
NRA's. In regard to the NRA, Romero said,

> They don't talk about [the Second Amendment] in legalistic or
> policy wonk terms. They talk about the gun culture. They talk
> about it in very personal, lifestyle terms. A light bulb went off
> in our heads. . . . "We can definitely to do that too." When we're
> talking about liberty, we're not talking about the First or the
> Fourth or the Fifth Amendment. We are, but we're not *only* talk-
> ing about that. We're talking about the ability for an individual to
> live the life she wishes to have with the dignity she's entitled to
> in our democracy. People really experience their freedom, their

autonomy, their agency, their self-actualization in deeply personal ways. They may not understand what the language of the Fourth or the Fifth Amendment is and it doesn't really matter.[30]

As Romero's comments make clear, the ACLU has learned from the NRA's ability to appeal to gun owners in a very personal way by focusing more on the values and ideals associated with particular debates than on the technicalities of specific policies.

The NRA also offers some lessons for its opponents, providing insights that may be useful for gun control advocacy groups. Of course, these groups face some major obstacles: while the NRA's alliance with the GOP presents some long-term risks, its place in the Republican Party is, in the near term, a major obstacle gun control advocates must overcome—a task made even more challenging by the status quo bias inherent in the US lawmaking process and the overrepresentation of rural constituencies in Congress discussed in the last chapter. Unified Democratic government may now be necessary to pass any sort of substantively meaningful gun control policies. And even when Democrats do have unified control of government, gun control advocates must convince them that gun control is a winning issue.

Nonetheless, the post-Sandy Hook and post-Parkland efforts of gun control activists have demonstrated a possible way forward, using—as discussed earlier this chapter—an approach that aligns closely with what both this project and Kristin Goss's work on the gun control movement would recommend. This study—especially chapter 3—suggests that gun control advocates can learn from the NRA by tying support for gun control to one or more important social identities held by potential movement participants, and creating or tapping into existing social networks that bring participants together. Similarly, Goss—in her previously mentioned study of gun control activism—found that gun control advocates have been most successful when they have framed gun regulations as a form of child protection.[31] The post-Sandy Hook and post-Parkland movements have taken exactly this sort of approach. Parkland activists have combined forces with organized groups created after Sandy Hook—led by Everytown for Gun Safety and Moms Demand Action—to create a genuine grassroots infrastructure built around shared identities and the protection of children.[32] The question moving forward is whether they can sustain momentum until the next time Democrats gain unified control of the federal government and then use their mobilization capabilities to get gun control on the legislative agenda.

Moving forward, future studies might fruitfully explore the extent to which other groups can successfully cultivate and use ideational resources like the NRA has. This might include a broader focus on the conditions under which group identities and ideologies can and cannot be developed, as well as the conditions that determine the extent to which they impact policy outcomes. It might also include a focus on whether and how the success—or failure—of groups in other policy domains at different points in time relates to their deployment of ideas and their ability to shape the political behavior of their members.

I hope the text-based methods I have developed here might be helpful in studying other groups, but this is by no means the only way to approach these questions. In-depth ethnographic work would also likely yield very useful insights; indeed, an ethnographic study of NRA members would enhance this study as well. Future studies might also collect new survey data that can more precisely measure the relationship between social identities, ideologies, and organized groups. The text-based approach used here enables a long-term analysis of the development of particular ideas, including during periods for which existing survey data is insufficient, but analyses of contemporary periods could use more fine-grained survey-based measures that would enable more precise measurements of the relationship between a group's rhetoric and its members' views.

The NRA and the Study of Organized Groups

In recent years, political scientists—tapping into rich but sometimes dormant scholarly traditions—have paid increased attention to the crucial role of groups in American politics. One area of focus has been on individuals: How do your group affiliations and identities—related to race, ethnicity, gender, occupation, place of residence, gun ownership status, and myriad other social groups—impact your political views, decisions, and actions? Another area of focus has been on the centrality of organized groups in politics: How do interest groups influence policy outcomes, and what role do they play in political parties?

For the most part, however, these lines of inquiry have proceeded separately, with scholars who are broadly interested in individual-level political behavior focused on the social and psychological impacts of individuals' group memberships and identities, and scholars broadly interested in political institutions focused on the scope and influence of organized groups.

This book—within the context of a single but substantively important case—helps unite these areas of inquiry by examining the connection between the NRA as an institution and gun ownership as a mass-level group identity associated with a broader ideological worldview. Put differently, the analysis of the NRA presented here helps us better understand the processes through which organized groups can alter individuals' political behavior and use that behavior to their advantage in the policymaking process.

Moreover, this work connects these lines of inquiry to the study of ideology by identifying the role that organized groups can play in cultivating ideologies and exploring the interrelated nature of parties, ideologies, and social identities. I have argued that the NRA cultivated an ideology among its supporters, which connected the gun owner identity to other politically relevant group identities and eventually enabled it to join a broader ideological movement and party coalition. This process further highlights the extent to which organized groups can alter mass behavior in ways that advance their interests and impact broader political developments.

More broadly, as noted in chapter 2, this project contributes to our understanding of how interest groups can use the third face of power to advance their political agendas—how they can influence politics by influencing the attitudes and actions of others. Further, it highlights the necessity of studying groups over long periods of time in order to understand their use of this dimension of power. As political scientist Paul Pierson notes, the third face of power "is likely to involve slow-moving processes that require a focus on group-based activity over a sustained period." Despite the analytical challenges associated with studying the third face of power, Pierson argues that a focus on the "ideational elements of power" is needed in order to fully understand how groups build and then entrench— often in hard-to-see ways—political advantages.[33]

The NRA's use of ideational resources to build and exercise power is a case in point: its development of a worldview around guns took place over the course of decades, and the full impact of that worldview on gun policy outcomes is only visible with attention to how the gun debate has played out over time. Future research can further extend our understanding of how other organized groups can and do use the third face of power by focusing on how they develop and disseminate ideas over time, and how they deploy ideas to gradually reshape policy debates that advance their interests.

The NRA and the Relationship between Groups and Parties

One important and exciting aspect of the renewed focus on the importance of groups in politics involves the study of their relationship with political parties. This body of scholarship—discussed in greater depth in chapters 2 and 6—has argued that organized groups are central to political parties, with some scholars arguing that durable coalitions of such groups are the defining feature of parties. This group-centric view of parties has raised lots of important questions, some of which are addressed—albeit partially—by this project.

The analysis of the NRA presented here helps develop our understanding of how groups join party coalitions, bringing attention to the underlying factors that make groups and parties compatible, the processes that produce those factors, and the conditions that determine the timing of party-group alignment. In identifying the mass-level inputs, institutional conditions, and entrepreneurial actions that led to the NRA's incorporation into the GOP coalition, this project presents one route through which party-group alignment can occur.

Further, by focusing in part on the importance of ideational factors in explaining the NRA's alignment with the GOP, this study helps elaborate connections between parties and mass-level identities and ideologies. My findings suggest that party coalitions can involve more than alliances between organized groups who often (but not always) advance a common ideology; they can also be characterized by an alignment of the *identities* associated with the groups included in the coalition.

Beyond helping us better understand the nature of party coalitions, this insight also helps explain otherwise puzzling group actions. This includes the NRA's failure to defend the rights of Black gun owners who have been mistreated by police; for instance, a strong defense of Philando Castile—an African American man who was killed by a police officer for legally carrying a firearm—might have caused a clash between the gun owner identity and other aligned identities, including white racial identity and Republican partisan identity, which could have, in turn, weakened its political position.

Future work might examine the extent to which the alignment of other organized groups with political parties has (or has not) followed a path that resembles the NRA's entry into the GOP, developing a broader understanding of the factors that lead to the alignment of parties and groups. More work is also needed to better conceptualize and measure the extent to which parties and groups are aligned. Chapter 6 includes a discussion of this and implements an initial set of measures, but a more systematic and generalizable approach would be useful. Lastly, additional focus might be placed on further conceptualizing the idea of parties as coalitions of aligned identities and on producing ways to empirically assess it. This might include collection of data that enables better analyses of alignments between group identities, as well as the development of tests that I did not consider or could not conduct given existing data.

The NRA, Biased Pluralism, and American Democracy

Finally, what can the NRA teach us about American democracy? And how should we think about the NRA's tactics in regard to the health of American democracy?

The notion that groups—and their relationships with each other and political institutions—structure, shape, and define politics can be traced back more than one hundred years. One school of thought—which gained prominence in the mid-twentieth century and was known as "pluralism"—recognized the important place of groups in politics and argued that political competition among them generally led to a healthy democracy. Building on the earlier work of important thinkers like Arthur Bentley and James Madison (who, in Federalist 10, effectively made a pluralist argument), political scientists including Robert Dahl and David Truman contended that open competition for political influence among groups in society enables power to be widely (if not entirely evenly) distributed, allowing a wide range of interests to be represented and preventing a small number of groups from dominating. Group competition, in short, leads to a democratically sound equilibrium in which the collective will is reflected in government.[34]

E. E. Schattschneider—a leading scholar writing in response to the optimism of pluralist scholarship—was among the first to identify and develop the concept of *biased* pluralism. Schattschneider agreed that organized groups are at the center of politics, but argued forcefully that the system of organized group conflict in the United States does not lead to widespread representation—that it is instead biased toward the interests of some Americans and against the interests of others. Schattschneider emphasized in particular the strong upper-class bias present in US group conflict, noting that power is heavily concentrated among wealthy interests in society.[35] And indeed, recent work has confirmed Schattschneider's suspicion, finding that interest groups and, in turn, policy outcomes do not equally represent all Americans.[36]

Although Schattschneider and others focused on the distorting effects of moneyed interests, this project shows that special interests can also deploy other resources—including ideas—to produce policy outcomes that conflict with the preferences of most citizens (who, in this case, favor stricter regulations on guns).

The NRA, in this sense, represents something of a democratic paradox: it subverts the will of the majority, but does so by working the levers of democracy. It has built power by encouraging its sup-porters—who are mostly average citizens, not elites—to partake in politics, but the outcomes they produce often conflict with what most Americans want (and, moreover, lead to a generally weak body of federal gun regulations that, in the views of many, contributes to the high rate of annual gun deaths in the United States). Moreover, when mobilizing its supporters, the NRA's identity-based appeals tend to rely on fear in a way that encourages polarization, discour-ages compromise, and—in some cases—advances conspiratorial views that are misleading and offensive. In the end, then, the NRA demonstrates that groups can be effective at using democracy to their advantage, even to the point of undermining it.

APPENDIX

Topic Modeling

Chapters 3 and 4 employ automated topic modeling, a text analysis technique that uses algorithms to infer the topics of documents within corpora based on word frequency and word co-occurrence. Analysts specify a number of topics, and then the model estimates both what those topics are and the proportion of each document that belongs to each topic. I use the Structural Topic Model (STM), a topic modeling technique that improves upon other approaches by allowing for the flexible incorporation of relevant document level covariates. More specifically, STM uses regression to incorporate covariates that are believed to influence (1) "the frequency with which a topic is discussed" (topical *prevalence* covariates) and/or (2) "the words used to discuss a topic" (topical *content* covariates).[1] For example, analysts can account for the possibility that different authors discuss the same topics using somewhat different words.

AMERICAN RIFLEMAN TOPIC MODELING

I estimated a model that fits the *American Rifleman* editorials into six topics,[2] and includes "Year" as a "prevalence" covariate—to account for the prevalence of topics changing over time—and "Author" as a "content" covariate—to account for different authors discussing the same topics using slightly different words. Table 3.1, in chapter 3, lists each topic's "Highest Probability" words—the words most likely to appear within a topic—and "FREX" words, which are words that are both common and *exclusive* to each topic. They are very useful

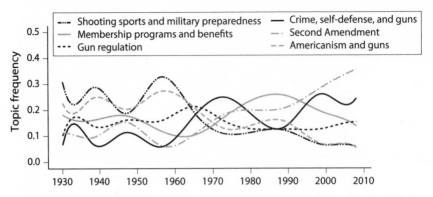

FIGURE A.1. Frequency of *American Rifleman* Editorial Topics over Time

in identifying the substantive, semantic meanings of topics because they not only frequently appear in a topic but also are relatively distinct to that topic.

I also calculated the proportion of each document comprised of each topic, which enabled me to read prototypical documents for each topic. I named and briefly described the topics based on close readings of example documents and their Highest Probability and FREX words (see table 3.1).[3] Four of the topics, as noted in chapter 3, pertain to gun control; I describe each of these in greater detail below. (Later in the appendix, I also describe how I identified gun control-related documents.)

I also examined how the prominence of each topic varies over time. All 6 topics are plotted together in figure A.1. The topics vary over time in sensible ways, which helps validate the model. *Shooting Sports and Military Preparedness*, for instance, is relatively prominent around World War II, reflecting both the environment of the time and the NRA's original mission of developing the marksmanship of American men. It declines following the postwar period and does not pick back up during later wars, likely because by those wars the organization had expanded its mission beyond marksmanship and its formal government ties had weakened. Similarly, *Crime, Self-Defense, and Guns* peaks at three main points: during (1) debates over gun regulation aimed at gangsters in the 1930s, (2) the rise of "law and order" politics in response to high crime rates in the 1960s and early 1970s, and (3) during the Clinton years, when both crime control and gun regulation were salient issues.

LETTERS TO THE EDITOR AND *AMERICAN RIFLEMAN* TOPIC MODELING

I estimated a separate topic model to assess a combined dataset containing the *American Rifleman* editorials and pro-gun letters to the editor, as described in chapters 3 and 4. I use this second model to examine both the content of the letters to the editor and the relationship of their content to the *American Rifleman* editorials. Because of a relative dearth of letters to the editor prior to the early 1960s and the resulting lack of statistical leverage during early time periods, the dataset used for this topic model (for both the letters and the editorials) begins in 1963. The number of letters to the editor printed about gun control increased substantially during this year—to the point that topic modeling of the dataset is viable—as a result of the President Kennedy's assassination and the long gun control debate that followed.

The model includes "Year," "Source" (*American Rifleman* or letters to the editor), and "Letter Type" as prevalence covariates and "Author/Newspaper" as a content covariate.[4] I landed on a model with five topics (a slightly reduced number of topics makes sense given that the letters to the editor—which are inherently political given my search criteria—have a narrower scope than the editorials). Table 4.1, in chapter 4, includes names and brief descriptions of each topic based on the Highest Probability and FREX words, as well as close readings of example documents; I describe each topic in greater detail below.

I again examined how each topic varies over time. All topics are plotted together in figure A.2 (again excluding confidence intervals for simplicity). As with the *American Rifleman*-only model, the relative prominence of each topic varies over time in a sensible way, providing validation for the model. The *Second Amendment* topic, for instance, becomes steadily more prominent over time, reflecting its increasing political relevance. It peaks in the first decade of the

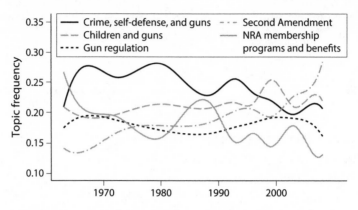

FIGURE A.2. Frequency of *American Rifleman* and Pro-Gun Letter to the Editor Topics over Time

twenty-first century, at which time the Supreme Court heard *D.C. v. Heller*—a landmark 2008 case in which it decided that the Second Amendment protects an individual right to own guns. And *Children and Guns* peaks at the end the 1990s, right around the time of the 1999 Columbine school shooting in Colorado, which spurred a large national debate about guns.

DESCRIPTION OF GUN CONTROL TOPICS FROM THE *AMERICAN RIFLEMAN* MODEL

Gun Regulation (figure A.3) addresses gun legislation in more general terms than other topics. Perhaps unsurprisingly given its generality, it is positively correlated with the *Crime, Self-Defense, and Guns* topic (correlation coefficient = 0.49). It is more stable over time than other topics—perhaps also due to its generality—and peaks during the 1960s, when gun regulation was debated and eventually enacted following several high-profile assassinations.

The January 1966 editorial, entitled "A Suggestion to Congress," is measured as a highly representative example:

> When Congress reconvenes . . . one of the questions to be answered . . . is what legislation, if any, is needed to further control firearms in interstate commerce. . . . Major attention has been

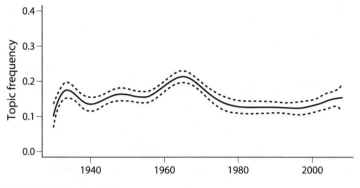

FIGURE A.3. Gun Regulation

given to "mail-order guns" and "destructive devices." Unfortunately, most of the proposed legislation has the wrong emphasis. It tends to harass the law-abiding citizen, while it would fail in its avowed purpose of denying firearms to those who violate the law. Unfortunately, also, much of the debate has been based upon emotion rather than reason, and upon impression rather than fact. This has led to gun control confusion and misunderstanding. Our Federal Government is one of limited or delegated powers. . . . The right to keep and bear arms is a fundamental personal freedom of the people of the United States of America. It should not be denied to citizens of good repute so long as they use them for lawful purposes.[5]

Crime, Self-Defense, and Guns (figure A.4) argues that guns are a *solution* to rather than a *cause* of crime and that gun regulation makes crime easier and self-defense more difficult. It advocates for harsh sentencing in lieu of restricting access to guns. It peaks at three points: during (1) debates over gun regulation aimed at gangsters in the 1930s, (2) the rise of "law and order" politics in response to high crime rates in the 1960s and early 1970s, and (3) during the Clinton years, when both crime control and gun regulation were salient issues.

The June 1997 editorial, in which Wayne LaPierre argues that new regulations would be unnecessary if existing regulations were better enforced, is a measured as a highly representative example:

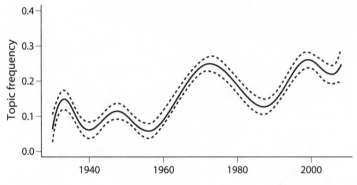

FIGURE A.4. Crime, Self-Defense, and Guns

"Gunrunning." It's Chuck Schumer's latest national media ploy and his biggest fraud yet. . . . Schumer's office released what the media called a "Congressional study" which he claimed showed a flow of guns from states with "weak" laws to states with "strong laws." The assertion that some states have weak gun laws and others have strong laws is patently false. . . . With his meaningless calls for new gun control, Charles Schumer would make it more difficult for peaceable people—you and me—to own and use firearms: Making the innocent pay the price for the guilty, when he won't make the guilty pay anything. . . . So, why is it that [Schumer] has never demanded that tough existing laws be enforced? Because—like his anti-gun soulmate, Bill Clinton—he knows the truth. Because if current Federal laws were enforced, and if the public knew that there were such laws, the call for gun control would be pointless. . . . Chuck Schumer, Janet Reno, Bill Clinton and their allies at the *Washington Post* and the *New York Times* and the national networks have to keep the lie alive. And every day they refuse to enforce the law—every day they keep the lie alive—innocent people suffer under the anvil of violent crime.[6]

Second Amendment (figure A.5) advocates for an individual rights interpretation of the Second Amendment. The Second Amendment, it argues, is critical to freedom because it enables the people to defend themselves against an abusive state; gun rights are the freedom that makes all other freedoms possible and that protect against

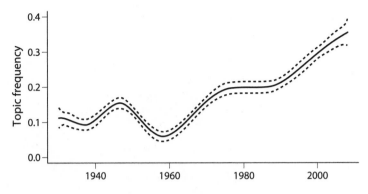

FIGURE A.5. Second Amendment

government tyranny. In general, the Second Amendment—and the protection of gun rights with which it is associated—is portrayed as a cornerstone of the American tradition. The topic has gradually—and very notably—increased in prominence since around 1960.

The editorial from August 1989 is a representative example:

> The right to own and use firearms is the preeminent individual right. Without the ability to physically defend the other provisions of our Constitution from encroachment, the remainder of the Bill of Rights become privileges granted by the government and subject to restrictions at the whim of government. . . . Whereas the Framers dreamed of a strong citizenry who could remove any threatening government, modern collectivists attempt to reduce the Second Amendment to a measure of the "sporting use" of firearms. . . . Self-defense, defense of country, and resistance to tyranny (the Second Amendment's triune) are not abstract principles. The right of the people to keep and bear arms guarantees the rest of our freedoms.[7]

Americanism and Guns (figure A.6) peaks earliest and describes the centrality of guns throughout US history and their importance to the American tradition. It was frequently used as a frame through which to oppose gun regulation attempts—including the Federal Firearms Act of 1934 and the National Firearms Act of 1938—and to rally support for war preparation measures involving civilian

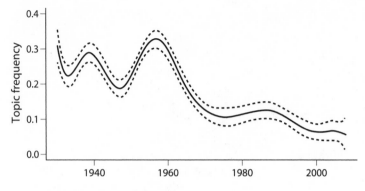

FIGURE A.6. Americanism and Guns

firearms training. It advocates limited government and hawkish foreign policy positions, and has been used to oppose gun regulations aimed at hunters and to more generally highlight the connection between gun owners and outdoor recreation. As discussed in chapter 4, it is similar to the *Second Amendment* topic in that it depicts guns as central to the American tradition and the protection of liberty, but differs in that it focuses on threats posed by foreign governments rather than on the threat of domestic tyranny posed by the US government.

The July 1947 editorial is a representative example. Written in celebration of Independence Day, it connects the American Revolution to contemporary (in 1947) battles against communism and fascism, and argues that perceived overreach by government officials is anti-American:

> The American Declaration of Independence was, in fact, a declaration of the principles of a form of government in which the majesty of the individual was recognized as the only foundation on which the majesty of the State properly could rest. . . . Americans, that is your heritage! . . . Today all over the world, Communism, Fascism, Nazism, Socialism feed upon and fertilize one another. All over the world the dignity of Man is being subordinated to the majesty of the State. . . . America is not untouched by the disease. American statesmen lack a clear chart to guide them on a consistent course toward the establishment of truly representative

forms of government. . . . Money alone will not do it. Armed might alone will not do it. . . . [The] principles set forth in the American Declaration of Independence . . . lighted the path to real freedom for the common man in 1776. They will do the same in 1947 if America itself leads the way in putting the State back into its proper relationship with the Citizen of the State—the State the servant of man, not man the servant of the State.[8]

OVERVIEW OF TOPICS FROM THE *AMERICAN RIFLEMAN* + LETTERS MODEL[9]

The *Crime, Self-Defense, and Guns* topic (figure A.7)—which is very similar to the identically named topic from the *American Rifleman*-only model—argues that gun control laws are unlikely to reduce crime. Further, documents from this topic argue that gun ownership is a *solution* to crime rather than a *cause* of it, with writers arguing that gun control laws hamper their ability to defend themselves against crimes. Finally, letters and editorials from this topic voice support for harsh criminal sentencing, blaming crime on what they see as a lack of strict law enforcement rather than a lack of sufficient regulations. The topic is fairly prominent throughout the period covered by the model, but is most prominent toward the beginning of that period; its prominence during the 1960s and 1970s makes sense given the crime-focused gun control debate that resulted from the high-profile political assassinations of the 1960s and the high rates of gun violence during both decades. In general, the topic rises and falls in ways that correspond to overall rates of gun violence, which dipped in the 1980s, increased in the early 1990s, then went back down in subsequent years.[10]

The following October 1974 letter to the editor printed in the *Chicago Tribune* is a highly representative example. The letter argues that gun control would harm law-abiding citizens without reducing crime, and also advocates for harsh enforcement of existing laws:

Anti-gun laws would only increase the crime rate, adding violations of the anti-gun laws to the total number of crimes and

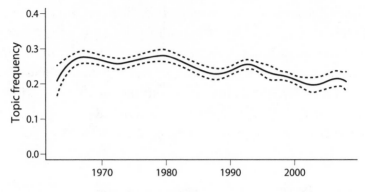

FIGURE A.7. Crime, Self-Defense, and Guns

making otherwise law-abiding citizens into criminals for their violations of the anti-gun laws. Nor would anti-gun laws discourage criminals who don't believe in obeying laws anyway, including laws against robbery, manslaughter, and murder. If all the time and effort that has been expended on trying to secure gun-ban laws had instead been expended towards the enforcement of laws on the books against criminals who use guns to commit crimes and towards the conviction and imprisonment of those who are guilty, then crime wouldn't be anywhere near the problem it is today.[11]

Children and Guns (figure A.8) discusses gun control in the context of both school shootings and firearms accidents in the home that lead to the deaths of children. Documents from this topic argue that gun-related accidents should be addressed through gun safety education, with some going as far as advocating that gun safety be taught in schools. The topic blames school shootings on factors other than access to guns, most notably what writers perceive to be poor parenting and a general breakdown of American society's moral fiber. It also criticizes the Million Mom March in 2000—a large rally that occurred in Washington and other cities in support of gun control—as misguided at best and as a cynical political stunt at worst. Finally, documents in this topic advocate for arming teachers and providing more armed security in schools as a way to stop future school shootings. As noted above, the topic unsurprisingly peaks

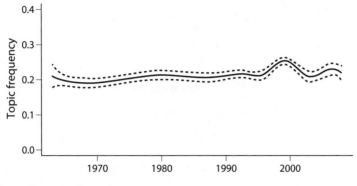

FIGURE A.8. Children and Guns

around the time of the 1999 school shooting at Columbine High School in Colorado.

The May 2000 letter to the editor from the *Arizona Republic* excerpted below is a representative example focused on the Million Mom March:

> The Million Mom March started out to be about moms and parents concerned about the safety issues with our kids. Somehow, magically, it was transformed into a political rally that had more to do with gun registration/confiscation than our kids' safety. I know the National Rifle Association offered $1 million for safety training in schools and challenged the MMM and Handgun Control to match them. The challenge was declined. Why? Because this was not about safety, it was once again a chance for Clinton/Gore to further their political goals and stand up on the soapbox against guns.[12]

A *New York Times* letter from that same month, excerpted below, also discusses the Million Mom March and does so while blaming school shootings on parents and schools:

> "Feel good" marches like the Million Mom March serve no constructive purpose (front page, May 15). In fact, the Million Mom March helped us evade the fact that fewer parents are doing a good job raising their children. It's the gun manufacturers they

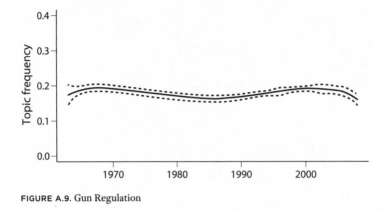

FIGURE A.9. Gun Regulation

scream. What about the parents who leave guns out for their children to take? Or the "self-esteem" obsessed schools, which teach children to go with their feelings instead of learning self-restraint?[13]

Finally, the following June 2007 letter from the *Arizona Republic* makes the case for arming teachers:

> I am for more people carrying concealed weapons. The restriction on how and where they can carry guns needs re-evaluating. In the school shootings, if the teachers could carry a concealed weapon there would have been a gunfight that could have saved many lives. In universities, reliable, tested people should be given permits. If the "crazy ones" do not know who may shoot back they will think twice before starting a slaughter. Utah permits concealed weapons on their campus grounds. Does anyone know of any adverse situations caused by their law?[14]

The *Gun Regulation* topic (figure A.9)—like the topic of the same name from the *American Rifleman*-only model—discusses gun control in more general terms than the other topics. As such, it—again, like the *American Rifleman*-only model's *Gun Regulation* topic—varies less over time than the other topics.

A representative example comes from the January 1999 *American Rifleman* editorial written by Wayne LaPierre, excerpted below, in which LaPierre discusses Clinton Administration gun regulations, arguing that they will create a slippery slope to gun confiscation:

"Insta-CHECK"—the Bill Clinton/Sarah Brady version—is a reality check for the nation's gun owners. . . . "Instant check" or "Insta-Check" as Clinton has styled it, is the ultimate White House spin. It is a far cry from the system Congress intended to create in 1993. In the 1999 reality, and in practice, the National Instant Check System (NICS) has been twisted by contorted FBI regulations into a firearms owner registration system that could be the baseline for future government action against peaceable citizens who choose to exercise their right to own and use firearms. Janet Reno and Bill Clinton, Al Gore and Sarah Brady ultimately want to be gun collectors. But the firearms they want to collect belong to the people. Those firearms are private property, owned by private citizens. They belong to you and me. But they can't collect your guns if they don't know you have them. And your lawful, private ownership of firearms is none of government's business. . . . The National Instant Check System—under Bill Clinton and Janet Reno's vision—would be the means to collect and keep unlawful files—dossiers on each of us, inaccessible to us—that could be used in the future to wipe out our civil rights. . . . I've got news for them. With respect to Instant Check, all bets are off. The NRA will use every power at our disposal to force the Federal government to obey the law. . . . Just as we rolled back portions of bad law with the passage of the Firearms Owners' Protection Act in 1986, we will roll back the sinister and devious effort to contort NICS into a system for subjecting gun buyers to enormous fees, government-sanctioned violations of privacy and civil rights, and centralized registration. Now is the time—help us fight.[15]

The *Second Amendment* topic (figure A.10)—again in similar fashion to the *American Rifleman*-only model's identically named topic—advocates for an individual rights interpretation of the Second Amendment. Gun rights are portrayed as crucial to freedom because they enable citizens to defend themselves against

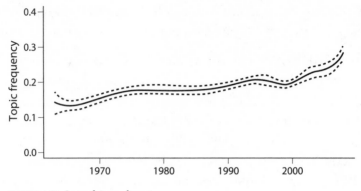

FIGURE A.10. Second Amendment

government tyranny. Gun rights—portrayed as the freedom that enables the protection of all other freedoms—are depicted as a centerpiece of liberty and the American tradition. Again, similar to the *American Rifleman*-only model's *Second Amendment* topic, this topic has dramatically increased in prominence since the 1960s, becoming the most prominent topic overall by the end of my period of study.

A representative example comes from a March 1980 letter printed in the *Atlanta Journal-Constitution*, in which the letter writer argues the Second Amendment is necessary as protection against government tyranny—a purpose tied back to the founding of the United States:

> I have just completed reading Robert Akerman's Sunday column entitled "The Right to Bear Arms." He presented the usual argument that the militia was "a body of citizens who could be called out in time of need to preserve order or repel an invasion." I suggest that this definition is dangerously incomplete since it misses the real point of the Second Amendment and fails to alert his readers to the essential reason for that amendment. When the founding fathers stated that the right of the people to keep and bear arms is "necessary to the security of a free state," the emphasis was on the word "free." Two-hundred years ago the oppression of big centralized government was still fresh in the memories of our founders, and they knew what seems to have been forgotten today—the lust for power by a few will lead to loss of freedoms

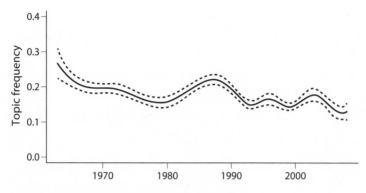

FIGURE A.11. NRA Membership Programs and Benefits

for the many unless the people are eternally vigilant and retain the means to preserve their liberties. So the Second Amendment was not added to protect us from foreign aggression but to protect us from the depredations of our own central government. And if you do not believe it is important to keep firearms unregistered, talk to a freedom lover from Czechoslovakia.[16]

The following March 1973 letter to the editor printed in the *Chicago Tribune* is another, similar representative example:

How long will the First Amendment rights of the press be secure if gun-owner rights under the Second Amendment are invalidated? I don't refer to the maintenance of arms by citizens for defense against government tyranny. That concept is as out of date as the Brown Bess musket. It is the legal aspect that concerns me. Once a clause of our Bill of Rights is nullified, all other clauses are correspondingly weakened. If our lawmakers outlaw one right and the courts uphold them, who can say which right will come next? The whole thing must hang together. We cannot guarantee just part of a constitution.[17]

Finally, the *NRA Membership Programs and Benefits* (figure A.11) topic is very similar to the *Membership Programs and Benefits* topic from the *American Rifleman*-only model, consisting mostly of editorials in which the NRA promotes new offerings designed to increase membership. It is prominent at the beginning of the 1960s, at which time the NRA ran several editorials discussing its plans to grow membership in the last decade of its first century of operation. It then peaks again during the 1980s and early 1990s when the NRA addressed its financial struggles by heavily promoting new revenue-generating programs and benefits.

A representative example comes from the October 1981 *American Rifleman* editorial written by Harlon Carter:

> With the last computer print-out at the close of business on July 31, 1981, NRA achieved a new landmark in its 110-year history. Our membership has now gone over the two million mark, and we are going on. That end of July count put NRA at exactly 2,008,011 individual dues-paying members. This marks a doubling of NRA's size and strength in just the last three years. . . . By doubling the number of members and thereby doubling the dues income, we came from a $24 million deficit in 1979 to a profit situation in 1981. This is what the increase in membership has done for you—for NRA. And, without you, the individual NRA member, we would never have achieved this phenomenal growth. . . . Under the wise and farsighted public affairs policy laid down by the NRA Board of Directors last October, we are now planning to put most of this additional money—your money never before available—into the development of a new program providing support, understanding and credibility for the real and active NRA and the worthy services it renders to all America.[18]

NOTES

Chapter 1: Introduction

1. The schedule was obtained using the Wayback Machine Internet Archive: see https://web.archive.org/web/20150418073556/http://www.nraam.org/special -events/seminars,-workshops-special-presentations.aspx; https://web.archive .org/web/20150419063330/http://www.nraam.org/attendee-info/celebrity -booth-appearances.aspx; and https://web.archive.org/web/20150418074949 /http://www.nraam.org/special-events/schedule-of-events.aspx.

2. In contemporary politics, "invisible primary" may be a somewhat mislead-ing phrase to describe the jockeying that occurs among potential candidates prior to the official start of an election. At this point, the process of sorting through a set of potential candidates to determine which are viable is actually rather visible. Moreover, potential candidates participating in the process no longer focus solely on gaining the support of elites, donors, and activists, but also on courting early support of the party's electoral base. Nonetheless, the term continues to be used to refer to the preprimary competition among potential candidates. See Kevin Reun-ing and Nick Dietrich, "Media Coverage, Public Interest, and Support in the 2016 Republican Invisible Primary," *Perspectives on Politics* 17, no. 2 (2019): 329–339; and Julia Azari, "The 2016 Primaries Were Weird. Will Things Get Even Weirder in 2020?," *FiveThirtyEight*, November 27, 2018, https://fivethirtyeight.com/features /the-2016-primaries-were-weird-will-things-get-even-weirder-in-2020/; Dave Boucher, Joey Garrison, and Mary Troyan, "GOP Heavyweights Fire Up the Base at NRA Event," *USA Today*, April 10, 2015, https://www.usatoday.com/story/news /politics/2015/04/10/nra-convention-2016-republican-candidates/25581489/; "2015 Nashville Annual Meetings," National Rifle Association, accessed April 23, 2019, https://www.nraam.org/past-meetings/2015-nashville-annual-meetings .aspx.

3. Aaron Blake, "Why Obama Invoked the Crusades—and What It Says about How He Views Terrorism," *Washington Post*, February 6, 2015, https://www .washingtonpost.com/news/the-fix/wp/2015/02/06/why-obama-invoked-the -crusades-in-re-islam-and-terrorism/.

4. Tessa Berenson, "Republican Candidates Didn't Just Talk Guns at NRA Event," *Time*, April 10, 2015, https://time.com/3818154/nra-conference-presidential -candidates/.

5. "Bobby Jindal: 2015 NRA-ILA Leadership Forum," YouTube video, NRA, April 10, 2015, https://www.youtube.com/watch?v=z8MARE7z65Y.

6. "Ted Cruz: 2015 NRA-ILA Leadership Forum," YouTube video, NRA, April 10, 2015, https://www.youtube.com/watch?v=OFgNLufR3ZE.

7. "Donald Trump: 2015 NRA-ILA Leadership Forum," YouTube video, NRA, April 10, 2015, https://www.youtube.com/watch?v=u7IDo_1a39w.

8. "1st Annual National Rifle Association Convention," *American Rifleman*, December 1948, 23–38.

9. Louis Menand, "He Knew He Was Right," *New Yorker*, March 19, 2001, https://www.newyorker.com/magazine/2001/03/26/he-knew-he-was-right.

10. Although the NRA and its supporters are also very active on the subnational level, the focus of this project is on federal level gun politics.

11. Frank R. Baumgartner and Beth L. Leech, *Basic Interests: The Importance of Groups in Politics and in Political Science* (Princeton, NJ: Princeton University Press, 1998); Terry Moe, "Power and Political Institutions," *Perspectives on Politics* 3, no. 2 (2005): 215–233; Paul Pierson, "Power in Historical Institutionalism," in *The Oxford Handbook of Historical Institutionalism*, ed. Orfeo Fioretos, Tulia G. Falleti, and Adam Sheingate (Oxford: Oxford University Press, 2016), 124–141.

12. A growing body of research suggests that such views may be well-founded: several studies have discovered that public policy responds disproportionately to the views of wealthy Americans and to the interest groups that represent them. Among others, see Larry M. Bartels, *Unequal Democracy: The Political Economy of the New Gilded Age* (Princeton, NJ: Princeton University Press, 2008); Martin Gilens, *Affluence and Influence: Economic Inequality and Political Power in America* (Princeton, NJ: Princeton University Press, 2012); Martin Gilens and Benjamin I. Page, "Testing Theories of American Politics: Elites, Interest Groups, and Average Citizens," *Perspectives on Politics* 12, no. 3 (2014): 564–581; Benjamin I. Page and Martin Gilens, *Democracy in America: What Has Gone Wrong and What We Can Do about It* (Chicago: University of Chicago Press, 2017); cf. Jeffrey R. Lax, Justin H. Phillips, and Adam Zelizer, "The Party or the Purse? Unequal Representation in the US Senate," *American Political Science Review* 113, no. 4 (2019): 917–940.

13. Insofar as it does not fit into predominant explanations of group influence, the NRA might be thought of as an outlier. Analytically, outliers are particularly useful for identifying new causal pathways to outcomes of interest because they share those outcomes with other cases that have different causes; put differently, an examination of the NRA is likely to be fruitful for developing new understandings of interest group influence because (1) it is a seemingly very influential group but (2) the causes of its influence appear to differ from those of other powerful groups. As such, although the theoretical framework and empirical investigation presented here are built around the case of the NRA, the insights produced here may shed light on other cases as well. See Jason Seawright, *Multi-Method Social Science: Combining Qualitative and Quantitative Tools* (Cambridge: Cambridge University Press, 2016); and Jason Seawright and John Gerring, "Case Selection Techniques

in Case Study Research: A Menu of Qualitative and Quantitative Options," *Political Research Quarterly* 61, no. 2 (2008): 294–308.

14. Nate Silver, "Party Identity in a Gun Cabinet," *FiveThirtyEight*, December 18, 2012, https://fivethirtyeight.blogs.nytimes.com/2012/12/18/in-gun-ownership-statistics-partisan-divide-is-sharp/.

15. Jarrett Murphy, "How the Gun Industry Got Rich Stoking Fear about Obama," *The Nation*, August 22, 2012, https://www.thenation.com/article/archive/how-gun-industry-got-rich-stoking-fear-about-obama/.

16. Robert Draper, "Inside the Power of the N.R.A," *New York Times Magazine*, December 12, 2013, https://www.nytimes.com/2013/12/15/magazine/inside-the-power-of-the-nra.html.

17. See Richard Harris, "If You Love Your Guns," *New Yorker*, April 20, 1968; Lee Kennett and James LaVerne Anderson, *The Gun in America: The Origins of a National Dilemma* (Westport, CT: Greenwood Press, 1975); Carol Skalnik Leff and Mark H. Leff, "The Politics of Ineffectiveness: Federal Firearms Legislation, 1919–1938," *ANNALS of the American Academy of Political and Social Science* 455, no. 1 (1981): 48–62; Robert J. Spitzer, *The Politics of Gun Control* (New York: Routledge, 2015).

18. Mark R. Joslyn, *The Gun Gap: The Influence of Gun Ownership on Political Behavior and Attitudes* (Oxford: Oxford University Press, 2020).

19. Howard Schuman and Stanley Presser, "The Attitude-Action Connection and the Issue of Gun Control," *ANNALS of the American Academy of Political and Social Science* 455, no. 1 (1981): 40–47; Kim Parker et al., "America's Complex Relationship with Guns," Pew Research Center report, June 22, 2017, http://www.pewsocialtrends.org/2017/06/22/americas-complex-relationship-with-guns/.

20. Lilliana Mason, "Guns and Abortion: How the Identities behind Issues Polarize American Politics," paper presented at the Annual Meeting of the American Political Science Association, San Francisco, CA, August 31–September 3, 2017.

21. Kristin A. Goss, *Disarmed: The Missing Movement for Gun Control in America* (Princeton, NJ: Princeton University Press, 2006).

22. Peter M. Aronow and Benjamin T. Miller, "Policy Misperceptions and Support for Gun Control Regulations," *The Lancet* 387, no. 10015 (2016): 23.

23. The National Firearms Act of 1934 still passed, but only after it was substantially watered down—or, as then-Assistant Attorney General Joseph Keenan described it, "emasculated" by the NRA. See Kennett and Anderson, *The Gun in America*, 211; and "Keep Those Letters and Telegrams Coming," *American Rifleman*, March 1934, 6.

24. Harris, "If You Love Your Guns."

25. Ibid., 57.

26. Draper, "Inside the Power of the N.R.A."; Laurent Bouton et al., "Guns and Votes," Working Paper (2016).

27. Although in recent times support for gun control is slightly less widespread when asked in general terms (as opposed to questions about specific gun control policies), majorities of Americans are still in favor of it. A Gallup poll in October 2018, for example, found that 61 percent of Americans believe that laws covering

the sale of firearms should be made stricter, with only 8 percent believing they should be less strict. Gallup has consistently asked that question since 1990 and has rarely found that less than a majority of Americans want stricter laws. See R. J. Reinhart, "Six in 10 Americans Support Stricter Gun Laws," Gallup News, October 17, 2018, https://news.gallup.com/poll/243797/six-americans-support-stricter-gun-laws.aspx.

28. Hazel Erksine, "The Polls: Gun Control," *Public Opinion Quarterly* 36, no. 3 (1972): 455–469.

29. "Continued Bipartisan Support for Expanded Background Checks on Gun Sales," Pew Research Center report, August 13, 2015, http://www.people-press.org/2015/08/13/continued-bipartisan-support-for-expanded-background-checks-on-gun-sales/; Parker et al., "America's Complex Relationship with Guns."

30. Roberto A. Ferdman, "The Unusual Story of America's First Mass Shooting," *Washington Post*, December 3, 2015.

31. Calculated using CDC data at https://wonder.cdc.gov/ucd-icd10.html.

32. "American Deaths in Terrorist Attacks, 1995–2016," National Consortium for the Study of Terrorism and Responses to Terrorism, November 2017, https://www.start.umd.edu/pubs/START_AmericanTerrorismDeaths_FactSheet_Nov2017.pdf.

33. Sarah Mervosh, "Nearly 40,000 People Died from Guns in U.S. Last Year, Highest in 50 Years," *New York Times*, December 18, 2018, A19.

34. Nicholas Kristof, "Kristof: Lessons from the Virginia Shooting," *New York Times*, August 26, 2015, A23.

35. Joe Palazzolo and Alexis Flynn, "U.S. Leads World in Mass Shootings," *Wall Street Journal*, October 3, 2015.

36. The Global Burden of Disease 2016 Injury Collaborators, "Global Mortality from Firearms, 1990–2016," *JAMA* 320, no. 8 (2018): 792–814.

37. German Lopez, "How Gun Control Works in America, Compared with 4 Other Rich Countries," *Vox*, March 14, 2018, https://www.vox.com/policy-and-politics/2015/12/4/9850572/gun-control-us-japan-switzerland-uk-canada; German Lopez, "A New, Huge Review of Gun Research Has Bad News for the NRA," *Vox*, https://www.vox.com/policy-and-politics/2018/3/2/17050610/guns-shootings-studies-rand-charts-maps.

38. Robert J. Spitzer, *Guns across America: Reconciling Rules and Rights* (Oxford: Oxford University Press, 2015); "The Effects of Stand-Your-Ground Laws," RAND Institute Research Review, April 22, 2020, https://www.rand.org/research/gun-policy/analysis/stand-your-ground.html#fn1; "The Effects of Concealed Carry Laws," RAND Institute Research Review, April 22, 2020, https://www.rand.org/research/gun-policy/analysis/concealed-carry.html.

39. Alexander DeConde, *Gun Violence in America: The Struggle for Control* (Boston: Northeastern University Press, 2001), 89.

40. James B. Trefethen and James E. Serven, *Americans and Their Guns: The National Rifle Association Story through Nearly a Century of Service to the Nation* (Harrisburg, PA: Stackpole Books, 1967).

41. "Speech Notes Memo from Lister to Edson," January 3, 1950, Box 15, Merritt Edson Papers, Library of Congress.

42. DeConde, *Gun Violence in America*, 99–103.

43. The surplus program, massively popular throughout much of the twentieth century, continues even today (although the NRA membership requirement was dropped in 1979). See Josh Sugarmann, *National Rifle Association: Money, Firepower & Fear* (Washington, DC: National Press Books, 1992), 109–113; and Spitzer, *The Politics of Gun Control*, 96.

44. Osha Gray Davidson, *Under Fire: The NRA and the Battle for Gun Control* (Iowa City: University of Iowa Press, 1998), 27–28; DeConde, *Gun Violence in America*, 102–103; Spitzer, *The Politics of Gun Control*, 94–96; Kennett and Anderson, *The Gun in America*, 138–140, 205–206.

45. Edward F. Leddy, *Magnum Force Lobby: The National Rifle Association Fights Gun Control* (Lanham, MD: University Press of America, 1987), 65.

46. John Scofield, "C. B. Lister Dies," *American Rifleman*, June, 1951, 12–13; "Build NRA," *American Rifleman*, January 1960, 14.

47. Leddy, *Magnum Force Lobby*, 72–73; Spitzer, *The Politics of Gun Control*, 94; "The NRA Accepts a Kennedy Challenge," *American Rifleman*, October 1972, 20.

48. "NRA Activities in 1969," *American Rifleman*, June 1970, 39–40.

49. George Dohrmann, "Split Leaves U.S. Team Short of Its Target," *Los Angeles Times*, July 8, 1995; "Competitive Shooting Programs," NRA website, accessed January 23, 2019, https://competitions.nra.org/.

50. Leddy, *Magnum Force Lobby*, 235.

51. "Shall-issue" states are those that require a permit to carry a concealed weapon, but do not give granting authorities any discretion to deny applicants (instead requiring that all individuals who meet specified criteria be issued a license). At the time of writing, most states have shall-issue laws.

52. Jennifer Carlson, *Citizen-Protectors: The Everyday Politics of Guns in an Age of Decline* (Oxford: Oxford University Press, 2015), 64.

53. In addition to its previously mentioned lobbying and political advocacy arm—the Institute for Legislative Action (NRA-ILA)—the NRA has a political action committee called the Political Victory Fund (NRA-PVF). The group also maintains several affiliated charitable organizations, which provide grants to organizations to develop shooting programs, administer a "Trigger the Vote" program geared toward voter registration, and provide support to individuals involved in firearms-related lawsuits. The original organization—central to all of these suborganizations and still chartered in New York—is legally established as a tax-exempt nonprofit, which is registered as the National Rifle Association of America. See https://www.nrapvf.org/about-pvf/; https://www.nrafoundation.org/; https://www.nrafaf.org/programs/; https://www.nradefensefund.org/; and https://www.nradefensefund.org/. Also see Samuel Brunson, "Is the NRA an Educational Organization? A Lobby Group? A Nonprofit? A Media Outlet? Yes," *The Conversation*, March 12, 2018, https://theconversation.com/is-the-nra-an-educational-organization-a-lobby-group-a-nonprofit-a-media-outlet-yes-92806.

54. See https://membership.nra.org/. Based on circulation of NRA magazines, some experts argue that this number is an overestimate; regardless of the exact number of current members, however, the NRA has continued to grow over time.

55. See https://stateassociations.nra.org/find-your-state-association/.

Chapter 2: Explaining the NRA's Power

1. Eric Lipton and Alexander Burns, "The True Source of the NRA's Clout: Money, Not Donations," *New York Times*, February 25, 2018, A1.

2. This idea is related to Daniel Carpenter's discussion of conceptual power in the context of regulatory policy—in which he describes how the Food and Drug Administration is able "to shape fundamental patterns of thought, communication, and learning" among a certain set of actors—except it is applied to an organized interest group rather than a government agency. See Daniel Carpenter, *Reputation and Power: Organizational Image and Pharmaceutical Regulation at the FDA* (Princeton, NJ: Princeton University Press, 2010), 64.

3. This argument extends Ken Kollman's "outside lobbying" concept—in which interest groups attempt to influence politics by altering mass behavior—by explaining how groups can build resources that enable them to shape their supporters' behavior in ways that have important impacts on policy outcomes. That is, this study helps explain how and why groups like the NRA are so effective at outside lobbying. See Ken Kollman, *Outside Lobbying: Public Opinion and Interest Group Strategies* (Princeton, NJ: Princeton University Press, 1998). The explanation of the NRA's influence offered here also extends prominent theories about the purpose of lobbying focused on information transmission and legislative subsidy. John Mark Hansen, in his study of the farm lobby, argues that interest groups are effective when they are able to provide reelection-minded legislators with useful, private information about voter preferences. In a related but different argument, Richard Hall and Alan Deardorff argue that successful interest groups give "legislative subsidies" designed to make their allies in Congress more effective legislators, providing their friends with "costly policy information, political intelligence, and labor." The NRA, however, not only provides policymakers with useful information about the preferences of a particular set of voters, but also alters those voters' preferences in ways that align with its policy agenda and make them more valuable to elected officials. See John Mark Hansen, *Gaining Access: Congress and the Farm Lobby, 1919–1981* (Chicago: University of Chicago Press, 1991); and Richard L. Hall and Alan V. Deardorff, "Lobbying as Legislative Subsidy," *American Political Science Review* 100, no. 1 (2006): 69–84.

4. A bit more specifically, Henri Tajfel—whose groundbreaking work launched social identity theory—argues that a social identity consists of the aspect of an individual's self-understanding that results from knowledge of his or her membership in a social group, combined with the personal significance the individual attaches to that group membership. See Henri Tajfel, *Human Groups and Social Categories: Studies in Social Psychology* (New York: Cambridge University Press, 1981).

5. Scholarly work on the importance of group memberships goes all the way back to Arthur Bentley in 1908 and continued through the seminal work of the Columbia and Michigan schools. See Arthur F. Bentley, *The Process of Government: A Study of Social Pressures* (Chicago: University of Chicago Press, 1908); Bernard R. Berelson, Paul F. Lazarsfeld, and William N. McPhee, *Voting* (Chicago: University of Chicago Press, 1954); Angus Campbell et al., *The American Voter* (New York: John Wiley and Sons, 1960). More recent scholarship by Christopher Achen and Larry Bartels—tapping into this long but sometimes dormant tradition in American politics—emphasizes the crucial importance of identity to political behavior. See Christopher H. Achen and Larry M. Bartels, *Democracy for Realists: Why Elections Do Not Produce Responsive Government* (Princeton, NJ: Princeton University Press, 2016) for both a contribution to and a review of literature on the importance of group memberships for political behavior.

6. Campbell et al., *The American Voter.*

7. Michael C. Dawson, *Behind the Mule: Race and Class in African-American Politics* (Princeton, NJ: Princeton University Press, 1994); Ismail K. White and Chryl N. Laird, *Steadfast Democrats: How Social Forces Shape Black Political Behavior* (Princeton, NJ: Princeton University Press, 2020).

8. Donald Green, Bradley Palmquist, and Eric Schickler, *Partisan Hearts and Minds: Political Parties and the Social Identities of Voters* (New Haven, CT: Yale University Press, 2002); Craig McGarty et al., "Collective Action as the Material Expression of Opinion-Based Group Membership," *Journal of Social Issues* 65, no. 4 (2009): 839–857.

9. Katherine J. Cramer, *The Politics of Resentment: Rural Consciousness in Wisconsin and the Rise of Scott Walker* (Chicago: University of Chicago Press, 2016).

10. Lilliana Mason, *Uncivil Agreement: How Politics Became Our Identity* (Chicago: University of Chicago Press, 2018).

11. Alexandra Filindra and Noah J. Kaplan, "Racial Resentment and Whites' Gun Policy Preferences in Contemporary America," *Political Behavior* 38 (2015): 255–275; Alexandra Filindra and Noah J. Kaplan, "Testing Theories of Gun Policy Preferences among Blacks, Latinos, and Whites in America," *Social Science Quarterly* 98, no. 2 (2017): 413–428; Scott Melzer, *Gun Crusaders: The NRA's Culture War* (New York: New York University Press, 2009); Jennifer Carlson, *Citizen-Protectors: The Everyday Politics of Guns in an Age of Decline* (Oxford: Oxford University Press, 2015); Jennifer Carlson and Kristin A. Goss, "Gendering the Second Amendment," *Law and Contemporary Problems* 80 (2017): 103–128; R. W. Connell, *Masculinities*, 2nd ed. (Berkeley: University of California Press, 2005); Mark R. Joslyn et al., "Emerging Political Identities? Gun Ownership and Voting in Presidential Elections," *Social Science Quarterly* 98, no. 2 (2017): 382–396.

12. An exception to this is Elisabeth Clemens's excellent study of the dawn of US interest group politics during the late nineteenth and early twentieth centuries. Describing organized groups as potential "templates for collective identity," Clemens argues that early groups representing workers, farmers, and women "promulgated delimited collective identities" related to membership in those groups,

which stood in contrast to broader partisan identities and helped drive collective action. My study builds on Clemens's by identifying and measuring more specific mechanisms through which organized groups can cultivate and disseminate identities before using them to their political advantage. See Elisabeth S. Clemens, *The People's Lobby: Organizational Innovation and the Rise of Interest Groups Politics in the United States, 1890–1925* (Chicago: University of Chicago Press, 1997), 11, 321.

13. Wayne LaPierre, "Standing Guard," *American Rifleman*, July 2002, 12.

14. According to social identity theory (SIT), individuals are motivated to categorize people into distinct groups and to identify with some of those groups in order to make sense of complex social situations and reduce uncertainty. Further, individuals desire a *positive* sense of self, motivating them to emphasize positive qualities of their group's identity and—especially when they sense that the group is threatened—to juxtapose those positive qualities with the perceived negative qualities of out-groups. See John C. Turner, "Towards a Cognitive Redefinition of the Social Group," in *Social Identity and Intergroup Relations*, ed. Henri Tajfel (Cambridge: Cambridge University Press, 1982), 15–40; Michael A Hogg, "Subjective Uncertainty Reduction through Self-Categorization: A Motivational Theory of Social Identity Processes," *European Review of Social Psychology* 11, no. 1 (2000): 223–255; Gordon W. Allport, *The Nature of Prejudice* (Cambridge, MA: Addison-Wesley, 1954); Marilynn B. Brewer, "The Psychology of Prejudice: Ingroup Love and Outgroup Hate?," *Journal of Social Issues* 55, no. 3 (1999): 429–444; Daniel Balliet, Junhui Wu, and Carsten K. W. De Dreu, "Ingroup Favoritism in Cooperation: A Meta-Analysis," *Psychological Bulletin* 140, no. 6 (2014): 1556–1581.

15. There actually is some evidence that sports can impact individuals' political attitudes under the right conditions. See Ethan C. Busby, James N. Druckman, and Alexandria Fredendall, "The Political Relevance of Irrelevant Events," *Journal of Politics* 79, no. 1 (2016): 346–350; and Andrew J. Healy, Neil Maholtra, and Cecilia Hyunjung Mo, "Irrelevant Events Affect Voters' Evaluations of Government Performance," *Proceedings of the National Academy of Sciences* 107, no. 29 (2010): 12804–12809.

16. Bernd Simon and Bert Klandermans, "Politicized Collective Identity: A Social Psychological Analysis," *American Psychologist* 56, no. 4 (2001): 319–331; Penelope Oakes, "The Salience of Social Categories," in *Rediscovering the Social Group*, ed. John C. Turner et al. (New York: Blackwell, 1987), 117–141; Jerome S. Bruner, "On Perceptual Readiness," *Psychological Review* 64, no. 2 (1957): 123–152.

17. "Unorganized Hunters Need Your Help," *American Rifleman*, December 1970, 16.

18. Leonie Huddy, Lilliana Mason, and Lene Aarøe, "Expressive Partisanship: Campaign Involvement, Political Emotion, and Partisan Identity," *American Political Science Review* 109, no. 1 (2015): 1–17; Peter Nauroth et al., "Social Identity Threat Motivates Science-Discrediting Online Comments," *PLoS ONE* 10, no. 2 (2015): e0117476; Samara Klar, "The Influence of Competing Identity Primes on Political Preferences," *Journal of Politics* 75, no. 4 (2013): 1108–1124; Claude M. Steele, *Whistling Vivaldi* (New York: W. W. Norton & Company, 2010); Diane M.

Mackie, Thierry Devos, and Eliot R. Smith, "Intergroup Emotions: Explaining Offensive Action Tendencies in an Intergroup Context," *Journal of Personality and Social Psychology* 79, no. 4 (2000): 602–616; Naomi Ellemers, "The Influence of Socio-structural Variables on Identity Management Strategies," *European Review of Social Psychology* 4, no. 1 (1993): 27–57; Matthew J. Lacombe, Adam J. Howat, and Jacob E. Rothschild, "Gun Ownership as a Social Identity: Estimating Behavioral and Attitudinal Relationships," *Social Science Quarterly* 100, no. 6 (2019): 2408–2424.

19. Mancur Olson famously argued that organized groups face substantial "free rider" problems in which potential members are tempted to coast on the efforts of others rather than contributing to a group's cause. Olson emphasized the *material*—tangible, often economic—selective incentives that groups offer to overcome these problems. Others, however, have suggested that groups might also offer nonmaterial, social and psychological incentives—including feelings of belongingness and social status, as well as the emotional, psychological benefits of publicly advancing a cause that one believes in—in order to overcome collective action problems. A group identity and ideology can be thought of as distinct types of social, psychological incentives that provide a reason to join the group. And beyond just assisting with the recruitment and retention of members (which is typically seen as the purpose of selective incentives), these resources are also useful for more directly advancing a group's policy agenda. Perceived threat to the gun owner identity, for example, likely motivates some gun owners to join the NRA. It can also, however, motivate them to take political action in defense of the group. In this sense, my analysis helps connect scholarship focused on interest group formation with scholarship focused on group influence. This perspective builds on Richard Skinner's discussion of the relationship between group membership incentives and electoral mobilization strategies, in which he notes that the NRA's appeal is largely related to purposive benefits and connects such benefits to its members' impact on elections. See Mancur Olson, *The Logic of Collective Action: Public Goods and the Theory of Groups* (Cambridge, MA: Harvard University Press, 1965); Peter B. Clark and James Q. Wilson, "Incentive Systems: A Theory of Organizations," *Administrative Science Quarterly* 6, no. 2 (1961): 129–166; Robert H. Salisbury, "An Exchange Theory of Interest Groups," *Midwest Journal of Political Science* 13, no. 1 (1969): 1–32; Richard M. Skinner, *More Than Money: Interest Group Action in Congressional Elections* (Lanham, MD: Rowman and Littlefield, 2007).

20. Alexander Hertel-Fernandez, Matto Mildenberger, and Leah C. Stokes, "Legislative Staff and Representation in Congress," *American Political Science Review* 13, no. 1 (2019): 1–18; David C. Broockman and Christopher Skovron, "Bias in Perceptions of Public Opinion among Political Elites," *American Political Science Review* 112, no. 3 (2018): 542–563.

21. On gun owner support for background checks: Kim Parker et al., "America's Complex Relationship with Guns," Pew Research Center report, June 22, 2017, http://www.pewsocialtrends.org/2017/06/22/americas-complex-relationship -with-guns/.

22. Robert Draper, "Inside the Power of the N.R.A," *New York Times Magazine*, December 12, 2013, https://www.nytimes.com/2013/12/15/magazine/inside-the -power-of-the-nra.html.

23. Mason, *Uncivil Agreement*; McGarty et al., "Collective Action as the Material Expression of Opinion-Based Group Membership."

24. Kim Parker, "Among Gun Owners, NRA Members Have a Unique Set of Views and Experiences," Pew Research Center report, July 5, 2017, http://www .pewresearch.org/fact-tank/2017/07/05/among-gun-owners-nra-members-have -a-unique-set-of-views-and-experiences/.

25. My definition of ideology is informed by Philip E. Converse, "The Nature of Belief Systems in Mass Publics," in *Ideology and Discontent*, ed. David E. Apter (New York: Free Press, 1964), 206–261; John Gerring, "Ideology: A Definitional Analysis," *Political Research Quarterly* 50, no. 4 (1997): 957–994; Hans Noel, *Political Ideologies and Political Parties in America* (Cambridge: Cambridge University Press, 2013), 41; Frances E. Lee, *Beyond Ideology: Politics, Principles, and Partisanship in the U.S. Senate* (Chicago: University of Chicago Press, 2009), 27; and Kathleen Knight, "Transformations of the Concept of Ideology in the Twentieth Century," *American Political Science Review* 100, no. 4 (2006): 619–626, 625.

26. "Marjorie Dannenfelser at #CPAC2019: Abortion, Human Dignity, and What Makes America Great," Susan B. Anthony List website, accessed March 26, 2020, https://www.sba-list.org/marjorie-dannenfelser-cpac-2019.

27. Noel, *Political Ideologies*; Hans Noel, "The Coalition Merchants: The Ideological Roots of the Civil Rights Realignment," *Journal of Politics* 74, no. 1 (2012): 156–173; David Karol, *Party Position Change in American Politics: Coalition Management* (Cambridge: Cambridge University Press, 2009); David Karol, *Red, Green, and Blue: The Partisan Divide on Environmental Issues* (Cambridge: Cambridge University Press, 2019).

28. John Gerring, *Party Ideologies in America, 1828–1996* (Cambridge: Cambridge University Press, 1998).

29. Noel, *Political Ideologies*.

30. My analysis builds on predominant existing theories of ideological development, most notably that of Hans Noel. While some (such as John Gerring) have argued that ideologies are created by politicians and/or party leaders, Noel argues that ideologies are formed by political thinkers—"ideologues" whom he describes as "coalition merchants"—consisting of intellectuals, pundits, and other advocates who package a set of issues together and then market those issue sets to parties in the hope that they will be adopted. My approach follows Noel's in the sense that it focuses on how political actors who were operating outside of parties created an ideology and disseminated it to individuals on the mass level. More specifically, in arguing that the NRA has successfully cultivated a political ideology among its supporters, I show that the NRA has served, in Noel's terms, as an ideologue—an ideological developer—by linking gun rights to a number of other political issues and beliefs, forming a coherent, differentiated political ideology in which support for gun rights is seen as one important part of a broader political worldview.

See Noel, *Political Ideologies and Political Parties in America*; and Gerring, *Party Ideologies in America*.

31. Mason, *Uncivil Agreement*; Lilliana Mason, "Distinguishing the Polarizing Effects of Ideology as Identity, Issue Positions, and Issue-Based Identity," paper presented at the Center for the Study of Democratic Politics Conference on Political Polarization: Media and Communication Influences, 2015; Lilliana Mason and Julie Wronski, "One Tribe to Bind Them All: How Our Social Group Attachments Strengthen Partisanship," *Political Psychology* 39, S1 (2018): 257–277.

32. See, among others, Marc Mauer and Ryan S. King, *Uneven Justice: State Rates of Incarceration by Race and Ethnicity* (Washington, DC: Sentencing Project, 2007); Michelle Alexander, *The New Jim Crow: Mass Incarceration in the Age of Colorblindness* (New York: New Press, 2010); Heather Ann Thompson, "Why Mass Incarceration Matters: Rethinking Crisis, Decline and Transformation in Postwar American History," *Journal of American History* 97, no. 3 (2010): 703–734; Bruce Western, *Punishment and Inequality in America* (New York: Russell Sage Foundation Publications, 2006), 49–50; Vesla M. Weaver, "Frontlash: Race and the Development of Punitive Crime Policy," *Studies in American Political Development* 21, no. 2 (2007): 230–265.

33. Wayne LaPierre, "Standing Guard," *American Rifleman*, December 1993, 7.

34. J. Warren Cassidy, "Here We Stand," *American Rifleman*, October 1987, 7.

35. Filindra and Kaplan, "Racial Resentment and Whites' Gun Policy Preferences."

36. Sheryl Gay Stolberg, Maggie Haberman, and Jonathan Martin, "Trump Weighs New Stance on Guns as Pressure Mounts after Shootings," *New York Times*, August 8, 2019, https://www.nytimes.com/2019/08/08/us/politics/gun-background-checks.html.

37. John Parkinson, "'We Have to Have Meaningful Background Checks' Trump Says, but NRA's 'Strong Views' Must Be 'Respected,'" *ABC News*, August 9, 2019, https://abcnews.go.com/Politics/trump-signals-support-gun-background-checks-nras-strong/story?id=64877305.

38. Maggie Haberman, Annie Karni, and Danny Hakim, "N.R.A. Gets Results on Gun Laws in One Phone Call with Trump," *New York Times*, August 21, 2019, A1.

39. Michael Zoorob and Theda Skocpol, "The Overlooked Organizational Basis of Trump's 2016 Victory," in *Upending American Politics: Polarizing Parties, Ideological Elites, and Citizen Activists from the Tea Party to the Anti-Trump Resistance*, ed. Theda Skocpol and Caroline Tervo (Oxford: Oxford University Press, 2020), 79–100.

40. See, among others, Kathleen Bawn et al., "A Theory of Political Parties: Groups, Policy Demands and Nominations in American Politics," *Perspectives on Politics* 10, no. 3 (2012): 571–597; Marty Cohen et al., *The Party Decides* (Chicago: University of Chicago Press, 2008); Katherine Krimmel, "The Efficiencies and Pathologies of Special Interest Partisanship," *Studies in American Political Development* 31, no. 2 (2017): 149–169; Karol, *Party Position Change*; Christopher Baylor, *First to the Party: The Group Origins of Political Transformation* (Philadelphia:

University of Pennsylvania Press, 2018). For classic scholarship that inspired some of this work, see V. O. Key, *Politics, Parties, and Pressure Groups* (New York: Thomas Y. Crowell Company, 1942); E. E. Schattschneider, *Party Government* (New York: Rinehart and Winston, 1942); Schattschneider, *The Semi-Sovereign People* (New York: Holt, Rinehart, and Wilson, 1960).

41. Anthony Downs, *An Economic Theory of Democracy* (New York: Harper & Row, 1957); John Aldrich, *Why Parties? The Origin and Transformation of Political Parties in America* (Chicago: University of Chicago Press, 1995).

42. Jacob S. Hacker and Paul Pierson, "After the Master Theory: Downs, Schattschneider, and the Rebirth of Policy-Focused Analysis," *Perspectives on Politics* 12, no. 3 (2014): 643–662.

43. Existing scholarship on party-group interactions has addressed some related questions, including why party-group relations have become increasingly strong in recent decades (Krimmel, "Efficiencies and Pathologies"), how ideological coalitions and party coalitions interact (Noel, *Political Ideologies*, 32–35), and the role that crucial "anchoring groups"—such as organized labor and the Christian Right—play in shaping "parties' long-term trajectories" and "ideological developments" (Daniel Schlozman, *When Movements Anchor Parties: Electoral Realignment in American History* [Princeton, NJ: Princeton University Press, 2015], 3). Finally, and perhaps most directly related, David Karol explores the processes through which parties change their issue positions over time, noting that new groups are sometimes incorporated into parties after party leaders adopt positions in the hope of attracting them—a process that Karol argues occurred in the case of gun control (Karol, *Party Position Change*). Issue evolution models—which describe processes in which political elites adopt stances on particular issues that are then adopted by the masses in ways that alter each political party—are also somewhat relevant, but often do not focus on the interactions between organized groups and parties themselves or on the conditions that lead to party elites adopting new stances in the first place. See Edward G. Carmines and James A. Stimson, *Issue Evolution: Race and the Transformation of American Politics* (Princeton, NJ: Princeton University Press, 1989).

44. Following Katherine Krimmel, my discussion defines parties as durable coalitions of politicians, their subordinates, and the individuals who comprise the organizations that support their election. Parties, in this view, manage coalitions of groups with which they have formed durable alliances, and these groups provide the parties with resources that help them win elections. This definition—which, unlike other group-centric definitions of parties, does not argue that groups themselves are parties—is useful because it enables me to examine the distinct incentives that lead, on the one hand, a particular party, and, on the other hand, a particular group to form an alliance. See Krimmel, "Efficiencies and Pathologies."

45. Paul Frymer, *Uneasy Alliances: Race and Party Competition in America* (Princeton, NJ: Princeton University Press, 1999); Paul Frymer and John David Skrentny, "Coalition-Building and the Politics of Electoral Capture during the Nixon Administration: African Americans, Labor, Latinos," *Studies in American*

Political Development 12 (1998): 131–161; J. David Greenstone, *Labor in American Politics* (New York: Knopf, 1969).

46. Schlozman, *When Movements Anchor Parties*, 19.

47. Indeed, Vermont Senator Bernie Sanders actually benefitted from the NRA's opposition to his Republican opponent in 1990. Sanders—at that time the ex-mayor of Burlington who had repeatedly been unable to win higher office—was a Socialist candidate for Vermont's only House seat. His opponent, incumbent Republican Peter Smith, supported an assault weapons ban, which led to intense retaliation from the NRA. Sanders beat Smith and then went on to become a senator and presidential contender. See David A. Farenthold, "How the National Rifle Association Helped Get Bernie Sanders Elected," *Washington Post*, July 19, 2015.

48. Harry Enten, "The NRA Used to Be Much More Bipartisan. Now It's Mostly Just a Wing of the GOP," CNN Politics, February 24, 2018 https://www.cnn.com/2018/02/24/politics/nra-partisan-bipartisan-republican/index.html; Center for Responsive Politics, "National Rifle Association Contributions," accessed January 20, 2019, https://www.opensecrets.org/orgs/totals.php?id=d000000082&cycle=2018.

49. David Karol, "Party Activists, Interest Groups, and Polarization in American Politics," in *American Gridlock: The Sources, Character, and Impact of Political Polarization*, ed. James A. Thurber and Antoine Yoshinaka (New York: Cambridge University Press, 2015), 68–85; Mark Hensch, "NRA Makes $1M Ad Buy to Tout Gorsuch: Report," *The Hill*, March 13, 2017, https://thehill.com/regulation/court-battles/323809-nra-makes-1m-ad-buy-to-tout-gorsuch-report; Nicole Gaudiano, "NRA Ad Campaign Urges Supreme Court Nominee Brett Kavanaugh's Confirmation," *USA Today*, August 7, 2018, https://www.usatoday.com/story/news/politics/onpolitics/2018/08/07/national-rifle-association-ad-brett-kavanaugh-confirmation/923026002/.

50. Ali Watkins, "How the N.R.A. Keeps Federal Gun Regulators in Check," *New York Times*, February 23, 2018, A12.

51. "NRA-PVF Endorses McCain," National Rifle Association, October 9, 2009, https://www.nraila.org/articles/20081009/nra-pvf-endorses-mccain; "NRA Endorses Bush for President," Fox News, October 13, 2004, https://www.foxnews.com/story/nra-endorses-bush-for-president; "NRA-PVF Endorses Mitt Romney and Paul Ryan for President and Vice President," National Rifle Association, October 4, 2012, https://www.nrapvf.org/articles/20121004/nra-pvf-endorses-romney-and-ryan (site discontinued); Ashley Parker, "Donald Trump Tells N.R.A. Hillary Clinton Wants to Let Violent Criminals Go Free," *New York Times*, May 20, 2016, A1.

52. Robert Maguire, "Audit Shows NRA Spending Surged $100 Million amidst Pro-Trump Push in 2016," *OpenSecrets News*, November 15, 2017, https://www.opensecrets.org/news/2017/11/audit-shows-nra-spending-surged-100-million-amidst-pro-trump-push-in-2016/.

53. Ana Santos and The Associated Press, "What Donald Trump Said during Atlanta's NRA Convention: 'No Longer Will Federal Agencies Be Coming

after Law-Abiding Gun Owners,'" *Atlanta Journal-Constitution*, October 2, 2017; Seung Min Kim, "At NRA Event, Trump Embraces Its Agenda in Campaign-Style Speech," *Washington Post*, May 4, 2018.

54. Brian F. Schaffner, Matthew Macwilliams, and Tatishe Nteta, "Understanding White Polarization in the 2016 Vote for President: The Sobering Role of Racism and Sexism," *Political Science Quarterly* 133, no. 1 (2018): 9–34; Diana C. Mutz, "Status Threat, Not Economic Hardship, Explains the 2016 Presidential Vote," *PNAS* 115, no. 9 (2018): E4330–E4339; John Sides, Michael Tesler, and Lynn Vavreck, "The 2016 U.S. Election: How Trump Lost and Won," *Journal of Democracy* 28, no. 2 (2017): 34–44; Lacombe, Howat, and Rothschild, "Gun Ownership as a Social Identity"; Parker et al., "America's Complex Relationship with Guns," 2; Filindra and Kaplan, "Racial Resentment and Whites' Gun Policy Preferences"; Kerry O'Brien et al., "Racism, Gun Ownership and Gun Control: Biased Attitudes in US Whites May Influence Policy Decisions," *PLoS ONE* 8, no. 10 (2013): e77552–e77552; Kristin A. Goss, "The Socialization of Conflict and Its Limits: Gender and Gun Politics in America," *Social Science Quarterly* 98, no. 2 (2017): 455–470; Melzer, *Gun Crusaders*; Carlson, *Citizen-Protectors*; Carlson and Goss, "Gendering the Second Amendment"; Angela Stroud, "Good Guys with Guns: Hegemonic Masculinity and Concealed Handguns," *Gender and Society* 26, no. 2 (2012): 216–238; Angela Stroud, *Good Guys with Guns: The Appeal and Consequences of Concealed Carry* (Chapel Hill: University of North Carolina Press, 2016); Connell, *Masculinities*; David Yamane, "Awash in a Sea of Faith and Firearms: Rediscovering the Connection between Religion and Gun Ownership in America," *Journal for the Scientific Study of Religion* 55, no. 3 (2016): 622–636; Stephen M. Merino, "God and Guns: Examining Religious Influences on Gun Control Attitudes in the United States," *Religions* 9, no. 6 (2018): 189–202; Andrew L. Whitehead, Landon Schnabel, and Samuel L. Perry, "Gun Control in the Crosshairs: Christian Nationalism and Opposition to Stricter Gun Laws," *Socius: Sociological Research for a Dynamic World* 4 (2018): 1–13; Andrew L. Whitehead, Samuel L. Perry, and Joseph O. Baker, "Make America Christian Again: Christian Nationalism and Voting for Donald Trump in the 2016 Presidential Election," *Sociology of Religion* 79, no. 2 (2018): 147–171; Parker, "Among Gun Owners."

55. This insight aligns with what Michele Margolis finds in her study of the relationship between partisan identity and religious identity. Whereas most scholars have argued that individuals' religious identities are a cause of their partisan identities, Margolis demonstrates that partisan identity can actually shape religious identity. In other words, an explicitly political group membership—party affiliation—can impact the other identities that individuals hold. My argument here is similar in terms of linking political factors—in this case, the alignment between groups that are included in a party coalition—to the identities that are held by members of each of those groups. See Michele F. Margolis, *From Politics to the Pews: How Partisanship and the Political Environment Shape Religious Identity* (Chicago: University of Chicago Press, 2018).

56. The importance of this is underscored by other recent work, including Eric Schickler's excellent study of the civil rights realignment. Eric Schickler, *Racial*

Realignment: The Transformation of American Liberalism, 1932–1965 (Princeton, NJ: Princeton University Press, 2016). Also see Neil A. O'Brian, "Before Reagan: The Development of Abortion's Partisan Divide," *Perspectives on Politics*, published online December 2, 2019, https://www.cambridge.org/core/journals/perspectives-on-politics/article/before-reagan-the-development-of-abortions-partisan-divide/64965291B3DFCD73A0E4F4451B4437E1.

57. Robert A. Dahl, *Who Governs?: Democracy and Power in an American City* (New Haven, CT: Yale University Press, 1961).

58. Peter Bachrach and Morton S. Baratz, "Two Faces of Power," *American Political Science Review* 56, no. 4 (1962): 947–952.

59. Steven Lukes, *Power: A Radical View* (London: Macmillan, 1974); John Gaventa, *Power and Powerlessness: Quiescence and Rebellion in an Appalachian Valley* (Urbana, IL: University of Illinois Press, 1982).

60. For a useful discussion of this, see Paul Pierson, "Power in Historical Institutionalism," in *The Oxford Handbook of Historical Institutionalism*, ed. Orfeo Fioretos, Tulia G. Falleti, and Adam Sheingate (Oxford: Oxford University Press, 2016), 124–141.

Chapter 3: The Political Weaponization of Gun Owners: The NRA and Gun Ownership as Social Identity

1. Quoted in Richard Lacayo, "Under Fire," *Time*, June 24, 2001, http://content.time.com/time/magazine/article/0,9171,153695,00.html.

2. David Keene, "Election 2012: On Guns . . . and Values," *American Rifleman*, August 2012, 14.

3. The NRA has gradually added additional publications, also "official journals," to its offerings. While the content of these publications differs, all contain some identical sections, including editorials, columns written by group leaders, and discussions of organizational matters. The *American Rifleman* is the oldest of these publications, has the most general focus, and is more circulated than the others combined.

4. The specific technique I used—discussed in the appendix—is the Structural Topic Model. See Margaret E. Roberts et al., "Structural Topic Models for Open-Ended Survey Responses," *American Journal of Political Science* 58, no. 4 (2014): 1064–1082.

5. I intentionally excluded letters to the editor that were written by political elites and/or paid NRA officials.

6. Using a combination of ProQuest databases and the newspapers' own online archives, I searched for "(gun OR firearm) AND (law OR legislation)." When using ProQuest, I limited my searches to letters to the editor. When using newspapers' own archives—which lacked the functionality to limit searches to particular sections of the papers—I added "AND (letter)" to the search terms above. I then manually went through each hit to eliminate false positives that either were not letters to the editor or did not actually pertain to gun control.

7. Never mind the fact that, as Robert Spitzer demonstrates, the early United States imposed substantial regulations on the ownership and use of guns; see *Guns across America: Reconciling Rules and Rights* (Oxford: Oxford University Press, 2015).

8. Wayne LaPierre, "Standing Guard," *American Rifleman*, July 1999, 10.

9. Identity salience is a product of *accessibility* (i.e., which identities does one value and frequently employ?) and *fit* (which identities are relevant to the situation currently being confronted?). See Jerome S. Bruner, "On Perceptual Readiness," *Psychological Review* 64, no. 2 (1957): 123–152; and Penelope Oakes, "The Salience of Social Categories," in *Rediscovering the Social Group*, ed. John C. Turner et al. (New York: Blackwell, 1987), 117–141.

10. See the appendix for more detailed discussion of coding rules.

11. Letters from gun control supporters would obviously refer to different in-groups and out-groups than the NRA editorials and pro-gun letters. The letters of gun control supporters were coded based on whether they describe gun control supporters collectively using positive characteristics and/or gun control opponents using negative characteristics.

12. Calling writers who favor gun control laws "anti-gun" is a bit of an oversimplification, as individuals who voice support for gun control laws may nonetheless enjoy firearms and support their use in certain contexts. Nonetheless, this phrase is useful shorthand for categorizing the letters to the editor I examine in this and the following chapter.

13. Gordon W. Allport, *The Nature of Prejudice* (Cambridge, MA: Addison-Wesley, 1954); Marilynn B. Brewer, "The Psychology of Prejudice: Ingroup Love and Outgroup Hate?," *Journal of Social Issues* 55, no. 3 (1999): 429–444; Daniel Balliet, Junhui Wu, and Carsten K. W. De Dreu, "Ingroup Favoritism in Cooperation: A Meta-Analysis," *Psychological Bulletin* 140, no. 6 (2014): 1556–1581.

14. Kim Parker et al., "America's Complex Relationship with Guns," Pew Research Center report, June 22, 2017, accessed January 7, 2019, http://www.pewsocialtrends.org/2017/06/22/americas-complex-relationship-with-guns/.

15. Matthew J. Lacombe, Adam J. Howat, and Jacob E. Rothschild, "Gun Ownership as a Social Identity: Estimating Behavioral and Attitudinal Relationships," *Social Science Quarterly* 100, no. 6 (2019): 2408–2424; Lilliana Mason, "Guns and Abortion: How the Identities behind Issues Polarize American Politics," paper presented at the Annual Meeting of the American Political Science Association, San Francisco, CA, August 31–September 3, 2017.

16. Bindu Kalesan et al., "Gun Ownership and Social Gun Culture," *Injury Prevention* 22, no. 3 (2016): 216–220.

17. I used Google's Ngram Viewer to measure the distinctiveness of each of the most frequently used in-group positive/out-group negative phrases. The more frequently a word is used in the Google corpus, the less distinctive it is.

18. Dichotomous variables (indicating whether a phrase appeared in each year) were used to address problems related to cross-time differences in the number of total documents per year (particularly in letters to the editor), which make the use of absolute counts of phrases by year or proportion of documents with phrases by

year untenable. Absolute counts are problematic because they misleadingly make the relative use of phrases seem to increase during years in which gun control was salient and, as a result, a large number of letters were printed. Proportions are problematic as well, however, because they misleadingly make the relative use of phrases seem high in years in which gun control was not salient and, as a result, few letters were printed; the proportion of letters with a particular phrase in such a year may be higher than in years with more letters, even if only one or two letters use the phrase. The use of dichotomous variables addresses both of these issues. I estimated linear probability models in which the dependent variable is usage of each phrase in pro-gun letters to the editor and the primary independent variables are lagged measures of usage in the *American Rifleman*. I controlled for contemporaneous *American Rifleman* usage and included lagged measures of the dependent variable to control for past usage in letters. I use a linear probability model rather than a logit or probit model, which generally produces similar results as maximum-likelihood models while requiring fewer assumptions and/or potentially arbitrary modeling decisions. See Joshua D. Angrist and Jorn-Steffen Pischke, *Mostly Harmless Econometrics: An Empiricist's Companion* (Princeton, NJ: Princeton University Press, 2009), 102–107. As a check, I also estimated the relationship between the variables in the dataset using a Firth penalized likelihood logistic regression, which is appropriate here as it helps with the problems of separation and rare outcomes. The results do not substantively differ from those produced by the linear probability model. See David Firth, "Bias Reduction of Maximum Likelihood Estimates," *Biometrika* 80, no. 1 (1993): 27–38. Finally, note that each row of the table presents a single model, which means that the coefficients for each lag are conditional on the other lags; the results are very similar when each lag year is estimated in a separate model.

19. As a robustness check, I also reversed the direction of these models to measure whether lagged usage of phrases in pro-gun letters predicts usage in the *American Rifleman* (while controlling for past use in the *American Rifleman* and contemporaneous use in letters). All results are null and/or inconsistent with just one exception ("anti-gunners," for which the three-year lagged variable is significant).

20. These arguments are in many ways akin to what Cook and Leitzel, adapting Hirschman, describe as "jeopardy" arguments. See Philip J. Cook and James A. Leitzel, "Perversity, Futility, Jeopardy: An Economic Analysis of the Attack on Gun Control," *Law and Contemporary Problems* 59, no. 1 (1996): 91–118; and Albert O. Hirschman, *The Rhetoric of Reaction: Perversity, Futility, Jeopardy* (Cambridge, MA: Belknap, 1991).

21. Cosine similarity is a bag of words technique for measuring the similarity of two texts or two groups of texts. It compares a vector of word frequencies from one text or group of texts and compares them to a vector of word frequencies from another text or group of texts by measuring the angle between the two vectors (which makes it useful for comparing documents or document sets of different lengths). It ultimately produces a similarity score ranging from 0 (no common language) to 1 (identical).

22. As figure 3.1 shows, the theoretically driven time periods are 1930–1945, 1946–1962, 1963–1976, 1977–1991, and 1992–2008. The first cut-point (1945/1946) corresponds to end of World War II, at which time the NRA diversified its programmatic offerings to appeal to veterans of the war. The second cut-point (1962/1963) corresponds with the return of gun control to the national agenda following high-profile political assassinations (the first of which, John F. Kennedy's assassination, occurred in 1963) and rising crime rates. The third cut-point (1976/1977) corresponds with the takeover of the NRA by a group of activist members at the 1977 annual meeting, which led to important changes to the organization. The last cut-point (1991/1992) corresponds to the beginning of Wayne LaPierre's tenure as the NRA's top executive and his authorship of its editorials. The relatively long length of the time buckets is appropriate due to the likely slow pace at which identities are disseminated; we would not expect the themes with which NRA supporters associate gun ownership to change overnight but rather to shift slowly as the NRA gradually alters its discourse. The length of the time buckets also reflects a practical consideration related to statistical power; some years—especially early on in the period of study—have relatively few letters to the editor, which makes it difficult to draw statistically meaningful inferences across short time periods.

23. I produced these confidence intervals using bootstrapping (with 1,000 iterations), resampling with replacement on the document level.

24. To deal with this further, aside from removing a standard set of stopwords from the corpus prior to analysis, I also removed some case-specific stopwords that are likely to appear in many documents in the corpus but do not provide useful information about the substantive contents of the documents or differences between document types (e.g., letter, columnist, gun, firearm, etc.).

25. C. B. Lister, "Pattern in Red," *American Rifleman*, April 1948, 10.

26. "The Constitutional Right to Bear Arms," *Chicago Tribune*, February 13, 1955.

27. Public Mail, June 1968, White House Central Files, LE-JL 3, Box 94, Lyndon B. Johnson Library.

28. Quote from Scott Melzer, *Gun Crusaders: The NRA's Culture War* (New York: New York University Press, 2009), 120.

29. "The Silent Protectors," *American Rifleman*, January 1971, 28.

30. "Gun Control Laws," *New York Times*, August 31, 1971.

31. Public Mail, June 1968, White House Central Files, LE-JL 3, Boxes 110–112, Lyndon B. Johnson Library.

32. "More Guns, Less Crime," *American Rifleman*, July 1998, 20–21.

33. Ian Ayres and John J. Donohue III, "Shooting Down the More Guns, Less Crime Hypothesis," *Stanford Law Review* 55 (2003): 1193–1312; John R. Lott Jr., "Piers Morgan's Revealing Rancor," *National Review*, February 24, 2014, https://www.nationalreview.com/2014/02/piers-morgans-revealing-rancor-john-r-lott-jr/#!.

34. "Guns Reduce the Crime Rate," *Atlanta Journal-Constitution*, August 1, 1999.

35. Angela Stroud, *Good Guys with Guns: The Appeal and Consequences of Concealed Carry* (Chapel Hill: University of North Carolina Press, 2016), 89–91.

36. "Guns, Papers: We Have Rights," *Arizona Republic*, February 25, 2000.

37. Public Mail, January 18, 1989, White House Office of Records Management FG051, George H. W. Bush Library.

38. Quote from Melzer, *Gun Crusaders*, 114.

39. Quote from Dan Baum, *Gun Guys: A Road Trip* (New York: Alfred A. Knopf, 2013), 132.

40. "NRA Firearm Training," NRA website, accessed January 23, 2019, https://firearmtraining.nra.org/.

41. Jennifer Carlson, *Citizen-Protectors: The Everyday Politics of Guns in an Age of Decline* (Oxford: Oxford University Press, 2015), 63; Wayne LaPierre, "Standing Guard," *American Rifleman*, March 2005, 10.

42. Katharine Q. Seelye, "Critics Say N.R.A. Uses Safety Campaign to Lure Children," *New York Times*, November 19, 1997, A24; "NRA Victories: Eighteen Million Safer Kids," NRA website, July 27, 2006, https://www.nraila.org/articles/20060727/nra-victories-eighteen-million-safer-k; "NRA's Eddie Eagle Gun-Safe Program Reaches 30 Million Children," *American Hunter*, September 2017, https://www.americanhunter.org/articles/2017/9/6/nras-eddie-eagle-gunsafe-program-reaches-30-million-children/.

43. See https://coach.nra.org/junior-shooting-camps/ and http://youth.nra.org/.

44. "Civilian Marksmanship Report," *American Rifleman*, March 1966, 14; C. B. Lister, "Hysteria Ahead," *American Rifleman*, June 1949, 12; C. B. Lister, "Call to Action," *American Rifleman*, March 1949, 10; Merritt Edson, "Our Association—Change and Growth," *American Rifleman*, May 1953, 12; "Unorganized Hunters Need Your Help," *American Rifleman*, December 1970, 16; Merritt Edson, "An Open Letter to the Membership," *American Rifleman*, September 1951, 12.

45. Quote from "Unorganized Hunters Need Your Help." Additional evidence from "C. B. Lister Memo to NRA Board of Directors," Box 15, Merritt Edson Papers, Library of Congress; Wayne LaPierre, "Standing Guard," *American Rifleman*, March 2005; S. M. Johnson, "Hunter Safety Education Never Out of Season," *American Rifleman*, June 1953, 12; Merritt Edson, "An Opportunity for All of Us," *American Rifleman*, May 1954, 16; "The Magnet," *American Rifleman*, August 1931, 6.

46. John Scofield, "C. B. Lister Dies," *American Rifleman*, June 1951, 12–13; "Build NRA," *American Rifleman*, January 1960, 14.

47. "Build NRA."

48. "NRA Activities in 1969," *American Rifleman*, June 1970, 39–40.

49. Ibid.

50. See https://membership.nra.org/. Based on circulation of NRA magazines, some experts argue that this number is an overestimate; regardless of the exact number of current members, however, the NRA has continued to grow over time.

51. "United We Stand," *American Rifleman*, January 1965, 16; "FIGHT!," *American Rifleman*, August 1932, 4; "Ten Thousand Boys," *American Rifleman*, August 1933, 4.

52. "FIGHT!"

53. Calvin Goddard, "How Illinois Organized to Fight Anti-Firearms Legislation," *American Rifleman*, November 1934.

54. Donald Stephen Cupps, "Bullets, Ballots, and Politics: The NRA Fights Gun Control" (PhD diss., Princeton University, 1970), 103; Edward F. Leddy, *Magnum Force Lobby: The National Rifle Association Fights Gun Control* (Lanham, MD: University Press of America, 1987), 115–116.

55. "The 'Debunkers,'" *American Rifleman*, February 1931, 6, 45.

56. "The Future of Firearms in America," *American Rifleman*, May 1960, 14.

57. Baum, *Gun Guys*, 35–36, 42.

58. Carlson, *Citizen-Protectors*, 28. Carlson tends to refer to it as "gun culture," but what she identifies can clearly be considered a group identity.

59. Ibid., 61.

60. Ibid., 68.

61. Ibid., chapter 3.

62. Lacombe, Howat, and Rothschild, "Gun Ownership as a Social Identity."

63. Melzer, *Gun Crusaders*, 181, 185.

64. I estimated a logistic regression in which "Call to Action" is the dependent variable and "Threat" is an independent variable (along with "Policy Discussion" and "Identity-Building Language"). I find that threat is a positive and highly statistically significant (p-value <0.001) predictor of calls to action within NRA editorials. See online appendix table 3A1.

65. "Zero Hour," *American Rifleman*, December 1940, 4.

66. Wayne LaPierre, "Standing Guard," *American Rifleman*, April 1997, 6–7.

67. "Can Three Assassins Kill a Civil Right?," *American Rifleman*, July 1968, 16.

68. Wayne LaPierre, "Standing Guard," *American Rifleman*, July 1999, 10.

69. "Firearms in the Senate," *American Rifleman*, February 1934, 4.

70. Lee Kennett and James LaVerne Anderson, *The Gun in America: The Origins of a National Dilemma* (Westport, CT: Greenwood Press, 1975), 211.

71. Kennett and Anderson, *The Gun in America*, 208–209; Alexander DeConde, *Gun Violence in America: The Struggle for Control* (Boston: Northeastern University Press, 2001), 143; "Firearms in the Senate"; "Keep Those Letters and Telegrams Coming," *American Rifleman*, March 1934, 6.

72. Mail Summaries, 1968, Mail Summaries, Box 1, Lyndon B. Johnson Library.

73. Richard Harris, "If You Love Your Guns," *New Yorker*, April 20, 1968, 127–128.

74. Special cover insert, *American Rifleman*, April 1989.

75. Mail Summaries, 1989–1991, WHORM WH004–01, Boxes 5–6, George H. W. Bush Library.

76. Howard Schuman and Stanley Presser, "The Attitude-Action Connection and the Issue of Gun Control," *The ANNALS of the American Academy of Political and Social Science* 455, no. 1 (1981): 40–47; Parker et al., "America's Complex Relationship with Guns"; Mark R. Joslyn, *The Gun Gap: The Influence of Gun Ownership on Political Behavior and Attitudes* (Oxford: Oxford University Press, 2020).

77. Peter M. Aronow and Benjamin T. Miller, "Policy Misperceptions and Support for Gun Control Regulations," *The Lancet* 387, no. 10015 (2016): 23.

78. That is, whether an individual actually owns a gun, which is separate from socially identifying with gun ownership.

79. Lacombe, Howat, and Rothschild, "Gun Ownership as a Social Identity."

80. Melzer, *Gun Crusaders*, chapters 4, 8.

81. Mason, "Guns and Abortion."

82. "Lawful Gun Owners," *Chicago Tribune*, May 2, 1999.

83. David Cole, *Engines of Liberty: The Power of Citizen Activists to Make Constitutional Law* (New York: Basic Books, 2016), 142, 143, 145.

84. Richard Feldman, *Ricochet: Confessions of a Gun Lobbyist* (Hoboken: Wiley, 2008), 75, 233.

85. "How Has the US Gun Lobby Been So Successful?," BBC News, January 27, 2016, https://www.bbc.com/news/world-us-canada-35355319.

Chapter 4: "America's First Freedom": The NRA's Gun-Centric Political Ideology

1. Charlton Heston, "Winning the Cultural War" (speech, Harvard Law School Forum, Boston, MA, February 16, 1999).

2. "Wayne LaPierre Remarks at Conservative Political Action Conference," C-Span, March 15, 2013, https://www.c-span.org/video/?311543-6/wayne-lapierre-remarks-conservative-political-action-conference&start=83.

3. This definition is informed by numerous studies of ideology, including Philip E. Converse, "The Nature of Belief Systems in Mass Publics," in *Ideology and Discontent*, ed. David E. Apter (New York: Free Press, 1964), 206–261; John Gerring, "Ideology: A Definitional Analysis," *Political Research Quarterly* 50, no. 4 (1997): 957–994; Hans Noel, *Political Ideologies and Political Parties in America* (Cambridge: Cambridge University Press, 2013), 41; Frances E. Lee, *Beyond Ideology: Politics, Principles, and Partisanship in the U.S. Senate* (Chicago: University of Chicago Press, 2009), 27; and Kathleen Knight, "Transformations of the Concept of Ideology in the Twentieth Century," *American Political Science Review* 100, no. 4 (2006): 619–626, 625.

4. "Zero Hour," *American Rifleman*, December 1940, 4.

5. "Firearms Restrictions Opposed," *New York Times*, March 19, 1941.

6. J. Warren Cassidy, "Here We Stand," *American Rifleman*, August 1989, 7.

7. Ibid.

8. Wayne LaPierre, "Standing Guard," *American Rifleman*, December 2004, 10.

9. Margaret E. Roberts et al., "Structural Topic Models for Open-Ended Survey Responses," *American Journal of Political Science* 58, no. 4 (2014): 1064–1082.

10. The anti-gun letters were coded based on whether they connect gun control to one or more distinct political issues. Because gun control has historically been discussed exclusively as a form of crime control, anti-gun letters were not automatically coded as having issue connections if they mentioned crime. Connection of

gun control to the prevention of gun crime—the exclusive impetus of calls for gun control—does not represent the sort of broader issue connection that collectively amounts to an ideology. Similarly, pro-gun letters and editorials that discuss crime but only do so while arguing that gun control will not effectively prevent it were also not coded as having issue connections. Instead, they must connect gun rights to crime prevention (e.g., argue that widespread gun ownership will reduce crime).

11. These issue sets are not treated as mutually exclusive; documents connecting gun rights to multiple issue sets were coded accordingly. See the appendix for coding and topic inclusion rules. Although liberty and limited government are related to each other, the NRA connects them to gun rights at different times and in different ways; this variation renders them appropriate to consider separately.

12. As noted elsewhere, not all documents that discuss crime (and, as a result, are then included in the *Crime* topic) are deemed to connect crime as a political issue to gun rights. Editorials or letters that simply argue that gun control is unlikely to be successful at reducing crime do not genuinely connect gun rights to crime prevention. To be included, documents must, in some way, connect guns to crime reduction (e.g., argue that increasing the number of guns in society will cause crime to drop).

13. Although limited government is an important issue set to which gun rights are connected by both the NRA and its supporters, it is substantially less prominent than liberty and crime issue connections. Examining the relationship over time between the NRA's discussion of this issue and pro-gun letter writers' discussion of it is not feasible. It is worth noting, however, that connections to limited government only began consistently appearing after the point at which gun rights became associated with partisan politics.

14. "Constitution Week," *American Rifleman*, September 1935, 6.

15. "The Attorney General Is Inconsistent," *American Rifleman*, January 1934, 4.

16. "The Sinister Influence," *American Rifleman*, April 1935, 6.

17. "Modification or Repeal of the Sullivan Act Is Urged," *New York Times*, February 18, 1932.

18. "A Sportsman's Reserve Corps," *Chicago Tribune*, February 7, 1935.

19. Scott Melzer, *Gun Crusaders: The NRA's Culture War* (New York: New York University Press, 2009), 16.

20. See, among others, "The National Rifle Matches," *New York Times*, September 2, 1931; "Objections Given to Gun Registration," *Atlanta Journal-Constitution*, January 27, 1962; "Possessing Firearms Upheld: Restrictive Legislation Is Opposed as Not Being Answer to Problem," *New York Times*, August 16, 1952; "$200,000—For What?" *American Rifleman*, January 1930, 6; "The Budget," *American Rifleman*, January 1930, 6; "The Twenty-fourth National Matches," *American Rifleman*, August 1930, 6; "The National Matches," *American Rifleman*, October 1930, 6; "Lest We Forget," *American Rifleman*, October 1936, 4.

21. "The 'Debunkers,'" *American Rifleman*, February 1931, 6, 45.

22. "Our Friends—The Policeman," *American Rifleman*, July 1930, 6.

23. C. B. Lister, "Invasion," *American Rifleman*, February 1943, 11.

24. "Possessing Firearms Upheld: Restrictive Legislation Is Opposed as Not Being Answer to Problem," *New York Times*, August 16, 1952.

25. See "Zero Hour"; "Behind the Headlines," *American Rifleman*, February 1941, 2; "Politics and Propaganda," *American Rifleman*, September 1940, 4; "Registration—Confiscation," *American Rifleman*, March 1946, 9; "Europe Can Be Wrong," *American Rifleman*, August 1941, 6.

26. "Zero Hour," 4.

27. See, for example, "Prohibiting Firearms," *Arizona Republic*, November 29, 1947; "Firearms Regulation," *Chicago Tribune*, February 18, 1956; "Use of Firearms Defended: Familiarity with Weapons Considered of Value under Present Conditions," *New York Times*, August 23, 1952.

28. "Firearms Restrictions Opposed," *New York Times*, March 19, 1941.

29. Constituent Letter to Dole, House of Representatives Papers, 1960–1969, Box 45, Folder 10, Robert J. Dole Archive.

30. "Let's Take the Offensive," *American Rifleman*, September 1958, 16.

31. "Arms Registration Queried," *New York Times*, September 18, 1949.

32. Philip J. Cook and Kristin A. Goss, *The Gun Debate: What Everyone Needs to Know* (Oxford: Oxford University Press, 2014), 36.

33. Lee Kennett and James LaVerne Anderson, *The Gun in America: The Origins of a National Dilemma* (Westport, CT: Greenwood Press, 1975), 242; Jack Raymond, "Rifle Clubs Grow as Leisure Rises: Youth Interest Is Also Called a Factor in Increase," *New York Times*, July 7, 1964, 17; Ben A. Franklin, "Aid to Rifle Club Stirs Opposition: Backers of Gun Control Bill Open Drive in Congress," *New York Times*, June 18, 1967, 30; "House Cuts Funds for Rifle Training," *New York Times*, October 1, 1975, 48.

34. "Memo from Basil to Edson on Second Amendment," June 18, 1955, Box 27, Merritt Edson Papers, Library of Congress.

35. "An Independent America," *American Rifleman*, July 1963, 16.

36. "Right to Bear Arms: Ownership of a Rifle Declared Part of Our National Heritage," *New York Times*, January 4, 1964.

37. See, for example, C. B. Lister, "The Greater Ranger," *American Rifleman*, January 1949, 8; and C. B. Lister, "Chipped Keystone," *American Rifleman*, April 1949, 12.

38. See, for example, "Handgun Hunting," *Chicago Tribune*, May 23, 1972; no title, *Chicago Tribune*, February 26, 1965; "Gun Control?," *Atlanta Journal-Constitution*, August 8, 1968; "Gun Controls," *Atlanta Journal-Constitution*, May 27, 1971; "Guns and the Law," *New York Times*, October 20, 1973.

39. Public Mail, June 27, 1968, White House Central Files, LE-JL 3, Boxes 107–109, Lyndon B. Johnson Library; Public Mail, July 2, 1968, White House Central Files, LE-JL 3, Boxes 105–106, Lyndon B. Johnson Library; Public Mail, June 17, 1968, White House Central Files, LE-JL 3, Boxes 107–109, Lyndon B. Johnson Library.

40. Carl Bakal, *The Right to Bear Arms* (New York: McGraw-Hill, 1966), 205.

41. Louis Lucas, "The Future of Firearms in America," *American Rifleman*, May 1960, 14.

42. "The NRA Police Shooting Program," *American Rifleman*, April 1961, 16.

43. J. Warren Cassidy, "Here We Stand," *American Rifleman*, August 1989, 7.

44. J. Warren Cassidy, "Here We Stand," *American Rifleman*, April 1987, 7.

45. "Guns a Necessary and Valuable Part of American Tradition," *Atlanta Journal-Constitution*, April 17, 1989.

46. "'Troublesome' Right?," *Atlanta Journal-Constitution*, May 23, 1991.

47. Melzer, *Gun Crusaders*, 114.

48. Ibid., 116.

49. Dan Baum, *Gun Guys: A Road Trip* (New York: Alfred A. Knopf, 2013), 157–158.

50. Angela Stroud, *Good Guys with Guns: The Appeal and Consequences of Concealed Carry* (Chapel Hill: University of North Carolina Press, 2016), 123.

51. Ibid.

52. Ibid., 126.

53. See online appendix table 4A1 for the full regression output.

54. See Marc Mauer and Ryan S. King, *Uneven Justice: State Rates of Incarceration by Race and Ethnicity* (Washington, DC: Sentencing Project, 2007); Michelle Alexander, *The New Jim Crow: Mass Incarceration in the Age of Colorblindness* (New York: New Press, 2010); Heather Ann Thompson, "Why Mass Incarceration Matters: Rethinking Crisis, Decline and Transformation in Postwar American History," *Journal of American History* 97, no. 3 (2010): 703–734; Bruce Western, *Punishment and Inequality in America* (New York: Russell Sage Foundation Publications, 2006), 49–50; Vesla M. Weaver, "Frontlash: Race and the Development of Punitive Crime Policy," *Studies in American Political Development* 21, no. 2 (2007): 230–265.

55. See Alexandra Filindra and Noah J. Kaplan, "Racial Resentment and Whites' Gun Policy Preferences in Contemporary America," *Political Behavior* 38 (2015): 255–275; Alexandra Filindra and Noah J. Kaplan, "Testing Theories of Gun Policy Preferences among Blacks, Latinos, and Whites in America," *Social Science Quarterly* 98, no. 2 (2017): 413–428.

56. Wayne LaPierre, "Standing Guard," *American Rifleman*, November 1993, 7.

57. "Handgun Owner Training Available," *American Rifleman*, August 1983, 50.

58. "Women and Gun Ownership," *New York Times*, February 24, 1986.

59. Harlon Carter, "Here We Stand," *American Rifleman*, November 1984.

60. J. Warren Cassidy, "Here We Stand," *American Rifleman*, January 1987, 7.

61. Wayne LaPierre, "Standing Guard," *American Rifleman*, September 2004, 10.

62. Melzer, *Gun Crusaders*, 125–126.

63. Baum, *Gun Guys*, 36.

64. Jennifer Carlson, *Citizen-Protectors: The Everyday Politics of Guns in an Age of Decline* (Oxford: Oxford University Press, 2015).

65. These time periods are 1930–1945, 1946–1962, 1963–1976, 1977–1991, and 1992–2008. The first cut-point (1945/1946) corresponds to end of World War II, at which time the NRA diversified its programmatic offerings to appeal to veterans of the war. The second cut-point (1962/1963) corresponds with the return of gun control to the national agenda following high-profile political assassinations (the

first of which, John F. Kennedy's assassination, occurred in 1963) and rising crime rates. The third cut-point (1976/1977) corresponds with the takeover of the NRA by a group of activist members at the 1977 annual meeting, which led to important changes to the organization. The last cut-point (1991/1992) corresponds to beginning of Wayne LaPierre's tenure as the NRA's top executive and his authorship of its editorials.

66. This consisted of (1) measuring the aggregate cosine similarity of lagged *American Rifleman* editorials from each period and pro-gun letters to the editor from the following period (producing "lagged *American Rifleman* scores"), (2) reversing the procedure to measure the similarity of lagged pro-gun letters from each period and *American Rifleman* editorials from the following period (producing "lagged letter scores"), (3) singling out the causal impact of *American Rifleman* editorials on pro-gun letters by subtracting the lagged letter similarity scores from lagged *American Rifleman* similarity scores for each period, (4) calculating the average difference across periods for each time grouping, and then (5) bootstrapping confidence intervals for each estimate; a positive, statistically significant result would indicate that pro-gun letters systematically respond to NRA editorials.

67. This figure uses 90 percent confidence intervals; there are fewer documents per bucket in this analysis than in last chapter's analyses, which reduces statistical power. The 16-year and theoretically driven buckets are also significant at the 95 percent confidence level.

Chapter 5: Gun Policy during the NRA's Quasi-Governmental Phase

1. "Democratic Study Group Research Memorandum 68–2," June 19, 1968, Legislative Background and Crises File, Gun Control Box 1, Lyndon B. Johnson Library.

2. A bill making it illegal to use US mail for handgun sales was signed into law in 1927. This bill, however, was meant to enhance rather than erode states' rights on the issue of gun control, as it "would prevent the U.S. Post Office from unintentionally aiding in breaking the laws of states with tougher gun regulations." Further, as Spitzer argues, the law was "little more than symbolic" because it did not prohibit the use of private shipping companies (e.g., UPS) for handgun sales. See Robert J. Spitzer, *The Politics of Gun Control* (New York: Routledge, 2015), 139.

3. Lee Kennett and James LaVerne Anderson, *The Gun in America: The Origins of a National Dilemma* (Westport, CT: Greenwood Press, 1975), 204.

4. Carol Skalnik Leff and Mark H. Leff, "The Politics of Ineffectiveness: Federal Firearms Legislation, 1919–1938," *ANNALS of the American Academy of Political and Social Science* 455, no. 1 (1981): 48–62; Alexander DeConde, *Gun Violence in America: The Struggle for Control* (Boston: Northeastern University Press, 2001), 146–147; J. M. Hakenjos, "Firearms Legislation," *American Rifleman*, May 1938, 30; M. A. Reckord, "Senate 3," *American Rifleman*, August 1938, 10–11.

5. Due in large part to the uneven availability and quality of data pertaining to different periods, not all cases receive equally detailed attention in the discussions that follow; I note my level of certainty about particular claims throughout.

6. Kennett and Anderson, *The Gun in America*, 206–207; DeConde, *Gun Violence in America*, 137–142.

7. "Firearms in the Senate," *American Rifleman*, February 1934, 4.

8. Carl Bakal, *The Right to Bear Arms* (New York: McGraw-Hill, 1966), 172.

9. The Franklin D. Roosevelt archive unfortunately does not contain samples of constituent mail.

10. "Guns for Racket Victims," *New York Times*, May 23, 1935.

11. "Concealed Weapons," *Chicago Tribune*, January 20, 1937.

12. Kennett and Anderson, *The Gun in America*, 208–209.

13. Leff and Leff, "The Politics of Ineffectiveness," 61.

14. DeConde, *Gun Violence in America*, 144.

15. Kennett and Anderson, *The Gun in America*, 211.

16. C. B. Lister, "Firearms Laws in the 73d Congress," *American Rifleman*, July 1934, 5.

17. Kennett and Anderson, *The Gun in America*, 209.

18. DeConde, *Gun Violence in America*, 143, 146–147; Reckord, "Senate 3"; Leff and Leff, "The Politics of Ineffectiveness," 55–56.

19. Spitzer, *The Politics of Gun Control*, 139–140; Leff and Leff, "The Politics of Ineffectiveness," 55–56, 61.

20. Leff and Leff, "The Politics of Ineffectiveness"; DeConde, *Gun Violence in America*, 146–147; Reckord, "Senate 3." Quote from Hakenjos, "Firearms Legislation," 30.

21. Patrick J. Charles, *Armed in America: A History of Gun Rights from Colonial Militias to Concealed Carry* (Amherst, NY: Prometheus, 2018), 216–217, 222–223.

22. Hakenjos, "Firearms Legislation."

23. Leff and Leff, "The Politics of Ineffectiveness"; DeConde, *Gun Violence in America*, 146–147.

24. DeConde, *Gun Violence in America*, 146.

25. "President Commends Association at Annual Meeting," *American Rifleman*, March 1938, 22; "Directors' Meeting, 1939," *American Rifleman*, March 1939, 9–11.

26. NRA Executive Vice President Milton A. Reckord stated this while testifying before Congress in 1934. Quoted in DeConde, *Gun Violence in America*, 141.

27. These include journalistic accounts of the NRA's early years too numerous to name, as well as some books written by academics. See, for instance, Adam Winkler, *Gunfight: The Battle over the Right to Bear Arms in America* (2011; New York: W.W. Norton, 2013).

28. Kennett and Anderson, *The Gun in America*, 225.

29. DeConde, *Gun Violence in America*, 151–152.

30. Ibid., 156.

31. Ibid., 163; Bakal, *The Right to Bear Arms*, 183.

32. DeConde, *Gun Violence in America*, 171; Hazel Erksine, "The Polls: Gun Control," *Public Opinion Quarterly* 36, no. 3 (1972): 455–469.

33. DeConde, *Gun Violence in America*, 168–169; Bakal, *The Right to Bear Arms*, 146.

34. Franklin E. Zimring, "Firearms and Federal Law: The Gun Control Act of 1968," *Journal of Legal Studies* 4, no. 1 (1975): 133–198, 145–146; DeConde, *Gun Violence in America*, 171.

35. On acceptance of the pre-assassination Dodd bill: Charles, *Armed in America*, 239.

36. Richard Harris, "If You Love Your Guns," *New Yorker*, April 20, 1968, 80; Bakal, *The Right to Bear Arms*, 201.

37. "Realistic Firearms Controls," *American Rifleman*, January 1964, 14.

38. David Cole, *Engines of Liberty: The Power of Citizen Activists to Make Constitutional Law* (New York: Basic Books, 2016), 146–147.

39. See "Realistic Firearms Controls"; and "The Misuse of Firearms," *American Rifleman*, March 1964, 16.

40. Bakal, *The Right to Bear Arms*, 197–198.

41. Harris, "If You Love Your Guns," 87; Kennett and Anderson, *The Gun in America*, 232; Charles, *Armed in America*, 248; Bakal, *The Right to Bear Arms*, 199.

42. DeConde, *Gun Violence in America*, 172–173.

43. Harris, "If You Love Your Guns," 79–80; DeConde, *Gun Violence in America*, 172; Bakal, *The Right to Bear Arms*, 199–200.

44. DeConde, *Gun Violence in America*, 173.

45. Quote from Sugarmann, *National Rifle Association*, 37; Bakal, *The Right to Bear Arms*, 208–209.

46. DeConde, *Gun Violence in America*, 174–175.

47. "Hearings Held on Administration Gun Control Bill," *CQ Almanac 1965* (Washington, DC: Congressional Quarterly, 1966), 640–645.

48. Harris, "If You Love Your Guns," 127–128.

49. "Letter from Orth to NRA members," April 9, 1965, James V. Bennett Personal Papers, Box 010, Firearms: Legislation: Dodd Bill: 1965: Testimony: Attorney General folder, John F. Kennedy Library.

50. Mail Summaries, 1965, Mail Summaries, Box 1, Lyndon B. Johnson Library.

51. Mail Summaries, 1965, Mail Summaries, Box 2, Lyndon B. Johnson Library.

52. Franklin Orth, "A Report to the Members on Federal Gun Legislation," *American Rifleman*, December 1965, 17–18.

53. Mail Summaries, 1965–1968, Mail Summaries, Boxes 1–4, Lyndon B. Johnson Library.

54. "Letter from Orth to NRA members," April 9, 1965, James V. Bennett Personal Papers, Box 010, Firearms: Legislation: Dodd Bill: 1965: Testimony: Attorney General folder, John F. Kennedy Library.

55. "Memo from Popple to Lamont," June 17, 1965, White House Central Files, Name File, National Ri, Lyndon B. Johnson Library.

56. Public Mail, June 1968, White House Central Files, LE-JL 3, Boxes 94–97, Lyndon B. Johnson Library.

57. Ibid.

58. Kennett and Anderson, *The Gun in America*, 235–236; Harris, "If You Love Your Guns," 144.

59. Charles, *Armed in America*, 266; "Gun Control Bills Stalled by Stiff Opposition," *CQ Almanac 1967* (Washington, DC: Congressional Quarterly, 1968), 08-859-08-863.

60. Harris, "If You Love Your Guns," 151–152.

61. Ibid., 57.

62. "Press Release on Gun Control," July 22, 1968, Senator Jacob K. Javits Collection, Box 41, Kiwanis Club of Ithaca, Gun Control folder, Stony Brook University Special Collections and University Archives.

63. "Democratic Study Group Research Memorandum 68–2," June 19, 1968, Legislative Background and Crises File, Gun Control Box 1, Lyndon B. Johnson Library.

64. "Congress Passes Extensive Anticrime Legislation," *CQ Almanac 1968* (Washington, DC: Congressional Quarterly, 1969), 09-225-9-226; DeConde, *Gun Violence in America*, 184; "Dodd & Co. Defeated, Block NRA Plan," *American Rifleman*, June 1968, 46–47.

65. DeConde, *Gun Violence in America*, 183–185; Spitzer, *The Politics of Gun Control*, 142.

66. DeConde, *Gun Violence in America*, 185.

67. Ibid., 184–185; Charles, *Armed in America*, 266–268; Walter Carroll, "Organizations Advocating Gun Control," in *Guns and Contemporary: The Past, Present, and Future of Firearms and Firearm Policy*, ed. Glenn Utter (Santa Barbara, CA: ABC-CLIO, 2016), 168–169.

68. Mail Summaries, 1968, Mail Summaries, Boxes 1–4, Lyndon B. Johnson Library.

69. Donald Stephen Cupps, "Bullets, Ballots, and Politics: The NRA Fights Gun Control" (PhD diss., Princeton University, 1970), 149–150, 160–161; "The Gun Under Fire," *Time*, June 21, 1968, http://content.time.com/time/subscriber/article/0,33009,900177,00.html.

70. Kristin A. Goss, *Disarmed: The Missing Movement for Gun Control in America* (Princeton, NJ: Princeton University Press, 2006), 110–111.

71. DeConde, *Gun Violence in America*, 185–186.

72. "Can Three Assassins Kill a Civil Right?," *American Rifleman*, July 1968, 16–17.

73. Cupps, "Bullets, Ballots, and Politics," 156.

74. Ibid., 152–153.

75. Ibid., 153.

76. Ibid., 174–176, 182–183, 202.

77. Ibid., 185–187.

78. Mail Summaries, 1968, Mail Summaries, Boxes 5, Lyndon B. Johnson Library.

79. NRA Staff, "Congress Threshes Out Gun Law Issue," *American Rifleman*, November 1968, 22.

80. Spitzer, *The Politics of Gun Control*, 143; Zimring, "Firearms and Federal Law," 151–153.

81. Cupps, "Bullets, Ballots, and Politics," 209–210; Rich Benjamin, "Gun Control, White Paranoia, and the Death of Martin Luther King, Jr.," *New Yorker*, April 3, 2018, https://www.newyorker.com/news/news-desk/gun-control-white-paranoia-and-the-death-of-martin-luther-king-jr.

82. "Effect of Gun Issue Seen in Vote Results," *American Rifleman*, January 1969, 28–29.

83. DeConde, *Gun Violence in America*, 182.

84. Alan C. Webber, "Where the NRA Stands on Gun Legislation," *American Rifleman*, March 1968, 22–23.

85. DeConde, *Gun Violence in America*, 175–176.

86. Charles, *Armed in America*, 254.

87. Ibid.

88. Kennett and Anderson, *The Gun in America*, 240.

89. "1966 Operating Report," National Rifle Association, 34.

90. Bakal, *The Right to Bear Arms*, 199.

Chapter 6: The Party-Group Alignment of the NRA and the GOP

1. Ana Santos and the Associated Press, "What Donald Trump Said during Atlanta's NRA Convention: 'No Longer Will Federal Agencies Be Coming after Law-Abiding Gun Owners,'" *Atlanta Journal-Constitution*, October 2, 2017, https://www.ajc.com/news/national-govt--politics/what-donald-trump-said-during-atlanta-nra-convention-longer-will-federal-agencies-coming-after-law-abiding-gun-owners/4jYnq5j1WacCVjBcUVJi2N/.

2. For further discussion of the relationship between the Democratic Party and organized labor, see J. David Greenstone, *Labor in American Politics* (New York: Knopf, 1969).

3. Daniel Schlozman, *When Movements Anchor Parties: Electoral Realignment in American History* (Princeton, NJ: Princeton University Press, 2015), 3.

4. David Karol, *Red, Green, and Blue: The Partisan Divide on Environmental Issues* (Cambridge: Cambridge University Press, 2019); Schlozman, *When Movements Anchor Parties*.

5. This definition is closely related to Katherine Krimmel's in "The Efficiencies and Pathologies of Special Interest Partisanship," *Studies in American Political Development* 31, no. 2 (2017): 149–169.

6. It is also not clear how to measure the extent to which particular groups are party groups. That is, although it is not difficult to imagine a spectrum in which anchoring groups are at one end and independent groups are at the other, it is unclear how to empirically place other groups along that spectrum. Because it is a study of a single group, this project is not well positioned to identify measures that could be used to determine the relative position of groups within party coalitions. Nonetheless, identifying such measures could be a fruitful topic of further research.

7. Not all of the indicators described above are available for the entirety of my period of study. As such, the following sections use the best measures available in each period.

8. Although it is difficult to locate measures of polarization on gun control covering the 1930s through the 1950s, as of the mid-to-late 1960s, gun control was cross-cutting on both the elite and mass levels. Secondary accounts provide no reason to think that the issue was partisan in earlier decades. See David Karol, *Party Position Change in American Politics: Coalition Management* (Cambridge: Cambridge University Press, 2009); and Hazel Erksine, "The Polls: Gun Control," *Public Opinion Quarterly* 36, no. 3 (1972): 455–469.

9. See chapter 1 for discussion of the NRA's support from the federal government. For the organization's discussion of itself as a quasi-governmental organization, see "Speech Notes Memo from Lister to Edson," Box 15, Merritt Edson Papers, Library of Congress.

10. "Letter from Goldwater to Edwards Brown," August 25, 1964, E. B. Mann Papers, Box 4, Folder 8, American Heritage Center.

11. Richard A. Viguerie, *The New Right: We're Ready to Lead* (Falls Church, VA: The Viguerie Company, 1981), 43, 83–86; Hans Noel, *Political Ideologies and Political Parties in America* (Cambridge: Cambridge University Press, 2013), chapter 6; Joseph E. Lowndes, *From the New Deal to the New Right: Race and the Southern Origins of Modern Conservativism* (New Haven, CT: Yale University Press, 2008); Jerome L. Himmelstein, *To the Right: The Transformation of American Conservatism* (Berkeley: University of California Press, 1990).

12. Viguerie, *The New Right*, 25–26, 71–77, 84; Himmelstein, *To the Right*, chapter 3.

13. Reva B. Siegel, "Dead or Alive: Originalism as Popular Constitutionalism in Heller," *Harvard Law Review* 122, no. 1 (2008): 213.

14. Paul Houston, "Gun Lobby Seeks Millions to Fight Its Foes at Polls," *Los Angeles Times*, April 25, 1976, A1.

15. Joan Burbick, *Gun Show Nation: Gun Culture and American Democracy* (New York: The New Press, 2006), 85–91.

16. "Memo to the Committee from Marc Tangner," October 10, 1975, Paul Weyrich Papers, Box 19, Folder 9, American Heritage Center.

17. Martin Durham, "Family, Morality and the New Right," *Parliamentary Affairs* 38, no. 2 (1985): 180–191.

18. "Franklin Orth, Gun Control Foe," *New York Times*, January 5, 1970, 37; Osha Gray Davidson, *Under Fire: The NRA and the Battle for Gun Control* (Iowa City: University of Iowa Press, 1998), 30–31, 35–36; Robert J. Spitzer, *The Politics of Gun Control* (New York: Routledge, 2015), 111–112; Richard Feldman, *Ricochet: Confessions of a Gun Lobbyist* (Hoboken: Wiley, 2008), 41–44; Siegel, "Dead or Alive," 211.

19. See "Shooting Clubs and National Defense," *American Rifleman*, August 1964, 16; "To Teach Our Men to Shoot," *American Rifleman*, October 1964, 16; "The Private Army Hoax," *American Rifleman*, September 1965, 20; "Civilian

Marksmanship Report," *American Rifleman*, March 1966, 14; "Shall We Export Firearms Instruction?," *American Rifleman*, October 1966, 18; "NRA Rifle Training as a Lifesaver," *American Rifleman*, November 1966, 16; "Voices of Authority on Civilian Marksmanship," *American Rifleman*, January 1968, 14; "U.S. Funds for a Lobby, None for DCM Shooters?," *American Rifleman*, August 1969, 19.

20. Carl Bakal, *The Right to Bear Arms* (New York: McGraw-Hill, 1966), 141.

21. The NRA's 1966 Operating Report indicates that 63 percent of its revenue that year came from membership dues, with similar proportions in the two prior years. The NRA's 1961 Operating Report indicates that 61 percent of its revenue that year came from dues, with, again, similar proportions in the two prior years.

22. John Scofield, "C. B. Lister Dies," *American Rifleman*, June 1951, 12–13; "Build NRA," *American Rifleman*, January 1960, 14.

23. Patrick J. Charles, *Armed in America: A History of Gun Rights from Colonial Militias to Concealed Carry* (Amherst, NY: Prometheus, 2018), 253–262; Lee Kennett and James LaVerne Anderson, *The Gun in America: The Origins of a National Dilemma* (Westport, CT: Greenwood Press, 1975), 239; Bakal, *The Right to Bear Arms*.

24. Kristin A. Goss, *Disarmed: The Missing Movement for Gun Control in America* (Princeton, NJ: Princeton University Press, 2006), 76; Ben A. Franklin, "Aid to Rifle Club Stirs Opposition: Backers of Gun Control Bill Open Drive in Congress," *New York Times*, June 18, 1967, 30.

25. Jack Raymond, "Rifle Clubs Grow as Leisure Rises: Youth Interest Is Also Called a Factor in Increase," *New York Times*, July 7, 1964, 17; Franklin, "Aid to Rifle Club Stirs Opposition"; "House Cuts Funds for Rifle Training," *New York Times*, October 1, 1975, 48; Goss, *Disarmed*, 76; "Army Cuts Help to Gun Programs of Civilian Clubs," *New York Times*, June 22, 1968, 1; Kennett and Anderson, *The Gun in America*, 242.

26. "Report from Maxwell E. Rich to NRA Executive Committee," Series 5, Box 14, Milton Reckord Papers, University of Maryland Special Collections and University Archives.

27. In 1968, the military slashed the program—excluding pistols from it entirely, severely restricting the type of ammunition available for purchase, and limiting participation to clubs whose members are likely to serve in the military in the future—which substantially weakened the incentives for clubs to maintain NRA affiliation. See "Army Cuts Help to Gun Programs."

28. Siegel, "Dead or Alive," 211; Joseph Tartaro, *Revolt at Cincinnati* (Buffalo, NY: Hawkeye, 1981), 21–22; Josh Sugarmann, *National Rifle Association: Money, Firepower & Fear* (Washington, DC: National Press Books, 1992), 48–52.

29. Siegel, "Dead or Alive," 211; Tartaro, *Revolt at Cincinnati*, 21–22; Sugarmann, *National Rifle Association*, 48–52.

30. Alexander DeConde, *Gun Violence in America: The Struggle for Control* (Boston: Northeastern University Press, 2001), 205; Siegel, "Dead or Alive," 211; Tartaro, *Revolt at Cincinnati*, 27; Davidson, *Under Fire*, 34; William J. Vizzard, *Shots in the Dark: The Policy, Politics, and Symbolism of Gun Control* (Lanham, MD: Rowman and Littlefield, 2000), 112.

31. Edward F. Leddy, *Magnum Force Lobby: The National Rifle Association Fights Gun Control* (Lanham, MD: University Press of America, 1987), 126–127.

32. Viguerie, *The New Right*, 38; Siegel, "Dead or Alive," 214, Jack Anderson, "Viguerie: A Modern Wizard of Oz," *Washington Post*, June 3, 1978, E43.

33. "Centennial Meetings Attract 14,000," *American Rifleman*, June 1971, 51–61.

34. For example, the August 1965 and January 1966 *American Rifleman* editorials make states' rights and limited government arguments against gun control, while numerous others advocate the "law and order" approaches to crime control advocated by the New Right and/or, as discussed throughout this section, tie gun rights to individual liberty.

35. As the codebook in the appendix notes, editorials and letters were coded in terms of drawing partisan connections based on whether they mention a major US political party or an ideology associated with a US party, or use the names of well-known party leaders to connote party. The upside of this scheme is that it captures how people in contemporary politics—which, as figure 6.1 indicates, is the period in which nearly all such connections were made—frequently discuss partisan politics; party and ideology are frequently conflated in nonacademic discussions, with references to "liberals," for example, substantively equivalent to references to "Democrats." The downside of this scheme is that it does not enable an examination of whether purely ideological references (e.g., "liberal" or "conservative") preceded explicitly partisan references.

36. These connections—as is discussed later—continued to grow throughout the rest of the period of study, albeit more slowly among letter writers than in NRA editorials. The gap between the frequency with which the NRA and letter writers draw partisan connections is probably the result of two factors. First (as discussed in chapter 3), the nature and length of editorials differ from that of letters to the editor; brief letters to the editor contain much less space to include information—such as mention of political parties—that is not directly related to the purpose of the letter. Second, it seems likely that the NRA is the driver of the explicit connection of gun rights—and the ideology that gun owners associate with it—to partisan politics. While pro-gun letter writers are likely to connect gun rights to conservative issue positions and to vote for conservative candidates, the NRA is more likely to make the connection to the Republican Party itself explicit. Given that nearly all of these connections were made after the point at which gun rights had become both a conservative and a Republican issue, this conflation is not particularly problematic.

37. "The G.O.P. Position on Control of Guns Stresses State Law," *New York Times*, August 8, 1968, 25; "Republican Party Platform of 1968," The American Presidency Project, accessed January 25, 2019, https://www.presidency.ucsb.edu /documents/republican-party-platform-1968.

38. "Republican Party Platform of 1972," The American Presidency Project, accessed January 25, 2019, https://www.presidency.ucsb.edu/documents /republican-party-platform-1972.

39. Viguerie, *The New Right*, 35–36; Diana Lambert, "Trying to Stop the Craziness of This Business: Gun Control Groups," in *The Changing Politics of Gun*

Control, ed. John M. Bruce and Clyde Wilcox (Lanham, MD: Rowman and Littlefield, 1998), 188–189; "George Gordon Liddy," *New York Times*, September 16, 1972, 12; "Nixon Conversation with Ehrlichman," June 29, 1972, Conversation 135–8, White House Tapes, Nixon Presidential Materials, National Archives. See http://www.nixontapes.org/chron3.html; "Gun Control Conversation," May 16, 1972, Conversation 725–11, White House Tapes, Nixon Presidential Materials, National Archives. See http://www.nixontapes.org/chron3.html; "Memo from Pat Buchanan to Other Staff Members," September 23, 1971, White House Special Files: Contested Materials Collection, Box 3, Folder 52, Richard Nixon Library.

40. "Korologos to Timmons," August 31, 1973, White House Central Files: Staff Member & Office Files: William Timmons, Box 30, Crime/Gun Control folder, Richard Nixon Library.

41. Ford, for instance, issued a press release following a mass shooting at the University of Texas in 1966 calling for state and federal laws making it harder to obtain guns. See "Statement by House Minority Leader Gerald R. Ford, R-Michigan," August 2, 1966, Gerald R. Ford Congressional Papers, Press Secretary and Speech File, Box D7, Firearms folder, Gerald Ford Library.

42. Davidson, *Under Fire*, 40–41.

43. "Mike Duval to Dick Cheney," June 4, 1976, Raoul-Duval Papers, Box 16, Gun Control, Gerald Ford Library; "Maxwell Rich to John Marsh," February 18, 1975, Geoffrey Shepard Files, Box 5, Gun Control, Gerald Ford Library; "Friedersdorf to President Ford," Max Friedersdorf Files, Box 11, Crime/Gun Control, Gerald Ford Library.

44. "Timmons to Callaway," President Ford Committee Records, Box H39, Gerald Ford Library.

45. "Ford to Halsey," September 14, 1976, Wayne H. Valis Files, Box 5, Gerald Ford Library.

46. "Ford to Carter," White House Central Files Name File, National Rifle Association, Box 2300, Gerald Ford Library.

47. "Republican Party Platform of 1976," The American Presidency Project, accessed January 25, 2019, https://www.presidency.ucsb.edu/documents/republican-party-platform-1976.

48. Ronald Reagan, "Ronald Reagan Champions Gun Ownership," *Guns & Ammo*, September 1975, 34–35.

49. Goss, *Disarmed*, 172; Viguerie, *The New Right*, 107; Tartaro, *Revolt at Cincinnati*.

50. Tartaro, *Revolt at Cincinnati*, chapter 10.

51. Siegel, "Dead or Alive," 211; Tartaro, *Revolt at Cincinnati*, 27; Davidson, *Under Fire*, 34; Leddy, *Magnum Force Lobby*, 127.

52. Spitzer, *The Politics of Gun Control*, 112; Sugarmann, *National Rifle Association*, 49.

53. Jeff Suess, "NRA: 'Revolt at Cincinnati' Molded National Rifle Association," *Cincinnati Enquirer*, March 8, 2018, https://www.cincinnati.com/story/news

/politics/2018/03/08/revolt-cincinnati-molded-nra-did-you-know-jeff-suess
-schism-within-national-rifle-association-led/404628002/.

54. Reginald Stuart, "Rifle Group Ousts Most Leaders in Move to Bolster Stand on Guns," *New York Times*, May 23, 1977, 16; Michael Waldman, *The Second Amendment: A Biography* (New York: Simon and Schuster, 2014), 90; Davidson, *Under Fire*, 35–36.

55. Waldman, *The Second Amendment*, 90; Davidson, *Under Fire*, 35–36.

56. "RSM to PW," January 29, 1982, Paul Weyrich Papers, Box 21, Folder 10, American Heritage Center; Siegel, "Dead or Alive," 212–215.

57. Viguerie, *The New Right*, 74–75.

58. A bit more specifically, Sheingate argues that political entrepreneurs (1) "exploit moments of instability, or speculative opportunities for innovation," (2) recombine elements of existing configurations in creative ways, and (3) "consolidate their innovations by creating new jurisdictions or boundaries that delineate the scope of regulative, normative, and cognitive constraints on action." Sheingate, "Political Entrepreneurship," 190. Sheingate's argument builds on earlier work by Mark Schneider and Paul Teske. See Mark Schneider and Paul Teske, "Toward a Theory of the Political Entrepreneur: Evidence from Local Government," *American Political Science Review* 86, no. 3 (1992): 737–747.

59. Leddy, *Magnum Force Lobby*, 98–100.

60. Feldman, *Ricochet*, 45.

61. Eric Schickler, *Disjointed Pluralism: Institutional Innovation and the Development of the U.S. Congress* (Princeton, NJ: Princeton University Press, 2001), 14–15.

62. Feldman, *Ricochet*, 46–47; Tartaro, *Revolt at Cincinnati*, chapters 5–6; Davidson, *Under Fire*, 36.

63. Spitzer, *The Politics of Gun Control*, 102; Leddy, *Magnum Force Lobby*, 102; Sugarmann, *National Rifle Association*, 50–51.

64. Waldman, *The Second Amendment*, 90.

65. Siegel, "Dead or Alive," 210–212.

66. Sugarmann, *National Rifle Association*, 45; Leddy, *Magnum Force Lobby*, 102–103.

67. Sugarmann, *National Rifle Association*, 51–54.

68. Mark R. Joslyn et al., "Emerging Political Identities? Gun Ownership and Voting in Presidential Elections," *Social Science Quarterly* 98, no. 2 (2017): 382–396.

69. The 40 percent Republican figure is more notable than it might sound; Republican Party identification was low during this period, with only 25 percent and 30 percent of Americans identifying as Republicans in 1976 and 1980, respectively. See "Party Affiliation Among Voters," Pew Research Center, accessed January 25, 2019, http://www.people-press.org/2016/09/13/2-party-affiliation-among-voters-1992-2016/; and "Party Identification by Year," *Washington Post*, accessed January 25, 2019, http://www.washingtonpost.com/wp-srv/politics/interactives/independents/data-party-identification.html.

70. When examining this period—in which the Republican Party was undergoing a shift in which it became more conservative—it is important to consider

both the party and the ideology with which survey respondents identified. Many self-described conservatives—particularly Southerners—who eventually "sorted" into the Republican Party still identified as Democrats at this time.

71. Leddy, *Magnum Force Lobby*, 241.

72. Original analysis of GSS data; Leddy, *Magnum Force Lobby*, 241.

73. In more analytical terms, the entrepreneurial actions of the new guard leaders during and after the revolt should be seen as a necessary condition for the NRA's shift into conservative and Republican politics.

74. Davidson, *Under Fire*, 36.

75. Adam Winkler, *Gunfight: The Battle over the Right to Bear Arms in America* (2011; New York: W.W. Norton, 2013).

76. Lambert, "Trying to Stop the Craziness of This Business," 188–189.

77. Nonetheless, Reagan signed into law a ban on open carry in California, which passed in response to the Black Panthers' open carry of firearms (see Winkler, *Gunfight*, 245). This is an instance that points to the alignment of the NRA—which essentially ignored the developments in California—and other gun rights supporters with racially conservative politics.

78. Reagan, "Ronald Reagan Champions Gun Ownership"; DeConde, *Gun Violence in America*, 212; Davidson, *Under Fire*, 213; Viguerie, *The New Right*, 173.

79. Davidson, *Under Fire*, 42.

80. Dan Baum, *Gun Guys: A Road Trip* (New York: Alfred A. Knopf, 2013), 62.

81. Scott Melzer, *Gun Crusaders: The NRA's Culture War* (New York: New York University Press, 2009), 190–191.

82. Davidson, *Under Fire*, 49.

83. "NRA Endorses Reagan: A Reagan Victory Equals Gun Owner Victory," *American Rifleman*, October 1980, 58.

84. "Republican Party Platform of 1980," The American Presidency Project, accessed January 25, 2019, https://www.presidency.ucsb.edu/documents/republican-party-platform-1980.

85. Joslyn et al., "Emerging Political Identities?"

86. Benjamin Taylor, "Reagan Speaks for Eased Gun Laws: Addresses NRA Meeting," *Boston Globe*, May 7, 1983, 1; DeConde, *Gun Violence in America*, 223.

87. Reagan also spoke to other groups that were clearly not part of the GOP coalition, such as the NAACP. Presidents of both parties, however, spoke to the NAACP both before and after Reagan's time in office; his decision to become the first sitting president to visit the NRA—as well as the fact that no Democrats have done so since then—suggests that this speech was different than those he delivered to other organizations.

88. See chapter 7 for more discussion of gun regulation battles during these years. See, for a helpful overview, Vizzard, *Shots in the Dark*.

89. Davidson, *Under Fire*, 45; Spitzer, *The Politics of Gun Control*, 145–149.

90. "Administration Position on McClure-Volkmer Bill," March 1982, James W. Cicconi Files, Box 11, McClure-Volkmer (Firearms Control Act), Ronald Reagan Library.

91. "Memo from Rob Keenan to John Denny," February 12, 1988, GHWB Vice President Files, Philip D. Brady Subject Files, OA-ID 14830, George H. W. Bush Library.

92. DeConde, *Gun Violence in America*, 235; Feldman, *Ricochet*, 157.

93. "Vice President Bush Becomes NRA Life Member," *American Rifleman*, July 1985, 50.

94. John Mintz, "George Bush Resigns NRA Membership—Cites 'Vicious Slander' against ATF Agents," *Seattle Times*, May 11, 1995, A3.

95. DeConde, *Gun Violence in America*, 237–240; Davidson, *Under Fire*, 207.

96. The Brady Bill was a gun control package eventually passed during the Clinton years, which was named after Reagan Press Secretary James Brady. Brady was paralyzed by a bullet during the assassination attempt on Reagan, and his wife, Sarah, later became a leading advocate of gun control.

97. Spitzer, *The Politics of Gun Control*, 156–158; Karol, *Party Position Change*, 90.

98. Feldman, *Ricochet*, 206; Spitzer, *The Politics of Gun Control*, 112.

99. Karol, *Party Position Change*; DeConde, *Gun Violence in America*, 246.

100. Karol, *Party Position Change*, 85–97; Aaron Blake, "Why Congress Still Won't 'Do Something' about Gun Laws after Las Vegas," *Washington Post*, October 2, 2017, https://www.washingtonpost.com/news/the-fix/wp/2017/10/02/why-congress-still-wont-do-something-about-gun-laws-after-las-vegas/?utm_term=.1b24cea292d8.

101. Mark Joslyn and Donald P. Haider-Markel, "Gun Ownership Used to Be Bipartisan. Not Anymore," *Washington Post*, May 9, 2017, https://www.washingtonpost.com/news/monkey-cage/wp/2017/05/09/gun-ownership-used-to-be-bipartisan-not-anymore/?utm_term=.b065db5ed811; Joslyn et al., "Emerging Political Identities?"

102. Melzer, *Gun Crusaders*, 117.

103. Baum, *Gun Guys*, 55.

104. Karoun Demirjian, "Senate Votes Down Gun Control Proposals in Wake of Orlando Shootings," *Washington Post*, June 20, 2016, https://www.washingtonpost.com/news/powerpost/wp/2016/06/20/senate-heads-for-gun-control-showdown-likely-to-go-nowhere/?utm_term=.3afa0e6fa7e7.

105. Support for a police permit requirement has been included more frequently in the General Social Survey (GSS) than any other gun control question, which makes it the most appropriate choice for examining over-time change. Other annual surveys lack consistently asked gun control questions going back to the 1970s.

106. For a discussion of the role that gender differences in support for gun control have played in driving this trend, see Kristin A. Goss, "The Socialization of Conflict and Its Limits: Gender and Gun Politics in America," *Social Science Quarterly* 98, no. 2 (2017): 455–470.

107. Kim Parker et al., "America's Complex Relationship with Guns," Pew Research Center report, June 22, 2017, http://www.pewsocialtrends.org/2017/06/22/americas-complex-relationship-with-guns/.

108. Thomas M. Carsey and Geoffrey C. Layman, "Changing Sides or Changing Minds? Party Identification and Policy Preferences in the American Electorate," *American Journal of Political Science* 50, no. 2 (2006): 464–477.

109. Ashley Parker, "Donald Trump Tells N.R.A. Hillary Clinton Wants to Let Violent Criminals Go Free," *New York Times*, May 20, 2016, A1.

110. "NRA-PVF Endorses McCain," NRA website, October 9, 2008, https://www.nraila.org/articles/20081009/nra-pvf-endorses-mccain; "NRA Endorses Bush for President," Fox News, October 13, 2004, https://www.foxnews.com/story/nra-endorses-bush-for-president; "NRA-PVF Endorses Mitt Romney and Paul Ryan for President and Vice President," NRA website, October 4, 2012, https://www.nrapvf.org/articles/20121004/nra-pvf-endorses-romney-and-ryan.

111. Robert Maguire, "Audit Shows NRA Spending Surged $100 Million amidst Pro-Trump Push in 2016," *OpenSecrets News*, November 15, 2017, https://www.opensecrets.org/news/2017/11/audit-shows-nra-spending-surged-100-million-amidst-pro-trump-push-in-2016/.

112. Joslyn and Haider-Markel, "Gun Ownership Used to Be Bipartisan"; Joslyn et al., "Emerging Political Identities?"

113. Parker, "Donald Trump Tells N.R.A. Hillary Clinton Wants to Let Violent Criminals Go Free."

114. Wayne LaPierre, "Armed Citizens Are America's Saving Grace," *American Rifleman*, October 2010, 12.

115. Brian Naylor and Domenico Montanaro, "Trump Appears to Read from the NRA's Script Hours after the Gun Lobby Chief's Speech," NPR, January 22, 2018, https://www.npr.org/2018/02/22/588038614/within-hours-of-an-nra-speech-trump-appears-to-read-from-largely-the-same-script.

116. The NRA, as of writing, had taken this video down. However, an excerpt of it, which includes the quoted section, can be found at "Viral NRA Ad Sparks Controversy," YouTube video, CNN, June 30, 2017, https://www.youtube.com/watch?v=9bBQq9GdeKI.

117. "Dana Loesch Has a New Show Coming to NRATV," YouTube video, NRA, February 14, 2018, https://www.youtube.com/watch?v=6dcFEAZQql8.

118. "NRA CEO Speaks at Conservative Forum after School Massacre; NRA Chief: Schools are 'Wide-Open' Target," CNN Newsroom transcript, February 22, 2018, http://www.cnn.com/TRANSCRIPTS/1802/22/cnr.03.html.

119. Charlotte Alter, "At the NRA's TV Network, Guns Are a Weapon in the Culture Wars," *Time*, November 27, 2017, https://time.com/5027071/nras-tv-network-guns-are-weapon-in-culture-wars/.

120. *Freedom's Safest Place*, season 2, episode 10, "We Stand for Our Flag," NRATV, accessed February 9, 2019, https://www.nratv.com/episodes/freedoms-safest-place-season-2-episode-10-we-stand-for-our-flag (site discontinued).

121. For a search of NRATV content discussing "Mueller," see https://www.nratv.com/search?q=mueller (site discontinued).

122. See the online appendix for the full output of this model and those that follow.

123. Santos and Associated Press, "What Donald Trump Said during Atlanta's NRA Convention."

124. Seung Min Kim, "At NRA Event, Trump Embraces Its Agenda in Campaign-Style Speech," *Washington Post*, May 4, 2018, https://www.wash ingtonpost.com/politics/trump-addresses-nra-members-for-first-time-since -parkland/2018/05/04/4fabe0e0-4faa-11e8-84a0-458a1aa9ac0a_story.html?utm _term=.3e61e9a2d344.

125. Kim Parker, "Among Gun Owners, NRA Members Have a Unique Set of Views and Experiences," Pew Research Center report, July 5, 2017, http://www .pewresearch.org/fact-tank/2017/07/05/among-gun-owners-nra-members -have-a-unique-set-of-views-and-experiences/.

126. Lilliana Mason, *Uncivil Agreement: How Politics Became Our Identity* (Chicago: University of Chicago Press, 2018), 14.

127. Brian F. Schaffner, Matthew Macwilliams, and Tatishe Nteta, "Understanding White Polarization in the 2016 Vote for President: The Sobering Role of Racism and Sexism," *Political Science Quarterly* 133, no. 1 (2018): 9–34; Diana C. Mutz, "Status Threat, Not Economic Hardship, Explains the 2016 Presidential Vote," *PNAS* 115, no. 9 (2018): E4330–E4339; John Sides, Michael Tesler, and Lynn Vavreck, "The 2016 U.S. Election: How Trump Lost and Won," *Journal of Democracy* 28, no. 2 (2017): 34–44.

128. German Lopez, "Donald Trump's Long History of Racism, from the 1970s to 2018," *Vox*, January 14, 2018, https://www.vox.com/2016/7/25/12270880 /donald-trump-racism-history; Stef W. Kight, "A List of Trump's Attacks on Prominent Women," *Axios*, October 16, 2017, https://www.axios.com/a-list-of -trumps-attacks-on-prominent-women-1513303964-8ef61562-4dcc-4cf0-aea6 -0ec89457fbc1.html.

129. Throughout this section, much of the discussion of social identification as a gun owner borrows from a separate project—discussed in chapter 3—that I coauthored with Adam Howat and Jacob Rothschild. We conducted a survey on Amazon's Mechanical Turk in which we measured gun owner identity among respondents using a prominent psychological group identification scale. We then examined the extent to which gun owner identification—as opposed to just gun ownership—predicts a range of political outcomes. See Matthew J. Lacombe, Adam J. Howat, and Jacob E. Rothschild, "Gun Ownership as a Social Identity: Estimating Behavioral and Attitudinal Relationships," *Social Science Quarterly* 100, no. 6 (2019): 2408–2424.

130. Lacombe, Howat, and Rothschild, "Gun Ownership as a Social Identity"; Parker et al., "America's Complex Relationship with Guns."

131. Alexandra Filindra and Noah J. Kaplan, "Racial Resentment and Whites' Gun Policy Preferences in Contemporary America," *Political Behavior* 38 (2015): 255–275; Angela Stroud, *Good Guys with Guns: The Appeal and Consequences of Concealed Carry* (Chapel Hill: University of North Carolina Press, 2016); Kerry O'Brien et al., "Racism, Gun Ownership and Gun Control: Biased Attitudes in US Whites May Influence Policy Decisions," *PLoS ONE* 8, no. 10 (2013): e77552–e77552.

132. Goss, "The Socialization of Conflict and Its Limits"; Parker et al., "America's Complex Relationship with Guns."

133. Melzer, *Gun Crusaders*; Jennifer Carlson, *Citizen-Protectors: The Everyday Politics of Guns in an Age of Decline* (Oxford: Oxford University Press, 2015); Jennifer Carlson and Kristin A. Goss, "Gendering the Second Amendment," *Law and Contemporary Problems* 80 (2017): 103–128; Angela Stroud, "Good Guys with Guns: Hegemonic Masculinity and Concealed Handguns," *Gender and Society* 26, no. 2 (2012): 216–238; Stroud, *Good Guys with Guns*; R. W. Connell, *Masculinities*, 2nd ed. (Berkeley: University of California Press, 2005).

134. Melzer, *Gun Crusaders*; Filindra and Kaplan, "Racial Resentment and Whites' Gun Policy Preferences"; Connell, *Masculinities*.

135. Melzer, *Gun Crusaders*, 158.

136. Avi Selk, "Gun Owners Are Outraged by the Philando Castile Case. The NRA Is Silent," *Washington Post*, June 21, 2017, https://www.washingtonpost .com/news/post-nation/wp/2017/06/18/some-gun-owners-are-disturbed -by-the-philando-castile-verdict-the-nra-is-silent/?utm_term=.510bde6a2716; Tim Harlow, "Drivers Get Repair Vouchers Instead of Tickets for Broken Car Lights," *Star Tribune*, April 18, 2017, https://www.startribune.com/drivers -get-repair-vouchers-instead-of-tickets-for-broken-car-lights/419693953/.

137. Michele F. Margolis, "Who Wants to Make America Great Again? Understanding Evangelical Support for Donald Trump," *Politics and Religion* 13, no. 1 (2020): 89–118.

138. David Yamane, "Awash in a Sea of Faith and Firearms: Rediscovering the Connection between Religion and Gun Ownership in America," *Journal for the Scientific Study of Religion* 55, no. 3 (2016): 622–636; Stephen M. Merino, "God and Guns: Examining Religious Influences on Gun Control Attitudes in the United States," *Religions* 9, no. 6 (2018): 189–202.

139. Merino, "God and Guns."

140. Andrew L. Whitehead, Landon Schnabel, and Samuel L. Perry, "Gun Control in the Crosshairs: Christian Nationalism and Opposition to Stricter Gun Laws," *Socius: Sociological Research for a Dynamic World* 4 (2018): 1–13.

141. Ibid.

142. Burbick, *Gun Show Nation*, 159–160.

143. Lacombe, Howat, and Rothschild, "Gun Ownership as a Social Identity"; Parker et al., "America's Complex Relationship with Guns."

144. Parker et al., "America's Complex Relationship with Guns."

145. Lacombe, Howat, and Rothschild, "Gun Ownership as a Social Identity"; Parker et al., "America's Complex Relationship with Guns."

146. Baum, *Gun Guys*, 183.

147. Parker, "Among Gun Owners, NRA Members Have a Unique Set of Views and Experiences."

148. Parker et al., "America's Complex Relationship with Guns."

149. Lacombe, Howat, and Rothschild, "Gun Ownership as a Social Identity."

150. Parker et al., "America's Complex Relationship with Guns."

151. Pew's identity question asked gun owning respondents, "How important, if at all, is being a gun owner to your overall identity?" It gave four response options ranging from "not at all important" to "very important." This is thus a coarser measure of gun owner identity than the measure used in the Lacombe, Howat, and Rothschild, "Gun Ownership as a Social Identity" MTurk survey (and analyses including it must exclude non-gun owning respondents), but it is nonetheless useful.

152. Sugarmann, *National Rifle Association*, 170.

153. "Administration Position on McClure-Volkmer Bill," March 1982, James W. Cicconi Files, Box 11, McClure-Volkmer (Firearms Control Act), Ronald Reagan Library.

154. The same might be true of the Democratic Party, but—given the compelling work on asymmetries between the two parties done by Matt Grossmann and David Hopkins—it is not safe to assume that this is the case. See Matt Grossmann and David A. Hopkins, *Asymmetric Politics: Ideological Republicans and Group Interest Democrats* (Oxford: Oxford University Press, 2016).

155. Schlozman, *When Movements Anchor Parties*, 3.

156. Ibid., 38.

157. Matea Gold, "Trump Stops Holding High-Dollar Fundraisers That Were Raising Big Cash for the GOP," *Washington Post*, October 25, 2016, https://www .washingtonpost.com/news/post-politics/wp/2016/10/25/trump-halts-big -money-fundraising-cutting-off-cash-to-the-party/?utm_term=.7bc11c10c83a; Tara Golshan, "Trump's Campaign Wants to Salvage His Ground Game. But an Expert Says 'The Damage Is Done,'" *Vox*, October 12, 2016, https://www.vox.com /policy-and-politics/2016/10/12/13228828/donald-trump-ground-game-expert -damage; Nick Corasaniti and Alexander Burns, "One Ally Remains Firmly behind Donald Trump: The N.R.A.," *New York Times*, August 10, 2016, A1; Mike Spies, "The Making of Donald Trump and the NRA's Marriage of Convenience," *The Trace*, April 28, 2017, https://www.thetrace.org/2017/04/donald-trump-nra-convention/.

158. Michael Zoorob and Theda Skocpol, "The Overlooked Organizational Basis of Trump's 2016 Victory," in *Upending American Politics: Polarizing Parties, Ideological Elites, and Citizen Activists from the Tea Party to the Anti-Trump Resistance*, ed. Theda Skocpol and Caroline Tervo (Oxford: Oxford University Press, 2020), 79–100; Spies, "The Making of Donald Trump and the NRA's Marriage of Convenience"; Mike Spies, "Documents Point to Illegal Campaign Coordination between Trump and NRA," *The Trace*, December 6, 2018, https://www.thetrace .org/2018/12/trump-nra-campaign-coordination/.

Chapter 7: Gun Policy during the NRA's Partisan Phase

1. "Statement by the President," The White House, Office of the Press Secretary, April 17, 2013, https://obamawhitehouse.archives.gov/the-press-office/2013/04/17 /statement-president.

2. Alexander DeConde, *Gun Violence in America: The Struggle for Control* (Boston: Northeastern University Press, 2001), 190, 193.

3. Ibid., 207.

4. Kristin A. Goss, *Disarmed: The Missing Movement for Gun Control in America* (Princeton, NJ: Princeton University Press, 2006), 39–44.

5. Osha Gray Davidson, *Under Fire: The NRA and the Battle for Gun Control* (Iowa City: University of Iowa Press, 1998), 56–58; Robert J. Spitzer, *The Politics of Gun Control* (New York: Routledge, 2015), 145–146; Congressional Quarterly, *Congress and the Nation, 1985–1988, Vol. VII: The 99th and 100th Congresses* (Washington, DC: Congressional Quarterly, 1989), Law and Justice chapter.

6. Davidson, *Under Fire*, 58.

7. DeConde, *Gun Violence in America*, 228; Congressional Quarterly, *Congress and the Nation, 1985–1988*, Law and Justice chapter.

8. "Federal Gun Law," *CQ Almanac 1985* (Washington, DC: Congressional Quarterly, 1986), 228–230; Davidson, *Under Fire*, 61.

9. David Karol, *Party Position Change in American Politics: Coalition Management* (Cambridge: Cambridge University Press, 2009), 88–89; Samuel C. Patterson and Keith R. Eakins, "Congress and Gun Control," in *The Changing Politics of Gun Control*, ed. John M. Bruce and Clyde Wilcox (Lanham, MD: Rowman and Littlefield, 1998), 71.

10. "Talking Points for NRA Meeting," September 20, 1985, Robert J. Dole Speeches Collection, Series 25, Box 39, Folder 34, Robert J. Dole Library.

11. "Subcommittee on Crime Continues Attack on S. 49," *American Rifleman*, January 1986, 47.

12. Davidson, *Under Fire*, 67.

13. Congressional Quarterly, *Congress and the Nation, 1985–1988*, Law and Justice chapter; Davidson, *Under Fire*, 66–67, 81; DeConde, *Gun Violence in America*, 228–229.

14. Congressional Quarterly, *Congress and the Nation, 1985–1988*, Law and Justice chapter; Samuel C. Patterson and Keith R. Eakins, "Congress and Gun Control," in *The Changing Politics of Gun Control*, ed. John M. Bruce and Clyde Wilcox (Lanham, MD: Rowman and Littlefield, 1998), 71.

15. Congressional Quarterly, *Congress and the Nation, 1985–1988*, Law and Justice chapter.

16. Spitzer, *The Politics of Gun Control*, 145–147.

17. "Administration Position on McClure-Volkmer Bill," March 1982, James W. Cicconi Files, Box 11, McClure-Volkmer (Firearms Control Act), Ronald Reagan Library.

18. Ibid.

19. "Annual Meetings Opened by Vice President Bush," *American Rifleman*, July 1986, 44–45; "Senate Leader Dole Keynotes NRA Banquet," *American Rifleman*, July 1986, 45.

20. Josh Sugarmann, *National Rifle Association: Money, Firepower & Fear* (Washington, DC: National Press Books, 1992), 168; Davidson, *Under Fire*, 80.

21. Linda Greenhouse, "House Passes Bill Easing Controls on Sale of Guns," *New York Times*, April 11, 1986; Laura I. Langbein and Mark A. Lotwis, "The

Political Efficacy of Lobbying and Money: Gun Control in the U. S. House," *Legislative Studies Quarterly* 15, no. 3 (1990): 413–440.

22. Davidson, *Under Fire*, 80; Larry J. Sabato, *PAC Power: Inside the World of Political Action Committees* (New York: W. W. Norton, 1984), 68.

23. DeConde, *Gun Violence in America*, 231.

24. Davidson, *Under Fire*, 199.

25. DeConde, *Gun Violence in America*, 237–238.

26. Davidson, *Under Fire*, 200–201.

27. DeConde, *Gun Violence in America*, 238; Davidson, *Under Fire*, 214.

28. Special cover insert, *American Rifleman*, April 1989.

29. Special cover insert, *American Rifleman*, May 1989.

30. Ibid.

31. Special cover insert, *American Rifleman*, September 1989.

32. Special cover insert, *American Rifleman*, July 1991.

33. James Jay Baker, "War for YOUR Guns," *American Rifleman*, September 1991, 36–39; NRA membership advertisement, *American Rifleman*, October 1991, 48.

34. Mail Summaries, 1989–1991, WHORM WH004–01, Boxes 5–6, George H. W. Bush Library.

35. "Memo on Gun Control Mail," April 22, 1989, WHORM JL003, George H. W. Bush Library.

36. Mail Summaries, 1989–1991, WHORM WH004–01, Boxes 5–6, George H. W. Bush Library.

37. "Constituent Letter to Bush," April 30, 1989, WHORM WH004–01, Boxes 5–6, George H. W. Bush Library.

38. "Society as a Whole Is Being Punished by Gun Control Hysteria," *Atlanta Journal-Constitution*, April 11, 1989.

39. "Craig Letter to Bush," May 16, 1989, WHORM CM009, Boxes 7–8 Elite, George H. W. Bush Library.

40. "Senate Letter to Bush," May 17, 1989, WHORM JL003, George H. W. Bush Library.

41. "Meeting Notes," April 4, 1989 or 1991, WHO Legislative Affairs Files, E. Boyd Hollingsworth, OA-ID 030889, George H. W. Bush Library.

42. "Stump Letter to Bush," April 25, 1991, WHORM JL003, George H. W. Bush Library.

43. "Constituent Letter to Bush," July 18, 1991, WHORM CM009, Box 7 Public, George H. W. Bush Library.

44. "Constituent Letter to Bush," April 6, 1991, WHORM JL003, George H. W. Bush Library.

45. "Bush Signs Stripped-Down Crime Bill," *CQ Almanac 1990* (Washington, DC: Congressional Quarterly, 1991), 486–499; "Anti-Crime Bill Falls Victim to Partisanship," *CQ Almanac 1991* (Washington, DC: Congressional Quarterly, 1992), 262–270; "Brady Bill Part of Stalled Crime Package," *CQ Almanac 1991* (Washington, DC: Congressional Quarterly, 1992), 271–273.

46. "No Compromise Forged on Crime Bill," *CQ Almanac 1992* (Washington, DC: Congressional Quarterly, 1993), 311–313.

47. Guy Gugliotta, "Senate GOP Stalling Defeats Crime Bill; House Passed Measure Bush Called Too Soft," *Washington Post*, November 28, 1991, A41; "Bush Says He'll Veto Crime Bill," *Austin American Statesman*, November 26, 1991, A1.

48. "Anti-Crime Bill Falls Victim to Partisanship"; "Brady Bill Part of Stalled Crime Package."

49. "Anti-Crime Bill Falls Victim to Partisanship"; "Bush Signs Stripped-Down Crime Bill."

50. "Gun Curbs Stall on Hill; Some Imports Banned," *CQ Almanac 1989* (Washington, DC: Congressional Quarterly, 1990), 262–265.

51. Ibid.

52. The NRA told members, for example, "While George Bush has not been a gun owner's dream, *Bill Clinton will be a gun owner's nightmare*." It then emphasized the importance of supporting pro-gun Congressional candidates. See "To Elect a 'Clinton-Proof' Congress," *American Rifleman*, October 1992, 1.

53. Spitzer, *The Politics of Gun Control*, 153, 159.

54. "President Signs 'Brady' Gun Control Law," *CQ Almanac 1993* (Washington, DC: Congressional Quarterly, 1994), 300–303; "Lawmakers Enact $30.2 Billion Anti-Crime Bill," *CQ Almanac 1994* (Washington, DC: Congressional Quarterly, 1995), 273–287.

55. John W. Kingdon, *Agendas, Alternatives, and Public Policies*, 2nd ed. (New York: Longman, 1995); Spitzer, *The Politics of Gun Control*, 149.

56. Goss, *Disarmed*, 17, 46–47; Philip J. Cook and Kristin A. Goss, *The Gun Debate: What Everyone Needs to Know* (Oxford: Oxford University Press, 2014), 36.

57. Goss, *Disarmed*, chapter 4, 176–179.

58. On the one hand, it makes sense that the waiting period would end once the computerized system was available, since part of the logic behind the waiting period was to allow time for a background check to be conducted. On the other hand, another major purpose of the waiting period was to provide "cooling off" time for individuals who sought to buy (and then immediately use) guns in fits of rage; in that sense, the five-year sunset provision substantially weakened the law. Spitzer, *The Politics of Gun Control*, 155–156, 159; "No Compromise Forged on Crime Bill"; "President Signs 'Brady' Gun Control Law."

59. "Lawmakers Enact $30.2 Billion Anti-Crime Bill."

60. Although Goss argues gun control advocates' incremental approach was useful for mobilizing support for gun control, other analysts, such as William Vizzard, argue that the laws passed in the early 1990s did not constitute significant policy shifts and were more notable for their "political acceptability and symbolic appeal than for their utility" in seriously addressing gun violence. In the end, given that this incremental approach was designed at least in part to help overcome the NRA's opposition, it again demonstrates the NRA's ability to reduce the severity

of laws that pass over its opposition. See William J. Vizzard, *Shots in the Dark: The Policy, Politics, and Symbolism of Gun Control* (Lanham, MD: Rowman and Littlefield, 2000), 83; and Goss, *Disarmed*, 148.

61. Congressional Quarterly, *Congress and the Nation, 1985–1988*, Law and Justice chapter; "National Rifle Association Profile for 1990 Election Cycle," Center for Responsive Politics, accessed February 9, 2019, https://www.opensecrets.org/orgs//totals?id=D000000082&cycle=1990.

62. "Handgun Control Inc Totals," Center for Responsive Politics, accessed February 9, 2019, https://www.opensecrets.org/orgs/totals.php?id=D000000424&cycle=2018; "National Rifle Association Totals," Center for Responsive Politics, accessed February 9, 2019, https://www.opensecrets.org/orgs/totals.php?id=D000000082&cycle=1990.

63. Norman J. Ornstein et al., *Vital Statistics on Congress* (Washington, DC: Brookings Institution, 2013), chapter 3.

64. "National Rifle Association Profile for 1992 Election Cycle," Center for Responsive Politics, accessed February 9, 2019, https://www.opensecrets.org/orgs//totals?id=D000000082&cycle=1992; Ornstein et al., *Vital Statistics*, chapter 3.

65. Congressional Quarterly, *Congress and the Nation, 1985–1988*, Law and Justice chapter; "Gun Curbs Stall on Hill"; Ronald G. Shaiko and Marc A. Wallace, "Going Hunting Where the Ducks Are: The National Rifle Association and the Grass Roots," in *The Changing Politics of Gun Control*, ed. John M. Bruce and Clyde Wilcox (Lanham, MD: Rowman and Littlefield, 1998), 165.

66. David Cole, *Engines of Liberty: The Power of Citizen Activists to Make Constitutional Law* (New York: Basic Books, 2016), 142–143.

67. Bill Clinton, *My Life* (New York: Random House, 2005), 630; Evelyn Theiss, "Clinton Blames Losses on NRA," *Plain Dealer*, January 14, 1995.

68. Christopher Kenny, Michael McBurnett, and David Bordua, "The Impact of Political Interests in the 1994 and 1996 Congressional Elections: The Role of the National Rifle Association," *British Journal of Political Science* 34, no. 2 (2004): 331–344.

69. Richard Feldman, *Ricochet: Confessions of a Gun Lobbyist* (Hoboken: Wiley, 2008), 228–229.

70. Cole, *Engines of Liberty*, 129.

71. "House Votes to Repeal Assault Weapons Ban," *CQ Almanac 1996* (Washington, DC: Congressional Quarterly, 1997), 5–32.

72. Allen Rostron, "The Dickey Amendment on Federal Funding for Research on Gun Violence: A Legal Dissection," *American Journal of Public Health* 108, no. 7 (2018): 865–867.

73. Spitzer, *The Politics of Gun Control*, 14, 162–164; "Juvenile Justice Bill Gets Hung Up on Dispute over Gun Control," *CQ Almanac 2000* (Washington, DC: Congressional Quarterly, 2001), 15-15-15-18.

74. "Gun Control Agreement Eludes Conferees, Derails Juvenile Crime Legislation," *CQ Almanac 1999* (Washington, DC: Congressional Quarterly, 2000),

18-3-18-26; Frank Bruni, "House Members Return to Fight over Gun Control, National Rifle Association Used Congress' Recess to Lobby against Pending Measures," *Austin American Statesman*, June 8, 1999, A3.

75. Spitzer, *The Politics of Gun Control*, 162–164.

76. "Gun Control Agreement Eludes Conferees"; Spitzer, *The Politics of Gun Control*, 162–164; Karen Hosler, "Republican Leaders Move to Slow Democrats' Momentum in House; 'Either Hang together, or Separately,' Speaker Warns Fractious GOP," *Baltimore Sun*, June 9, 1999, A3.

77. Bruni, "House Members Return to Fight over Gun Control"; DeConde, *Gun Violence in America*, 286.

78. Wayne LaPierre, "Standing Guard," *American Rifleman*, July 1999, 10.

79. Spitzer, *The Politics of Gun Control*, 164; DeConde, *Gun Violence in America*, 286.

80. "LaPierre: 'The NRA Has Always Supported the Instant Check,'" *CNN Early Edition*, June 15, 1999.

81. Rob Hotakainen, "House Rejects Plan to Target Media Violence," *Minneapolis Star Tribune*, June 17, 1999, A1; Tamara Lytle, "House Gives Up on Gun Law," *Orlando Sentinel*, June 19, 1999, A1; Ken Foskett, "Gun Control: Issue Splitting Georgia GOP's Solid Front," *Atlanta Journal-Constitution*, June 13, 1999, A13; "Gun Control Agreement Eludes Conferees."

82. "Guns Not Focus," *Atlanta Journal-Constitution*, May 6, 1999.

83. "Right to Bear Arms," *Atlanta Journal-Constitution*, May 8, 1999.

84. Karol, *Party Position Change.*

85. Spitzer, *The Politics of Gun Control*, 162–164; "Juvenile Justice Bill Gets Hung Up on Dispute over Gun Control."

86. "Gun Control Agreement Eludes Conferees"; Spitzer, *The Politics of Gun Control*, 162–164; "Juvenile Justice Bill Gets Hung Up on Dispute over Gun Control."

87. "Gun Control Agreement Eludes Conferees"; Spitzer, *The Politics of Gun Control*, 162–164; "Juvenile Justice Bill Gets Hung Up on Dispute over Gun Control."

88. Spitzer, *The Politics of Gun Control*, 164; DeConde, *Gun Violence in America*, 286.

89. "National Rifle Association Totals," Center for Responsive Politics, accessed February 9, 2019, https://www.opensecrets.org/orgs/totals.php?id=D000000082&cycle=1998.

90. Goss, *Disarmed*, chapter 4.

91. Paul Nowell, "Gun-Control Fear Boosts Membership and Donations. NRA Eagerly Awaits Gathering," *Pittsburgh Post-Gazette*, May 19, 2000, A11.

92. Spitzer, *The Politics of Gun Control*, 155; "Republicans Victorious on Gun Liability," *CQ Almanac 2005* (Washington, DC: Congressional Quarterly, 2006), 14-13-14-14.

93. Alexander C. Hart, "Off-Target," *New Republic*, February 2, 2011, https://newrepublic.com/article/82421/gun-control-democrats-obama-congress.

94. Philip Rucker and Sari Horwitz, "On Gun Control, Obama's Record Shows an Apparent Lack of Political Will—Until Now," *Washington Post*, December 23, 2012.

95. One piece of gun legislation did pass following the Virginia Tech shooting with the cooperation of both the NRA and Brady Campaign. The legislation authorized Congress to spend money to make the NICS instant background check system's mental health records more complete and incentivizes states to help with the process. There was no guarantee, however, that Congress would actually follow through and appropriate the authorized funding. Moreover, the legislation also made it substantially easier for some individuals previously ruled mentally incompetent to have their gun rights restored. The NRA cheered the law as a victory, while some gun control advocacy groups—such as the Violence Policy Center—described it as a "pro-gun Trojan Horse." See Josh Sugarmann, "Trojan Horse Gun Control: The NRA Wins on the NICS Bill," *Huffington Post*, December 20, 2007; and Richard Simon, "Bush Signs Bill Geared to Toughen Screening of Gun Buyers," *Los Angeles Times*, January 8, 2008.

96. Peter Wallsten, "Massacre at Virginia Tech: Democrats Hesitant to Push Gun Laws," *Los Angeles Times*, April 20, 2007, A20; Adam Nagourney and Jennifer Steinhauer, "Sadness Aside, No Shift Seen on Gun Laws," *New York Times*, January 14, 2011, A1.

97. Ron Harris, "NRA's Muscle Feared," *St. Louis Dispatch*, April 22, 2007, B1.

98. Robert Draper, "Inside the Power of the N.R.A.," *New York Times Magazine*, December 12, 2013, https://www.nytimes.com/2013/12/15/magazine/inside-the-power-of-the-nra.html; Rucker and Horwitz, "Obama's Record Shows an Apparent Lack of Political Will."

99. "Gun Control Effort Has Little Power, Even in Wake of Newtown Shootings," *CQ Almanac 2013* (Washington, DC: Congressional Quarterly, 2014), 9-3-9-6; Spitzer, *The Politics of Gun Control*, 168.

100. Dave Kopel, "Siege," *American Rifleman*, February 2013, 46–53; Wayne LaPierre, "Standing Guard," *American Rifleman*, February 2013, 12–14; Wayne LaPierre, "Stand and Fight," *American Rifleman*, February 2013, 54–60.

101. Wayne LaPierre, "Stand and Fight," *American Rifleman*, February 2013, 59–60.

102. Wayne LaPierre, "Why America's Gun Owners Must Stand and Fight," *American Rifleman*, April 2013, 58–63.

103. *American Rifleman*, February 2013; *American Rifleman*, March 2013; *American Rifleman*, April 2013.

104. Spitzer, *The Politics of Gun Control*, 167–168; Draper, "Inside the Power of the N.R.A."; "Gun Control Effort Has Little Power, Even in Wake of Newtown Shootings."

105. Draper, "Inside the Power of the N.R.A."

106. Spitzer, *The Politics of Gun Control*, 169.

107. Cole, *Engines of Liberty*, 140–141.

108. Gary C. Jacobson and Jamie L. Carlson, *The Politics of Congressional Elections*, 9th ed. (Landham, MD: Rowman and Littlefield, 2016), 21–24; Frances E.

Lee and Bruce I. Oppenheimer, "Senate Apportionment: Competitiveness and Partisan Advantage," *Legislative Studies Quarterly* 22, no. 1 (1997): 3–24.

109. Kristin A. Goss, "Whatever Happened to the 'Missing Movement'? Gun Control Politics over Two Decades of Change," in *Gun Studies: Interdisciplinary Approaches to Politics, Policy, and Practice*, ed. Jennifer Carlson, Kristin A. Goss, and Harel Shapira (New York: Routledge, 2019), 136–150.

Chapter 8: Conclusion

1. Katie Zezima and Beth Reinhard, "NRA's Top Lobbyist Resigns amid Chaos at the Gun Rights Organization," *Washington Post*, June 26, 2019, https://www.washingtonpost.com/national/nras-top-lobbyist-resigns-amid-chaos-at-the-gun-rights-organization/2019/06/26/235447ec-9835-11e9-916d-9c61607d8190_story.html; Patrick Coffee, "Ackerman McQueen Moves to Terminate 38-Year Contract with the NRA," *Adweek*, May 29, 2019, https://www.adweek.com/agencies/ackerman-mcqueen-moves-to-terminate-38-year-contract-with-the-nra/.

2. Danny Hakim, "New York Deepens Its Investigation into the N.R.A.," *New York Times*, December 9, 2019, https://www.nytimes.com/2019/12/09/us/nra-investigation-new-york.html; Carol D. Leonnig and Tom Hamburger, "New York Attorney General Seeks to Dissolve NRA in Suit Accusing Gun Rights Group of Wide-Ranging Fraud and Self-Dealing," *Washington Post*, August 6, 2020, https://www.washingtonpost.com/politics/nra-lapierre-ny-attorney-general/2020/08/06/8e389794-d794-11ea-930e-d88518c57dcc_story.html.

3. Tim Mak, "Secret Recording Reveals NRA's Legal Troubles Have Cost the Organization $100 Million," NPR, April 21, 2020, https://www.npr.org/2020/04/21/839999178/secret-recording-reveals-nras-legal-troubles-have-cost-the-organization-100-mill.

4. Lisa Marie Pane, "NRA Cutting Staff and Salaries amid Coronavirus Pandemic," ABC News, May 3, 2020, https://abcnews.go.com/Politics/wireStory/nra-cutting-staff-salaries-amid-coronavirus-pandemic-70479845.

5. Kristin A. Goss, *Disarmed: The Missing Movement for Gun Control in America* (Princeton, NJ: Princeton University Press, 2006); Kristin A. Goss, "Whatever Happened to the 'Missing Movement'? Gun Control Politics over Two Decades of Change," in *Gun Studies: Interdisciplinary Approaches to Politics, Policy, and Practice*, ed. Jennifer Carlson, Kristin A. Goss, and Harel Shapira (New York: Routledge, 2019), 136–150.

6. Danny Hakim and Rachel Shorey, "Gun Control Groups Eclipse N.R.A. in Election Spending," *New York Times*, November 16, 2018, https://www.nytimes.com/2018/11/16/us/politics/nra-gun-control-fund-raising.html; German Lopez, "The 2018 Midterm Elections May Have Exposed a Shift on Gun Control," *Vox*, November 8, 2018, https://www.vox.com/2018/11/7/18072146/midterm-election-gun-control-ballot-initiative-congress-results.

7. Mary Thornton, "Bloodletting at the Gun Lobby," *Washington Post*, May 20, 1986, https://www.washingtonpost.com/archive/politics/1986/05/20

/bloodletting-at-the-gun-lobby/6219c341-f88c-474f-95b5-c0aae22a2217/; Osha Gray Davidson, *Under Fire: The NRA and the Battle for Gun Control* (Iowa City: University of Iowa Press, 1998), 185–188.

8. Steven A. Holmes, "Rifle Lobby Torn by Dissidents and Capitol Defectors," *New York Times*, March 27, 1991, A20; Michael Isikoff, "NRA Selects Hard-Liner as Gun Bill Battle Nears," *Washington Post*, April 16, 1991, https://www.washington post.com/archive/politics/1991/04/16/nra-selects-hard-liner-as-gun-bill-battle -nears/a5deb355-ab18-490d-b82d-943bfeb22c1d/; Davidson, *Under Fire*, 237–239.

9. Paul Frymer, *Uneasy Alliances: Race and Party Competition in America* (Princeton, NJ: Princeton University Press, 1999); Paul Frymer and John David Skrentny, "Coalition-Building and the Politics of Electoral Capture during the Nixon Administration: African Americans, Labor, Latinos," *Studies in American Political Development* 12 (1998): 131–161.

10. Harry Enten, "The NRA Used to Be Much More Bipartisan. Now It's Mostly Just a Wing of the GOP," CNN Politics, February 24, 2018, https://www .cnn.com/2018/02/24/politics/nra-partisan-bipartisan-republican/index .html; "National Rifle Association Contributions," Center for Responsive Poli- tics, accessed January 20, 2019, https://www.opensecrets.org/orgs/totals .php?id=d000000082&cycle=2018; Maggie Astor and Weiyi Cai, "The N.R.A. Has Trump. But It Has Lost Allies in Congress," *New York Times*, August 26, 2019, https://www.nytimes.com/interactive/2019/08/26/us/politics/nra-congress -grade.html.

11. R. J. Reinhart, "Record U.S. Partisan Divide on Views of the NRA," Gallup, June 28, 2018, https://news.gallup.com/poll/236315/record-partisan-divide-views -nra.aspx; Jeffrey M. Jones, "Americans' Views of NRA Become Less Positive," Gallup, September 13, 2019, https://news.gallup.com/poll/266804/americans -views-nra-become-less-positive.aspx.

12. Maggie Astor, "Bearing F's from the N.R.A., Some Democrats Are Cam- paigning Openly on Guns," *New York Times*, November 2, 2018, https://www .nytimes.com/2018/11/04/us/politics/gun-control-candidates-election.html; Maggie Astor, "We Surveyed the 2020 Democrats on Gun Control. Here Are the New Dividing Lines," *New York Times*, October 13, 2019, https://www.nytimes .com/2019/10/13/us/politics/democrats-gun-control.html.

13. Kate Samuelson, "A Lot of Gun Owners Really Dislike This NRA Ad," *Time*, June 30, 2017, https://time.com/4841051/gun-owners-nra-advertisement/; Jay Willis, The Precipitous Collapse of NRATV," *GQ*, November 15, 2019, https:// www.gq.com/story/nratv-collapse.

14. Stephen Skowronek, *The Politics Presidents Make: Leadership from John Adams to Bill Clinton* (Cambridge, MA: Harvard University Press, 1997).

15. William D. Adler, "Whose President? Donald Trump and the Reagan Regime," in *American Political Development and the Trump Presidency*, ed. Zachary Callen and Philip Rocco (Philadelphia: University of Pennsylvania Press, 2020), 101–113; Julia Azari, "Trump's Presidency Signals the End of the Reagan Era," *Vox*,

December 1, 2016, https://www.vox.com/mischiefs-of-faction/2016/12/1/13794680/trump-presidency-reagan-era-end.

16. Robert Griffin, Ruy Teixeira, and William H. Frey, "America's Electoral Future Demographic Shifts and the Future of the Trump Coalition," Center for American Progress and Brookings Institution report, April 2018.

17. Daniel J. Galvin, "Party Domination and Base Mobilization: Donald Trump and Republican Party Building in a Polarized Era," *The Forum* 18 (2020).

18. Adler, "Whose President?"

19. Indeed, I may be writing about the NRA at a point in its history that is in some ways similar to the point in organized labor's history captured by J. David Greenstone in his classic work, *Labor in American Politics* (New York: Knopf, 1969).

20. John Haughey, "Report: What's Next for America's Public Land?," *Outdoor Life*, March 17, 2017, https://www.outdoorlife.com/report-next-for-americas-public-land/; John Haughey, "How an Advocacy Hashtag Got a Bill Scrapped in 7 Days," *CQ*, September 22, 2017, https://info.cq.com/resources/advocacy-hashtag-got-bill-scrapped-7-days/; Juliet Eilperin, "Facing Backlash, Utah Rep. Jason Chaffetz Withdraws Bill to Transfer Federal Land to the States," *Washington Post*, February 2, 2017, https://www.washingtonpost.com/news/energy-environment/wp/2017/02/02/facing-backlash-utah-rep-jason-chaffetz-withdraws-bill-to-transfer-federal-land-to-the-states/.

21. Andrea Louise Campbell, *How Policies Make Citizens: Senior Political Activism and the American Welfare State* (Princeton, NJ: Princeton University Press, 2003).

22. Robert Pear, "In Ads, AARP Criticizes Plan on Privatizing," *New York Times*, December 30, 2004, A16; Jill Zuckman, "AARP: Don't Mess with Social Security," *Chicago Tribune*, January 30, 2006, https://www.chicagotribune.com/news/ct-xpm-2005-01-30-0501300337-story.html.

23. Campbell, *How Policies Make Citizens*; "You've Earned a Say in the Future of Medicare and Social Security," AARP, January 2012, https://www.aarp.org/politics-society/advocacy/info-04-2011/AARP-fights-against-threats-to-medicare-and-social-security.html.

24. Campbell, *How Policies Make Citizens*.

25. To be sure, the NRA does not speak for all gun owners, and there are rival organizations that exist on both its political right and left. Nonetheless, the NRA is more dominant in its issue area than many other groups are in their issue areas.

26. Hahrie Han, *How Organizations Develop Activists: Civic Associations and Leadership in the 21st Century* (Oxford: Oxford University Press, 2014). For a discussion of how this study relates to gun politics, see Hahrie Han, "Want Gun Control? Learn from the N.R.A.," *New York Times*, October 4, 2017, A23. For a somewhat related study focused on the decline of federated civic organizations, see Theda Skocpol, *Diminished Democracy: From Membership to Management in American Civic Life* (Norman: University of Oklahoma Press, 2003).

27. Ziad Munson, *The Making of Pro-Life Activists: How Social Movement Mobilization Works* (Chicago: University of Chicago Press, 2008).

28. Feldman quoted in Marc Fisher, "Businesses Spurn the NRA, but Gun Group Doesn't Much Care," *Chicago Tribune*, March 2, 2018, https://www.chicago tribune.com/business/ct-nra-businesses-20180302-story.html.

29. For a discussion of how homeschooling advocates have also used a similar approach, see Heath Brown, "How Do Policy Organizations Frame Issues and Shape Identity? Exploring the Case of School Choice," *Administration & Society* 52, no. 7 (2020): 1038–1068.

30. "Why the A.C.L.U. Wants to Be More Like the N.R.A," *The Daily* (podcast), July 30, 2018, https://www.nytimes.com/2018/07/30/podcasts/the-daily/aclu-nra -trump.html.

31. Goss, *Disarmed*.

32. For a discussion of this movement, see the following interview with Goss: James Burnett, "What's Next for the Parkland Activists? The Questions One Gun Politics Expert Is Asking Now," *The Trace*, March 27, 2018, https://www.thetrace .org/rounds/parkland-activists-gun-reform-kristin-goss/.

33. Paul Pierson, "Power in Historical Institutionalism," in *The Oxford Handbook of Historical Institutionalism*, ed. Orfeo Fioretos, Tulia G. Falleti, and Adam Sheingate (Oxford: Oxford University Press, 2016), 124–141.

34. Robert A. Dahl, *Who Governs? Democracy and Power in an American City* (New Haven, CT: Yale University Press, 1961); Arthur F. Bentley, *The Process of Government: A Study of Social Pressures* (Chicago: University of Chicago Press, 1908); James Madison, "Federalist #10: The Utility of the Union as a Safeguard against Domestic Faction and Insurrection (1787)," in *The Federalist Papers*, ed. Clinton Rossiter (New York: Signet Classics, 2003), 71–78; David Truman, *The Governmental Process: Political Interests and Public Opinion* (New York: Alfred A. Knopf, 1951). For a useful discussion of these works, see Christopher H. Achen and Larry M. Bartels, *Democracy for Realists: Why Elections Do Not Produce Responsive Government* (Princeton, NJ: Princeton University Press, 2016).

35. E. E. Schattschneider, *The Semi-Sovereign People* (New York: Holt, Rinehart, and Wilson, 1960).

36. Kay Lehman Schlozman, Sidney Verba, and Henry E. Brady, *The Unheavenly Chorus: Unequal Political Voice and the Broken Promise of American Democracy* (Princeton, NJ: Princeton University Press, 2012); Martin Gilens and Benjamin I. Page, "Testing Theories of American Politics: Elites, Interest Groups, and Average Citizens," *Perspectives on Politics* 12, no. 3 (2014): 564–581; Martin Gilens, *Affluence and Influence: Economic Inequality and Political Power in America* (Princeton, NJ: Princeton University Press, 2012).

Appendix

1. Margaret E. Roberts et al., "Structural Topic Models for Open-Ended Survey Responses," *American Journal of Political Science* 58, no. 4 (2014): 1064–1082, 1067.

2. There is not a single set of criteria to use to determine a "correct" number of topics. Following others, I tried specifications with more and less topics and "evaluated their semantic coherence and exclusiveness independently from each other," as Bauer and his coauthors did in their 2016 application of STM. I also used the STM R package's selectModel function to confirm that the topics identified here as a whole are not artifacts of modeling choices. Finally, I used the topicQuality function to examine the sematic coherence of each topic; all topics scored well. See Paul C. Bauer et al., "Is the Left-Right Scale a Valid Measure of Ideology? Individual Level Variation in Associations with 'Left' and 'Right' and Left-Right Self-Placement," *Political Behavior* 39, no. 3 (2017): 553–583.

3. The FREX and Highest Probability words are generally intuitive descriptors of the semantic meaning of each topic. The *Americanism and Guns* topic is the only exception; however, after reading numerous example documents, I am confident I have appropriately labeled its semantic meaning. The difficulty of interpreting its FREX and Highest Probability words may be a result of it having more content variation over time than other topics.

4. "Letter Type" is a code assigned to each document to account for the nature of the letter writer's motivation for sending in a letter. The format and language of letters varies based on whether they are written in response to a column/letter previously published by the paper, to a notable instance of gun violence (e.g., school shootings), to a piece of legislation, and so on. Since these differences impact the contents of the letters, incorporating this variable into the model enables better topic estimation. The variable is comprised of the following categories and combinations of them: response to a pro-gun letter/editorial/ article, response to an anti-gun letter/editorial/article, response to a neutral letter/editorial/article, response to a tragedy/notable instance of gun violence, response to proposed legislation, and other/unprompted. All *American Rifleman* editorials—which, unlike the letters to the editor, do not vary substantially in format based on whether they are motivated by particular events—are assigned the letter type "Editorial." As in the *American Rifleman*-only model, I account for different authors discussing the same topics using slightly different words by including the author of each editorial as a content covariate; as a point of reference, eleven different people authored *American Rifleman* editorials between 1963 and 2008. Unlike the *American Rifleman* editorials, most of the letters to the editor have unique authors. Because of the way that STM uses content covariates (essentially producing separate models for each value of the covariate and then marginalizing over those values), it does not make sense (and is not computationally feasible) to have a distinct value for each letter author. I include the newspaper in which the letter appears instead, which enables me to account for cross-newspaper differences.

5. "A Suggestion to Congress," *American Rifleman*, January 1966, 14.

6. Wayne LaPierre, "Standing Guard," *American Rifleman*, June 1997, 10–11.

7. J. Warren Cassidy, "Here We Stand," *American Rifleman*, August 1989, 7.

8. C. B. Lister, "Declaration of Independence," *American Rifleman*, July 1947, 6.

9. With the exception of the *NRA Membership Programs and Benefits* topic, all of the topics from this model have highly representative examples from both newspaper letters to the editor and *American Rifleman* editorials. However, most of the examples I chose to include here come from letters to the editor, since the previous section contains several example documents from NRA editorials. The *NRA Membership Programs and Benefits* topic is the exception; this topic is mostly comprised of *American Rifleman* editorials that discuss and promote NRA offerings, which the model likely fits into their own topic because they are relatively distinct from other documents in the corpus.

10. Philip J. Cook and Kristin A. Goss, *The Gun Debate: What Everyone Needs to Know* (Oxford: Oxford University Press, 2014), 36.

11. "Against Anti-Gun Laws," *Chicago Tribune*, October 13, 1974.

12. "Mom March a Misfire," *Arizona Republic*, May 19, 2000.

13. No title, *New York Times*, May 16, 2000.

14. "Let Concealed Weapons on Campus," *Arizona Republic*, June 2007.

15. Wayne LaPierre, "Standing Guard," *American Rifleman*, January 1999, 10.

16. "Point Missed," *Atlanta-Journal Constitution*, March 2, 1980.

17. "Gun Owners' Rights," *Chicago Tribune*, March 3, 1973.

18. Harlon B. Carter, "A Bigger and Better NRA," *American Rifleman*, October 1981, 50.

INDEX

Page numbers in *italics* refer to figures and tables.

Princeton Studies in American Politics
Historical, International, and Comparative Perspectives

Suzanne Mettler, Eric Schickler, and
Theda Skocpol, Series Editors
Ira Katznelson, Martin Shefter,
Founding Series Editors (Emeritus)

A NOTE ON THE TYPE

This book has been composed in Adobe Text and Gotham.
Adobe Text, designed by Robert Slimbach for Adobe,
bridges the gap between fifteenth- and sixteenth-century
calligraphic and eighteenth-century Modern styles.
Gotham, inspired by New York street signs, was designed
by Tobias Frere-Jones for Hoefler & Co.